£5.99

TWILIGHT
of the
BWANAS

TWILIGHT
of the
BWANAS

An account of life in East Africa
during the colonial period

GORDON DYUS

Library of Congress Control Number: 2011918675
ISBN: Hardcover   978-1-4653-6654-2
                   Softcover   978-1-4653-6653-5
                   Ebook   978-1-4653-6655-9

To order additional copies of this book, contact:
Xlibris Corporation
0-800-644-6988
www.XlibrisPublishing.co.uk
Orders@XlibrisPublishing.co.uk
302979

CONTENTS

DEDICATION

This book is dedicated to the memsahibs of East Africa,
without whom the bwanas would never have survived.

PREFACE

Many books have been written about East Africa and there is obviously something about the region which brings out the literary side of people who have come into contact with it. The books vary considerably in content and range from bodice-ripping novels about sex in the bush to scholarly dissertations on the migratory habits of the wildebeest. Whatever the angle of approach, however, one thing is common to them all—their authors loved East Africa. You don't have to have been born there to experience this feeling, either. The magic seems to rub off on visitors of all descriptions, and even the most hardened tourist will think longingly of the time he or she spent there.

The reason for yet another book about East Africa arises from the need to document the traditions, customs, hopes and fears of a tribe which is now on the verge of extinction. Like so many instances in history, this vanished tribe played no small part in why things are the way they are now and it would be a shame for its brief history to be lost to future generations. Who were the members of this tribe? None other than the white men who ruled East Africa for approximately seventy years, beginning in the 1890s and ending in the 1960s. Call them colonials, imperialists, empire-builders, exploiters, land-grabbers, whatever your view of history persuades you is accurate, but I propose to use the plural of the Swahili term *bwana* as a generic description. This word (pronounced bw-ar-na) is a courtesy title, generally used as a term of respect to a stranger in the way that one would say *Mister* or *Sir.* Politeness in greeting is deeply entrenched in African culture and bwana is used to anybody in authority—a custom which automatically included adult males of non-indigenous extraction during the colonial era.

In case this sounds chauvinist, it is. There is no female equivalent of bwana in Swahili and the early white settlers had to import the Indian expression *memsahib,* (a combination word derived from the English *ma'am* and the Hindi *sahib*) as a suitable mode of address for the fair sex. At the same time, they quickly adopted the word bwana as a common figure of speech and white males would use it on each other. Newcomers to East Africa soon got used to being addressed as 'Bwana Jones' or 'Bwana Smith' and many an argument would be conducted with its assistance, as in 'Listen, Bwana, you've got hold of the wrong end of the stick.' The Americans, introduced to East Africa by hunting and movie-making expeditions, found this so amusing that Bob Hope eventually made a movie entitled 'Call Me Bwana', which gave him an excuse to be funny while wearing a pith helmet.

For reasons which will be explained, the bwanas and their memsahibs left East Africa a long time ago and while a few of them may still be found there, the majority are scattered over the world in an elderly condition. The purpose of this book is to tell you about them—who they were, how they got there, how they lived and finally, why and when they left. As a specialised part of the British Empire story, it is also aimed at the vexed subject of colonialism and analyses its benefits and weaknesses. Like so many sudden disappearances of a social order which have occurred during different periods of history, the bwanas were unaware until late in the day that their days were numbered and did not realise that their twilight time had begun when World War Two ended. They were still full of confidence in the late 1950s and the cataclysmic year of 1960 came as a shock to many of them. Thereafter, they were quick to react but by that stage, the world had irrevocably changed and there was nothing for it but to move on. This was done with a degree of urgency and by 1970, the process was more or less complete.

This book must therefore be viewed as a popular history—not necessarily popular in the sense of generating vast sales but popular from the aspect of being informal. Not only will there be an absence of footnotes or quotations from official documents but there will be a considerable input of reminiscence. I was part of the bwana scene from birth onwards and while I have no intention of inflicting an autobiography on the world, there are many instances in the narrative on which my personal recollection has a bearing. In this regard, I am aware of the commonly-held theory that the last person to know the truth about a country is someone who actually lived there but members of the up-and-coming generation seem to have little idea of East Africa's history and may find a firsthand account helpful. Modern visitors may take a package tour round the game parks and think they have learned something about the country, but by and large, there is little realisation of the incredible effort that went into East Africa's early development.

Thanks are due to many people for their help in compiling this book. As a lot of them helped without realising it, however, it would plainly be an intrusion of their privacy to refer to them without their express permission and I have adopted the policy of not dropping the names of people still living into the narrative unless they happen to be public figures. I have also assumed that bwanas and memsahibs who are dead and gone need not be protected in this manner and indeed, would be glad to be remembered as they look down on earth at celestial sundowner time.

As to the content and appearance of the book, I must firstly thank my wife, Alex, who not only features in many different episodes but has been a wonderful source of advice and support. Invaluable contributions were received from Jenny O'Toole (née Hill), Patricia Doy (née Bailey) and Johnny Johnston, treasured friends of my youth; and the warmest thanks are due to the ex-Ugandans who were so helpful on the subject of the Tank Hill party, namely Brian McMurray, John Steed, John Tucker and David Kemp. Brian's untimely death in California during the early part of 2011 was a great shock and his inimitable style of phrasing a pithy comment is sadly missed.

Finally, my thanks are due to the people who lived in East Africa during the time of which I have written. Irrespective of ethnic background or tribe, there was always a high degree of individuality about them and every day could be guaranteed to reflect this. Nobody was ordinary and though this gave rise to many strange situations, they were normally solved with goodwill on all sides. Being a bwana in this environment was a privilege and I feel lucky to have been one.

G. D.
South Australia, 2011.

CHAPTER 1

BACKGROUND HISTORY

As used within the context of the British Empire on which the sun never set, the generic label *East Africa* did not actually apply to the eastern part of the continent of Africa. It applied specifically to Kenya, Uganda, Tanganyika, and Zanzibar, the last two of which now form Tanzania. Other countries such as Ethiopia and Somalia, though demonstrably eastern in situation, were not part of 'East Africa', nor were the adjacent countries of Rwanda and Burundi, which were regarded as part of the Congo. Similarly, Mozambique, though taking up a long stretch of Africa's eastern coastline, was not part of the East African bloc and had more to do with Central Africa than its neighbours to the north.

At the time this story started, however, none of these countries had any special identity and indeed, the whole African continent south of the Sahara was a large expanse of grassland and forest, full of wild animals and sparsely populated by wandering tribes. It was unknown territory to Europeans and would have probably stayed that way if the Renaissance had not educated people's palates as well as their minds. The quality of food suddenly became important and the fifteenth century saw a burgeoning desire for pepper and spices with which to enliven the winter diet of salted meat. This led Europeans to seek closer contact with the fabled countries of the East, and though travellers like Marco Polo managed to get there by going overland, it was plainly easier to go by ship if you could get round the continent of Africa. So the Portuguese, who were the leading seafarers of the time, decided to have a crack at it and sent off an expedition captained by Bartholomew Dias de Novaes in 1488. It was pioneering work of the most venturesome kind because Dias didn't know how far south he would have to go before getting round the corner—if, in fact, there was a corner to be got round. As history records, he did indeed keep going and succeeded in reaching the Cape of Good Hope at the southern tip of what is now South Africa. It was a truly epic voyage and though he only went a limited distance round the corner, the path had been laid for others to follow, and another famous Portuguese seafarer named Vasco da Gama finally reached India in 1498.

This success fired up the Portuguese to no small extent and they traded vigorously with their new Indian friends, establishing Goa and other outposts in the process. It was a long voyage to and from Portugal, however, and the East African coast proved to be an important staging post for their fleets of galleons. This led them into conflict with the Arabs of Oman and the Persian Gulf, who had enjoyed a long association with the same stretch of coast. The two opposing cultures fought each other vigorously, and the Portuguese established forts at various places to constitute a series of strongholds. The most notable of these is probably Fort Jesus in Mombasa, erected at the end of the sixteenth century. It still dominates the old harbour and legend has it that the walls are stained with blood. It certainly saw its share of fighting, and the great siege of 1696-98 is one of the most poignant stories of human conflict. Sadly for the Portuguese, it ended with the defenders being slaughtered by the besieging Arabs one day before the relief fleet of galleons arrived. The fort, now a National Park, will be mentioned again later in this chronicle but for the time being, it should be noted as well worth a visit.

As Portuguese influence along the East African coast gradually waned due to a decrease in trade, the Arab influence became stronger and by the beginning of the nineteenth century, the coastal strip was almost entirely under their control. By this time, they were deeply engaged in the slave trade, and their excursions into the interior resulted in many thousands of young blacks being forcibly rounded up and marched down to the slave markets on the coast. Shocking though it may sound to modern ears, the slave trade was one of the biggest games the world had to offer at this time and the activities of the Arabs in the eastern part of Africa easily rivalled the better-known activities of the European traders on the western side of the continent, who exported slaves to America and the West Indies. The British themselves were foremost in the slave trade for a considerable period and only achieved redemption in the eyes of history by being the first to outlaw it, abolishing slavery throughout the King's possessions in 1833 and taking active steps thereafter to enforce cessation. Even in America—the land of the free-slavery was fully accepted during the early period of development and it was so firmly entrenched in the southern part of the USA that a bitter four-year civil war had to be fought before abolition could be introduced in 1865. This still did not mean a universal end to the practice, however, and the Arabs continued their depredations in East Africa until the Royal Navy finally discouraged them in the early years of the twentieth century. To this day, it is still possible to trace the great slave routes which led from the central parts of the continent to the sea by the bleached bones of the captive slaves who perished on the way.

Though it might have been thought Africa's problems were over when slavery was extinguished, this was unfortunately not the case because the rush for colonies started at roughly the same time that slavery finished. The British, having taken over the Cape from the Dutch in 1795 and thereafter establishing themselves in South Africa, were probably foremost in the colonisation stakes but various other countries had also established their zones of influence. Started somewhat reluctantly as an extension of trading interests, the grab for Africa soon became frenetic and the European powers began to bump into each other. This made life rather tricky for both diplomats and explorers, and it was decided to convene a conference at which the overlaps could be sorted out and the conflicting claims could be settled. So in 1884—ironically, the same year that the Fabian Society was founded—a whole group of whiskered statesmen met together in Berlin and agreed to a set of boundary lines, drawn in an arbitrary fashion on grossly inaccurate maps. It must have been like playing *Monopoly* on a grand scale and one wonders at the extent of geographical knowledge at the time. Livingstone and Stanley had had their celebrated meeting only a few years earlier, and darkest Africa was still in the process of being explored.

There was, one gathers, a lot of heated debate behind the scenes but at the end of the day, the carve-up tended to reflect existing trading and exploration patterns. The French were confirmed to be masters of most of the northern and western parts of the continent, the Belgians took the middle, and the Portuguese took what are now Angola and Mozambique. The British, who had already secured their western interests in the shape of Nigeria, the Gold Coast (now Ghana), and Sierra Leone, were awarded Egypt, the Sudan, British East Africa (Uganda and Kenya), the Rhodesia's, Nyasaland and Bechuanaland. Germany, a late starter to come to the party, ended up with the countries presently known as Tanzania, Namibia and Cameroon, while Italy nobbled Libya, Somalia and Eritrea. Italy did in fact get Ethiopia allocated to them as well but nobody told the Ethiopians about this and the latter resisted so violently when occupation was attempted that its conquest was deferred for some forty years until Mussolini had another go at it in the 1930s.

It was truly a feast of imperial power, and what is so striking about it is the absence of any concern over the morality of colonisation as a process. Africa was simply regarded as virgin territory, ripe for the taking, and no one worried about the rights of its indigenous peoples, who were deemed to be in need of enlightenment. They weren't Christians, they couldn't read or write, and in addition to this, they didn't have any guns with which to repel invaders. Furthermore, the missionaries wanted to save their souls and the politicians saw it as their duty to export the benefits of European civilisation to them. What the indigenous people thought was never discussed—firstly, because it was assumed they wouldn't have understood what was planned for them and secondly, because the wondrous nature of European culture was deemed to be self-evident and no greater benefit could be visualised than to confer it on a lot of poor savages.

Some historians will assert it was naked exploitation that drove colonisation, and that European countries were set on acquiring raw materials to supply their factories. There are grounds for doubting this, however, because the early colonists had a very lean time of it and the politicians at home in Europe kept baulking at the amount of money that was needed to create something viable in the wilderness. It was far more a case of energy being directed towards a perceived vacuum and unfortunately for Africa's inhabitants, a vacuum was clearly perceived. Many adventurous people were fed up with the feudal flavour of Europe, and were only too glad to shake its dust off their boots. In the ethos of the time, might was right and it was an accepted part of life that the strong would triumph over the weak and lord it over them. Neither can one discount the proselytising zeal of the missionaries, who were only too keen to console the dispossessed indigenes with the promise of everlasting life and get the local maidens to cover up their bosoms.

As an example of the prescriptive way in which Africa was carved up, there is a famous story about the peculiar kink in the boundary between Kenya and Tanzania in the vicinity of Mount Kilimanjaro. The truth of the story is disputed but it is such a good one that it bears repeating. The kink, according to the story, is not a legacy of the Berlin Conference but reflects a later amendment occasioned by Kaiser Wilhelm II grumbling to his grandmother, Queen Victoria, that Germany didn't have any high mountains in its colonies. 'Never mind, dear,' said his grandmother,' I'll give you one of mine as a birthday present.' So the boundary was re-drawn, and the highest mountain in Africa suddenly found itself in Deutsch Ostafrika instead of British East Africa. Personally, I tend to believe it because if you put a ruler on a modern map of East Africa and run the edge along the section of the Kenya-Tanzania boundary adjacent to the coast, you will find an extension of that line hits Lake Victoria at the very same point from which the diversion takes off.

While this may sound high-handed in the extreme, it must be pointed out that the subdivision of Africa did not happen in isolation. The grab for Africa coincided with a global trend towards the expansion of settlement. The era of exploration was drawing to a close and as more became known about the remote regions of the world, migration was quick to follow. At this very same time, the United States and Canada were busy expanding westwards, Argentina was being opened up, and Australians and New Zealanders were branching out far beyond their original settlements. Railways were being built everywhere, the local fauna was being shot out and indigenous people were lucky if they did not endure the same fate. The masses of Europe were on the move and there was little the displaced indigenes could do to prevent it, though some of them opposed the invasion with vigour. The American Indians, for example, resisted stoutly, as did the Maoris in New Zealand and the Zulu, Xhosa and Matabele nations in Southern Africa. The Hereros fought the Germans in South-West Africa, the Riffs fought the French and the Ethiopians fought the Italians. In the end, they were all beaten and had to learn how to co-exist with their conquerors.

It wasn't only people with black or olive skins, either, who fought to preserve their way of life. The white Afrikaner farmers of the Transvaal and the Free State in South Africa—who had a plentiful supply of guns given to them by Germany—felt so threatened by the British that they went to war with them in 1899 and nearly drove them into the sea before being overwhelmed by the combined forces of the British Empire. Popularly known as the Boer War, (*boer* being the Afrikaans word for farmer), the struggle constituted the first modern war of the new era and it is both sad and remarkable that it should have been fought on African soil. Much has been written about the ebb and flow of events during its progress but inevitably, imperial power triumphed in the end and the Boers finally surrendered in 1902. The two fledgling republics then became colonies like the rest of Africa and were absorbed into the imperial system.

In East Africa, the Berlin Treaty sparked off all sorts of interesting repercussions. It was all very well having a whole chunk of Africa delineated in your favour but Britain had its hands full elsewhere and in consequence, fell back on the time-honoured expedient of entrusting trade and development to a merchant company in much the same way that East India Company had originally administered India. The British East Africa Company thus came into being under the leadership of Sir William Mackinnon and was granted a royal charter by Queen Victoria in 1888. Initially focussed on Mombasa, the agents of the company went about their business with considerable energy but found it was not easy to get trade off the ground. Soon, they began punting the idea of building a railway to Uganda, perceiving this might make commerce easier. They also complained vociferously about the coastal strip falling under the control of the Sultan of Zanzibar and claimed this was limiting their freedom of action.

Zanzibar thus had considerable nuisance value and though it may have smelled sweetly of cloves, it was not in good odour with Britain for the additional reason of its involvement in slavery. Increasingly, it began to be felt the Sultan should be subject to greater British influence and might require administrative assistance. The only snag was that Germany was beginning to feel the same way. Zanzibar was directly opposite the German sphere of interest, and the Germans felt that if anyone should clip the Sultan's wings, it should be them. Feelings on the issue began to get heated and the cruisers of both imperial powers were beginning to exchange dirty looks as they steamed past each other on their flag-showing patrols up and down the coast.

It is a tribute to the diplomacy of that era that the matter was settled without any shooting. The world may have subsequently lurched into a state of massive conflict but at this point, jaw-jaw was still deemed preferable to war-war. Not deterred by the fact that Zanzibar was an independent sultanate, the parties simply got together and agreed to do a swap. Germany had always wanted to get its hands on Helgoland—a small island in the North Sea which Nelson had acquired on behalf of Britain some eighty years earlier—and one of Bismarck's bright young men recognised the Zanzibar crisis as an opportunity to set matters right. So a deal was done. In terms of the Helgoland-Zanzibar Treaty of 1890, Zanzibar was agreed to be a British responsibility and Helgoland was ceded to Germany. But that was not all—the French, who had been sitting in on the meeting and also claimed to have established a presence on the spice island, were given a free hand with Madagascar provided they left Britain to it in Zanzibar. All eminently sensible, with something in it for everyone!

Unfortunately for the British East Africa Company, this triumph of diplomacy wasn't much help in generating revenue. Uganda became difficult and in 1892, the Company found itself involved in a squabble between the Kabaka—the king of Buganda—and the missionaries which escalated into a minor civil war. Peace was restored but only at a cost which nearly bankrupted the Company and made its continued operation highly questionable. By 1894, the British Government found it had to step in and declare protectorate status over Uganda, following this a year later with a similar declaration over what is now known as Kenya. The Company then went out of business and the administration of British East Africa became an official function of the Crown.

Interestingly enough, Zanzibar—which was declared a protectorate in 1890 after the treaty had been signed—continued to function under the authority of the Sultan but in 1896, the pro-British incumbent of the office died and a new Sultan who didn't like the British took over. Plainly, this called for some friendly persuasion and in the August of that year, ships of the Royal Navy starting shelling the Sultan's palace, only desisting when a white flag denoting surrender was run up on the shore. Historians refer to this action as the Anglo-Zanzibar War and it is said to have been the shortest war ever fought—lasting 38 minutes from start to finish.

Meanwhile, much forcible pacification had been proceeding in the other component parts of Africa and it took until 1908 or thereabouts for Europe's new colonies to reach a state of enforced peace. Both the British and the Germans had trouble with their new East African possessions, the latter having particular difficulty with what was known as the Maji-Maji Rebellion in the southern part of Deutsch Ostafrika. The Swahili word for water is *maji* and the theory had spread among the tribes that if you were sprinkled with a few drops of magic water obtainable from the witchdoctor, you would be immune to European bullets. Needless to say, this proved to be fallacious and many people died as a result of German military efficiency. The British weren't far behind in their methods of suppressing unrest, either, and Kenya's early history contains more than one gory instance of spear-wielding tribesmen coming up against rifles and machine guns.

With hindsight, one can see it was inevitable for the first stages of colonisation to have generated resistance. Many of the newly subject peoples of Africa came from a warrior tradition and did not take kindly to the white tribes who had come upon them. It took some years for the period of initial conflict to die down and for the administration of colonial territories to become more benevolent and enlightened. Once this had happened, however, there was an influx of European settlers and the establishment of towns and farms proceeded at a fast pace. Railways were built, harbours were developed and crops were harvested. Indigenous folk were introduced to the pleasure of working for a wage and the process of government became more structured. No one talked about democracy, of course, but it was generally assumed—at some unspecified time in the far-off future—that there would be some form of local representation.

Strangely enough, it was only in South Africa that anything resembling democracy was introduced, which occurred in 1910 when the four British colonies of the Cape, Transvaal, Natal and the Free State were formed into a self-governing Dominion within the British Empire. In many ways, this was a great piece of statesmanship since it reconciled two parties who had recently been at war with each other and provided them with a common political platform. Unfortunately, however, no one thought to include the indigenous black population of the country in the new dispensation and thereby hangs a long and bitter tale. It wasn't a deliberate omission—it was just not an issue and nobody thought of it. The mindset of the era held that blacks could run their own tribal affairs in land reserved for them and leave the complex business of running a country to the whites. It didn't matter if the latter were numerically in a minority—this was irrelevant in the face of their greater knowledge and ability. And if this sounds odd to modern ears, it was in fact a fair conclusion to have reached at this time because South Africa's black population was nowhere near ready to run a modern government. Universal voting eligibility is a fairly modern concept and it was not only blacks who were excluded from the franchise in 1910 but women as well—on roughly the same grounds.

East Africa certainly saw some major developments from the close of the nineteenth century onwards. The British were the first to kick off when they finally decided to go ahead with the proposed railway line from Mombasa to Lake Victoria with the aim of facilitating access to Uganda. While it was plainly one of the most adventurous projects of the late Victorian age, it was fiercely opposed in Britain as a waste of money and its detractors labelled  it *The Lunatic Line*, pointing to the fact that no one knew whom it was meant to serve or what benefits could be expected once the line reached Uganda. There was much dissent in the House of Commons and in the press of the day but fortunately for Kenya, the line did get built and was an incredible feat of engineering. Commencing in 1896, construction took five years and many problems were encountered before the line reached Kisumu on the lakeshore. Aside from the terrain proving rougher than anticipated, difficulties arose from the lack of technical aptitude exhibited by local tribesmen and the entire labour force had to be imported from India. No sooner had work progressed to a place called Tsavo, however, when the project was brought to a grinding halt by a pair of man-eating lions, who had developed a taste for railway workers. Predatory and cunning beyond belief, these animals caused complete chaos in the construction camp and no work was possible until they had been tracked down and shot. This in itself was a gripping adventure story and *The Man-eaters of Tsavo* by Colonel Patterson, the man who hunted down the lions, is a wonderful book. (It is also the subject of a wildly inaccurate movie which resulted in my wishing the lions had eaten the actor who played Colonel Patterson).

Further inland, construction of the railway paused again when it got to what is now Nairobi and what began as a construction camp soon turned into a thriving town. By that stage, however, the railway line had gone ahead and made its way through the highlands, crossing the equator a couple of thousand metres above sea level and finally reaching Lake Victoria as planned. A ferry boat was then transported to Kisumu in pieces, was re-assembled, and duly launched. A short length of track linking Port Bell to Kampala was laid on the far shore of the lake and voila, the dream of reaching Uganda became a reality.

Further south in Deutsch Ostafrika, the Germans also went into the railway business and constructed not just one but two railway lines leading from the coast into the interior. The first, known as the Usambara Railway, ran inland from the port of Tanga along the foothills of the Usambara and Pare Mountains to Moshi, a pleasant town which nestled at the foot of Mount Kilimanjaro. Shorter than the British effort, its route followed the Pangani River and formed the backbone of German administration in the northern part of the country. Important though it was, however, it was quite dwarfed by the second line, the Central Line, which ran from Dar es Salaam to Kigoma on Lake Tanganyika. Also an excellent feat of engineering, it had several purposes in that it not only linked the regional centres of Morogoro, Dodoma and Tabora with the capital city of Dar es Salaam, but gave the Belgian Congo an eastward outlet to the sea as well as providing a rapid means of moving goods and people from one end of the country to the other.

These railways enabled substantial development to occur in both British and German parts of East Africa and attracted substantial immigration from Europe. Several thousand new arrivals in the years preceding the outbreak of the First World War laid the foundation of the bwana species, and a mixture of farmers, officials and commercial wallahs spread quickly over the landscape. Most of the prospective farmers headed for the highland areas where coffee and tea could be profitably grown but sisal was also popular with the Germans, who cultivated the spiky crop in large plantations. In British East Africa, the incoming settlers established a huge enclave that became known as *The White Highlands* and Nairobi grew rapidly in size, supplanting Mombasa as the largest town in the country and becoming the capital by virtue of its central situation and cool climate. Hunting was a regular occupation for almost everybody, and the possibility of being taken on safari by professional 'white hunters' lured many well-known people to visit East Africa in order to shoot big game and take a bag of trophies home with them.

One of the most significant arrivals during this period was someone who can best be described as the granddaddy of the bwanas. This was none other than Lord Delamere, an English aristocrat who moved to British East Africa in 1901 and thereafter played a formative role in local agriculture and politics. An autocratic character who would brook no nonsense from anyone, he acquired large land holdings in the heart of the 'White Highlands' and conducted much pioneering work on the production of cattle, wheat and maize. Though serious in outlook, there was a fun-loving side to him, too, and he is commonly credited with having founded the Happy Valley set—a clique of wealthy colonists whose social and sexual activities became a byword for frivolous behaviour. The Norfolk Hotel was one of his haunts when he came into town and it is related that he once rode his horse into the dining room, where he proceeded to jump over the tables. A man of great influence and one of the giants of the colonial era, the main street of Nairobi was called after him and his descendants are still in the country.

Unfortunately for East Africa, the boom in settlement which had got off the ground in 1910 came to an abrupt halt in 1914 with the onset of the Great War or World War One, call it what you will. (Some optimists at the time even called it the War to End All Wars). With Germany, Austria-Hungary, and Turkey on one side and the other European powers, the British Empire and eventually the USA on the other side, this was war like the world had never seen and though the action took place mainly in Europe and the Middle East, there were a couple of sprightly side-shows on the African continent as well—including a very lively one in East Africa. What this did to the perceptions of the local population is a matter for conjecture and one might well ask why the Germans in Deutsch Ostafrika, being surrounded by enemies and vastly outnumbered, chose to make a fight of it. It would have made far more sense to have kept East Africa neutral and though this was seriously contemplated by them at one point, the decision to fight was eventually prompted by a desire to distract Allied effort from other theatres. This aim was achieved but only by the expedient of training black troops to fight against white soldiers—a proposition which many people said was impossible. In point of fact, General von Lettow Vorbeck, the commander of German forces in Deutsch Ostafrika, managed it with conspicuous success and raised several locally trained battalions of *askari,* (a commonly used Swahili word for soldier or policeman), which he formed into a unified *Schutztruppe* (defence force) with the aid of a handful of serving and retired officers.

The first actions of the war were not fought on land but by the German cruiser *Konigsberg,* which had been gracing the placid waters of Dar es Salaam harbour when war was declared on 4 August 1914. Slipping out of Dar in her role as a sea raider, she soon sank a British merchant ship near the Gulf of Aden, and followed this up by making a surprise attack on the *Pegasus,* an elderly British cruiser anchored at Zanzibar. The spice island echoed again to the noise of naval gunfire as the out-gunned *Pegasus* was sunk, and the victorious *Konigsberg* then headed south with the intention of rounding the Cape and getting back to Germany. Unfortunately for her, she developed engine trouble before she had gone very far and Kapitan Loof had to seek refuge in the delta of the Rufiji River, approximately 100 kilometres south of Dar es Salaam. By this time, the Royal Navy, stung by the loss of the *Pegasus,* were looking for her in strength and succeeded in finding her just before the engine repairs were completed. A full blockade by several British ships was mounted to stop the *Konigsberg* escaping and eventually, the cruiser was crippled by gunfire from a couple of flat-bottomed monitor gunboats which had been specially towed all the way from the Mediterranean. Remarkably, the monitors' gunfire had been directed from the air by two British spotter aircraft—probably the first time this technique had been used.

Kapitan Loof then had his ship scuttled but this was not the end of the *Konigsberg's* influence on the subsequent campaign. Not only did her crew join von Lettow's forces, but they dismantled her 4-inch guns and dragged them through the bush by ox-cart to Dar es Salaam where they were mounted on railway trucks and subsequently used to good effect in von Lettow's operations. As later remarked by a British officer in his diary, it was a bizarre experience to be at the receiving end of naval high explosive shells in the middle of tropical Africa.

Von Lettow, in the meantime, had used his *Schutztruppe* to good effect in a series of cross-border raids into British East Africa. Suitably provoked but without the military manpower to do much about it, the British authorities sent for help from the Indian Army, who attempted a seaborne landing at

Tanga. Thinking that von Lettow's black soldiers would be a walkover, it was not deemed necessary to use first grade troops in the assault and the invading force was ignominiously routed. It was a major defeat and one which made the British Government sit up sharply. Plainly something must be done about von Lettow but who would lead the Allied forces in British East Africa, which had been hastily reinforced by two brigades from South Africa? The initial choice fell on a General named Smith-Dorrien who had African experience but the latter fell ill as he was leaving London and the British then invited Jan Smuts, the South African Minister of Defence, to take charge personally. It was a brilliant choice. Jan Christian Smuts—arguably the most famous son of South Africa until the advent of Nelson Mandela—was still a relatively young man at this time and had been instrumental in getting the new Union of South Africa up and running. A Cambridge graduate, a lawyer, and a daring guerrilla leader who had led the British a merry song and dance during the Boer War, Smuts had played a decisive role in defeating the Germans in South West Africa and was Prime Minister Louis Botha's right hand man. Not bad going for someone who only started school at the age of twelve!

Once the question of command had been settled, a further detachment of South African mounted troops and infantry was raised and Smuts took ship for Mombasa in early 1916. (As chance would have it, I met a delightful old gentleman many years later in Johannesburg, who had been on the same ship and had stood sentry-go outside Smuts' cabin). The South Africans arrived just in time for news of another British defeat in the hilly border country near Moshi and Smuts summarily took charge. History could play no stranger tricks and indeed, the subsequent campaign proved to be one of the most fascinating of the whole war. With two skilful commanders up against each other in tropical country under the snows of Mount Kilimanjaro, the script had everything—heat, dust, torrential rains, wild animals, incredible marches, sickness and heroism. As there were very few roads and the railway system was so limited, the logistics of supply were a nightmare and many thousands of horses, oxen and porters were involved. The widespread presence of tsetse fly made life very difficult for horses, however, and it was no easier to manage thousands of porters, who kept needing to be fed. This led to further columns of porters carrying food for the first lot of porters and so on.

The subsequent story of the war in German East Africa is told in many excellent books but in brief summary, the South African and British forces invaded from the north and slowly pushed von Lettow and his men away from the main towns into the southern parts of the country. Striving for a decisive victory but conscious of the unpopularity which a heavy casualty list would involve, Smuts kept trying to outflank and encircle von Lettow but the wily Prussian general always succeeded in evading the trap in classic guerrilla style. Remarkably, when he was pushed to the southern limits of the country, he even invaded Mozambique and caused considerable alarm to the Portuguese before doubling back and marching into Northern Rhodesia, which he reached in late 1918. He then had to be persuaded that the war was over before he agreed to lay down his arms—truly a gallant gentleman and a magnificent soldier. He and his troops had the distinction of being the last undefeated German army in the field when peace was finally declared.

Smuts, meanwhile, had not stayed in German East Africa until the end of the war but had gone back to South Africa after Dar es Salaam had been liberated in late 1916. His intellectual stature had so impressed the British Government that he was invited to join the Imperial War Cabinet and played a formative role in founding the League of Nations, the predecessor of the United Nations. As is well-known, he became the Prime Minister of South Africa on two separate occasions and played an even greater role in the Second World War than he had in the First, becoming a Field-Marshal and an intimate colleague of Winston Churchill.

The quality of Smuts and von Lettow can be gauged from an incident which occurred when Smuts went to visit his troops in the Morogoro area. Unknowingly, he came within range of the German positions at precisely the same time that von Lettow happened to be in one of the German trenches. It was indeed the long arm of coincidence but neither knew the other was there until von Lettow took a look through his binoculars at the South African lines and realised he was looking at Smuts, whom he recognised by his hat and red beard. Most people in this situation would have had no hesitation in grabbing a rifle and shooting such a notable opponent but the General decided this would be unsportsmanlike. So he held his fire and Smuts proceeded back to his base camp, where word of von Lettow's forbearance eventually reached him through a captured askari a few days later. Never the sentimentalist, this apparently moved Smuts to comment in his brusque way that von Lettow was a fool—but a gentleman.

There are many other stories worth telling about the East African campaign but one which really appeals is the epic journey of the airship, which was despatched from Germany in 1917 with a cargo of essential supplies (including some schnapps and Iron Crosses) for von Lettow and his men. There was no way a ship could have broken the British naval blockade and though it was a long shot, an airship must have seemed to the High Command in Berlin to be the only way of supporting their beleaguered troops in far-off Africa. Incredibly, a long-distance Zeppelin was despatched with instructions to fly down the Nile until it reached Deutsch Ostafrika—a fearsome aerial journey for those days. Fearsome it may indeed have been but apparently, the initial parts of the journey went well and the airship had flown as far as Khartoum when the crew received a message over the radio to say that von Lettow had surrendered. So they turned round and managed to get themselves back to Germany—little realising that the message was a fake which had been sent to them by British Intelligence. Not cricket perhaps but what a triumph for the cloak-and-dagger boys!

Talking of which, no account of the war in East Africa would be complete without mention of Colonel Richard Meinertzhagen, who was surely one of the most colourful and controversial characters ever to advance the cause of the British Empire. As a young officer with the King's African Rifles, he had played a considerable role in pacifying British East Africa before being transferred to the Indian Army, from whence he returned to be Chief Intelligence Officer to Smuts. Involved in many extraordinary incidents in later phases of the war in Egypt and Palestine, Meinertzhagen ran a whole network of black spies behind the German lines in East Africa and was able to monitor the instructions that von Lettow issued to his field commanders with considerable success. How you might ask was this accomplished? Well, you must remember that the German officers of the *Schutztruppe* had no supplies of toilet paper and any instruction or movement order which came their way was eventually utilised for personal purposes. Meinertzhagen's men specialised in collecting such pieces of paper after they had been used and their boss obtained much valuable information from studying them.

A personal part of this narrative goes back to Smuts' triumphant return to South Africa in 1916, leaving a large contingent of South African troops in Dar es Salaam awaiting repatriation. The port, however, was in a state of chaos and the job of getting the South African soldiers and their equipment back home was severely hindered by the Germans having partially blocked the harbour entrance by sinking a dry dock and a small steamer across it. The usual process of loading cargo into lighters and towing them out to the waiting ships was extremely difficult in consequence and a bottleneck had built up. Acutely conscious of this, Smuts made haste to get in touch with the leading figure of the South African waterfront as soon as he arrived home. This gentleman was none other than TB Davis, founder of the largest stevedoring group in the country and extremely wealthy as a result. 'TB',

known to several generations of budding mariners for having established
a training ship named the *General Botha* in Cape Town and to generations
of university students as the donor of Howard College in Durban, was a
remarkable man in any day and age. As I heard the story, he was a seafaring
Channel Islander who fell overboard in a shipping mishap near Jersey and
was picked up by another ship bound for South Africa. The ship couldn't turn
back for the sake of one person, and so TB went all the way and subsequently
made a fortune in his new and somewhat unexpected setting. His life was
not without sadness, however, because his elder son Howard was killed in
the Great War and it was in his memory that he endowed the University.

TB was certainly a forceful character because I am told he immediately
despatched a fleet of tugs and lighters to Dar es Salaam, where they managed
to squeeze past the obstructions in the main channel and clear the backlog of
men and cargo in double quick time. Never slow to recognise an opportunity,
TB then decided to open for business in East Africa and this is how the
East African Lighterage and Stevedoring Company came into being—a
fact which was responsible for my father going to East Africa and spending
his working life there. As both he and my mother belong to a later stage of
being a bwana, however, I will tell you about their arrival in East Africa in
a later chapter.

The end of World War One heralded major changes everywhere and this
state of flux was only partially resolved at the 1919 Peace Conference. As far
as East Africa was concerned, it was confirmed that Britain would take over
what had been Deutsch Ostafrika, after first chopping off Ruanda-Urundi
and allocating it to Belgium as part of the spoils of war. It was also agreed
that German settlers would be stripped of title to their estates and shipped
back to Germany—a decision which left the British facing the prospect
of setting up a new administration in a large tropical country which had
been ravished by warfare and denuded of managerial skills. This was a tall
order but due to the efforts of Political Officers seconded from the Army,
the country was running again by the time formal authority was granted
by the League of Nations. In terms of this, the country was to be known as
Tanganyika and administered as a mandated territory held in trust on behalf
of its indigenous population until they were capable of self-government at
some unspecified date in the future.

How seriously the authorities took the terms of the mandate is a matter
for debate. Most people, I think, held the view that self-government was
a millennium away and the administration of the country could be safely
conducted along normal colonial lines. Admittedly, there was a commitment

to doing it in an enlightened way but it must have seemed to many as if Cecil Rhodes' dream of uninterrupted British sovereignty all the way from the Cape to Cairo had finally been fulfilled.

In British East Africa, there were no apparent concessions to enlightened thought in the way of mandates or future self-rule. The country was re-named Kenya (pronounced Keen-ya) and proclaimed to be a full colony as from 1920. At the same time, a decision was taken to develop the concept of East Africa as a unified bloc, and a common currency was introduced. As Uganda and Zanzibar retained their status as protectorates, it was a very mixed bag from a constitutional point of view but no one saw this as a problem. In practice, no one could tell the difference and it was probably only in the fields of land tenure and local government that divergences were appreciable. Uganda got the full colonial treatment complete with Governor and supporting administration, while the Sultan of Zanzibar was made answerable to a sharp-eyed British Resident.

The stage was thus set for an influx of bwanas. A surge of British ex-servicemen migrated to Kenya and were rewarded with farms. Others set up for themselves in business and the commercial scene in Nairobi grew rapidly in the hands of the Indian community. The same pattern was repeated in Tanganyika, save that the incoming settlers were more cosmopolitan and featured several European nationalities with a strong Greek contingent, who were particularly active in buying up ex-German sisal estates. Uganda, too, got its share of planters, traders and officials, and by the mid-1920's, it could be said that the show was really on the road. A common postal service was introduced and in 1927, Tanganyika joined the Customs Union which had already existed between Kenya and Uganda. The stamps issued by the new Post Office were splendid and my favourite was the standard 10 cent issue labelled 'Kenya, Uganda, Tanganyika' with King George V's head above a lion at sunset. It must, one imagines, have been a considerable relief to the authorities to be able to dispense with the unwieldy label *Mandated Territory of Tanganyika* on the stamps it had previously been issuing.

There was, during those early post-war years in East Africa, a distinct sense of the world being young. Everything was new and whether it was a farm, a career or a filing system, it was virtually being started from scratch. Having survived the war was additional cause for feeling good about life and a lot of the memsahibs began to have babies, thereby conferring the first locally-born bwanas on the East African landscape. The indigenous population weren't too unhappy, either, and their original defiance gave way to acceptance as the new administration proved it could be trusted to preserve the peace and see they didn't starve. Later on, the Kikuyu in Kenya began to resent having been shunted off to a defined reserve but initially, there was enough room for everybody and there was little tension. As government was conducted according to the principle of indirect rule, the chiefs of the various tribes retained their authority and administration was largely conducted through them. There was mutual respect between the races and crime was so low that most people didn't bother to lock their doors at night—except as protection against marauding animals.

So there was generally a go-getting atmosphere at this time. The Union Jack flew proudly at all the flag-staffs, Governors complete with white uniforms and ostrich feathers represented His Majesty the King, Lord Delamere watched over settlers' interests with an eagle eye, and back in London, who else but Winston Churchill presided over the Colonial Office.

It was not a bad time to be a bwana.

CHAPTER 2

THE EARLY YEARS

In the aftermath of war and with a wave of new people arriving, it took the first part of the 1920's for East Africa to settle down. This process was even more marked in Tanganyika because a whole new Governmental structure was necessary and new laws had to be written to replace the German way of doing things. Simultaneously, all the properties which had been confiscated from the departing German settlers had to be listed and made available for acquisition. The railways, which von Lettow and his men had blown up during their retreat, had to be put into working order again and the Brewery had to be re-vitalised. The German Governor's palace in Dar es Salaam, which had been shelled by the British Navy, needed to be re-built and the officials of the incoming British administration had to be housed and given premises in which to work.

In Kenya, the process of post-war readjustment was much easier because nothing had been destroyed and the existing administration was intact. Nairobi grew rapidly in size and gracious suburbs began stretching out towards Muthaiga and the Rift Valley. Other towns grew as well and many public buildings, hotels, churches, hospitals and clubs came into existence, together with such essential facilities dear to British hearts as golf courses and sport fields. Thousands of acres of coffee were planted in the farming areas, and the port of Mombasa began to handle an increased amount of imports and exports. It was quite frenetic and not to be left out of the action, the Happy Valley set wound up their gramophones and danced the Charleston with abandon, stopping only to recharge their glasses and dally with each other's wives.

Uganda did not get a large influx of settlers taking up new farms but did receive a goodly share of officials and business men. Kampala not only became a lively commercial centre, but also an educational one with the establishment in 1922 of the technical school which was later to become Makerere University. Entebbe, however, remained the administrative capital and all the functions of the Uganda Government were concentrated there. The country may have contained some very disparate tribes but they all seemed content to co-exist and Uganda acquired the reputation of being the pearl of Africa.

As already pointed out, this post-war influx of people into the three East African countries wasn't solely European in origin. The Indian community, which had established itself during the building of the railways, had been augmented by large scale migration from India to fill the need for workers, civil servants and artisans. The more enterprising ones, blessed with inherent commercial spirit, became traders and it took only a short while before most of the shops in East Africa were owned and run by Indians. The British might once have been described as a nation of shopkeepers but this certainly did not apply in East Africa and it is doubtful whether economic viability would ever have been achieved without the enterprise of its Indian inhabitants. The Indian *duka* (shop) became an institution and every centre of population was served by at least one of them.

The introduction of the new currency was interesting, too. Previously, all the countries involved—including the Germans—had worked on the basis of the rupee which had established itself along the coast as a result of the passing trade with India. The new system was beautifully simple, however, and rested on one basic relationship, namely 100 cents = 1 shilling. The pound was not recognised as a unit of currency and though 20 shillings was worth one pound and could be readily exchanged as such throughout the sterling area, prices were only quoted in pounds as a form of shorthand. With great practicality, the copper coins of the system, namely the ten cent piece, the five cent piece and the one cent piece, were designed with a hole in the middle in recognition of the fact that few members of the populace had any pockets and had to carry their coins by threading them on to a piece of string which they hung round their necks.

As a further aid towards a fresh start, each country in the East African bloc was allocated a national emblem to encourage a sense of identity. Kenya was allocated the lion, Tanganyika was given the giraffe, and Uganda the crested crane. Presumably, the choice of these creatures was based on the fact they were common within their respective countries but there is something dominant about the lion which carries the suggestion of Kenya seeing itself as a cut above the others. Whether this was true may be arguable but the emblems were adopted without demur and no time was lost in inscribing them on school exercise books and government property.

Inevitably, as the new order settled down, getting around became a first priority. Motor cars had become an accepted fact of life by this time and roads capable of being used by them had to be built. Do not let the word 'road' lead you into visualising a series of tarred or gravel highways, however. In most cases, the surface of the earth was simply stumped and scraped by gangs of labourers and their handiwork was often washed away. The black cotton soil of the Kenya Highlands was especially notorious for impeding progress when wet, and bridges over rivers were a luxury. Goods and people could only be moved reliably by rail and several branch lines were added to the railway network as a matter of urgency. The longest of these was the connection between Tabora on the Tanganyika Central Line and Mwanza on Lake Victoria, but an equally important link between the Kenya and Tanganyika systems was also laid between Voi and Moshi.

A good picture of these early days is given by a German map of Dar es Salaam which I have in my possession. According to the title, it was compiled by the German Survey Department in April 1913 but it also has the stamp of a Berlin bookseller on it, which implies it was freely available in Europe as well. How it was acquired by the Geographical Section of the British General Staff is not clear but it was obviously issued to His Majesty's Armed Forces, because it bears a military-type grid and an English reference legend. A further note confirms it was reprinted by the Ordnance Survey in 1915, from which one assumes that it was just in time for Smuts to use it during his campaign. A fascinating document, it confirms that Dar was still a small town at this time, and many areas which are now well-known suburbs were simply described as *palmen* (palms), *lichter busch* (light bush), or *dichter busch* (dense bush).

Certainly, Dar had a continental feel to it and the built-up area reflected a rectangular pattern of tree-lined streets. There were some fine buildings, too, prominent among which was the hospital on the sea front, the Lutheran Church overlooking the harbour, and the Kaiserhof Hotel, which subsequently became the New Africa Hotel. Many business buildings and residential houses were also of good quality and were excellent examples of German tropical architecture, their thick walls and shuttered windows giving off a distinct ambience. The incoming British officials must have been a bit stuffy, however, because the Casino—where the Germans had frolicked with enthusiasm—was turned into a government office and allocated to the Lands and Surveys Department. In later years it still felt strange to see the dance-floor full of drawing tables and it wasn't difficult to imagine Teutonic endearments being muttered into shell-like ears over a background of ghostly waltz music.

Fortunately, the new street names reflected a more romantic frame of mind and the main road in the middle of town, which was lined with flowering acacia trees, was happily christened Acacia Avenue. Other streets received names like Burton Street and Speke Street in honour of the well-known British explorers but some names were more contemporary and the liberating efforts of the South African Army were recognised by the creation of Smuts Street and van Deventer Street, the latter being named after the sturdy Boer general who had marched all the way from Moshi to Dodoma in 1916. Needless to say, these relics of South African military muscle caused much consternation among the ranks of local politicians when the heady days of independence arrived many years later and South Africa was perceived to be a racist threat to the African continent.

Urgent attention was also necessary in Dar to several pressing matters. As no self-respecting British colony could function without a golf course, immediate steps were taken to rectify this omission, using the ground behind the German cemetery on which the Allied troops had been camping. The Dar es Salaam Gymkhana Club thus came into being and an 18-hole golf course was laid out round it. The very name of the club is redolent of Empire, and it is a tribute to the architecture of the day that the clubhouse is still giving satisfaction to numerous members. The golf course wasn't bad, either, and though it suffered from the available ground being flat without any potential for water features, it was made very playable and the difficulty of getting grass to grow on the greens was solved by substituting 'browns' of brushed sand. The other matter, of course, was the absence of an Anglican church and similar energy was displayed in getting a handsome cathedral built in tropical style. The church was christened St. Albans and here again, it has catered for the community's needs in exemplary fashion for many years.

The first British Governor of Tanganyika was Sir Horace Byatt, who presided over the initial sorting-out until it was time to hand over to Sir Donald Cameron—a red-headed go-getter who gingered up the country to no small extent during his years at the helm between 1924 and 1931. My old friend, Geoff Baker, who arrived in Tanganyika in 1925, remembered him well and confirmed how energetically he stirred up slow-moving officials. He was also an exponent of indirect rule and was no great lover of the new settlers, who had either headed for the highland areas in the northern and southern parts of the country or had opted to grow sisal in the vicinity of Tanga and Morogoro. Cameron did encourage development, however, and his tenure saw the new town of Arusha being founded and the Great North Road being pushed southwards through the Southern Highlands, which stretched from Iringa on the edge of the escarpment to Tukuyu in the vicinity of Lake Nyasa.

Geoff himself went to the tea plantations in the Mufindi area and made his monthly journeys into Iringa on horseback. On the one occasion he visited Dar, he told me how he happened to meet Capt. Wilson—the surveyor who had surveyed the tea estates—and how the latter took him for the hottest and most vigorous walk of his life round the Oyster Bay area, which was still undeveloped bush in those days. Selander Bridge (named after the head of the Public Works Department) had still to be constructed over the Msimbazi Creek at that time and Oyster Bay showed little sign of becoming a major suburb.

A sense of the newness of the situation in East Africa in the years which followed World War One can be obtained from the papers of Walter Fryer, who was one of the first District Officers to begin work in Tanganyika when hostilities were concluded. Although English by birth and originally a schoolteacher by profession, Walter had a fair degree of African experience under his belt by the time he took up his appointment, having emigrated to South Africa before the war and subsequently taken part in the German South West Africa campaign—a dashing affair which saw South African troops led by Botha and Smuts defeat the incumbent Germans. Returning from this, he then volunteered to fight the Germans in East Africa and joined the South African contingent which fought its way across Tanganyika under the command of Smuts and van Deventer. During this process, the need for administrative control of the newly-conquered territory was soon felt and Walter became what was termed a 'Political Officer'. Naturally, this led to the possibility of staying on after the war was over and since he really liked what he had seen of East Africa, he lost no time in taking up the opportunity and made haste to bring his wife and children up from South Africa to join him. Initially based in Tabora, he was subsequently posted to a variety of stations and served in the Provincial Administration until his retirement in the 1930's.

It must have been a fascinating job because the first of the duties which he and his fellow District Officers had to fulfil was to make sense of the way the Germans had run their colony and to discover the customs and traditions of the various tribes which inhabited the country. Charged with the task of running a vast territory about which little was known, the Colonial Office and the Governor were desperate to find out more about the people they had to govern. At the same time, the flag had to be shown and the people had to be introduced to the British way of exercising authority.

Walter was thus in the position of being an administrative pathfinder in outlying parts of the country and on one of his early safaris, he found himself exploring the native kingdom of Ufipa, which lay between Lake Tanganyika and Lake Rukwa. Still a relatively unknown part of Tanzania, this area was difficult to get to and the only means of ingress was to take the train to Kigoma and then sail down the southern shore of Lake Tanganyika. This in itself was no mean feat as the lake was known for sudden storms and the local dhows were renowned for their propensity to capsize. Even the ambience of the lake was a little sinister and Walter noted that the blue hills surrounding the lake formed a huge and mysterious amphitheatre in which—to use his own words—*one unconsciously allows the mind to wander from the dark tragedies of the past enacted thereon to the fascinating possibilities which the future holds for this still little known corner of the world.*

Fortunately, on this safari he was able to avail himself of the services of HMS *Fifi*—a substantial 30-foot vessel which had been captured from the Germans. Powered by steam and mounted with a 2 pounder gun, it must have been a fine sight as it cruised the deep blue waters of the lake, though conditions on board must have been somewhat crowded during this particular trip. To start off with, there were 11 members of the crew in addition to the bwana and his retinue of 3 servants. But this was not all. The latter had brought their wives with them and there was a large quantity of stores, food and bedding. There must have been standing room only and the matter was apparently complicated by HMS *Fifi* being extremely skittish on the water and the ladies in question being poor sailors who apparently prayed non-stop to be back on the shore.

Eventually reaching a village on the southern shore of the lake, Walter relates how he and his servants marched inland, only pausing to exchange greetings with a couple of White Fathers who ran a mission nearby. There were no soldiers or police with him, and nothing could have been less representative of militant colonialism. As they marched, there were frequent pauses to talk to the indigenous locals and Walter made exhaustive notes as they went on the geography, vegetation, and customs of each village. His account of his travels makes lively reading, and his arrival at a place called Ngongo is worth recounting—again in his own words.

I was met by the chief man of the village and escorted in for the last half-mile by several hundred women, old and young. It was a point of honour with the Wakwa that every woman who could stand on her feet must turn out to welcome a visitor and while doing so, make that peculiar noise obtained by rolling the digit of the right hand between the lips and screaming to the full extent of their powerful lungs. Hence, headed by a capering horde of leaping and screaming dusky females, I arrived at the village and took my seat under the shade of an enormous baobab tree, by which time all the women had marshalled themselves into lines and got down on their knees with heads bowed to the ground and bodies moving from side to side in perfect rhythm as they continued to chant their songs of welcome, including my praises. I then had to call a halt to this as there appeared no chance of them pulling up of their own accord.

Once in the Rukwa Valley, one gets the distinct impression that Walter Fryer was conscious of treading in an undisturbed part of the Garden of Eden—save, of course, for the persistent presence of the tsetse fly, which he noted as one of biggest problems to face the new territory. He would have had vivid memories of the way that thousands of horses, oxen and mules had died during Smuts' campaign and spoke longingly of the day on which the fly menace might be eradicated. You cannot have game without the tsetse fly being near, however, and Walter found the Rukwa area to be a sportsman's paradise where game was spread in wanton profusion. (He actually typed *confusion* which one assumes was a slip of the mind or finger but could, one supposes, have also been factual. Can there not be a *confusion of elephants?*) Intentional or not, elephants were certainly there in great numbers and not only elephants but rhino, hippo, lion, leopard, and vast herds of zebra, whilst wild geese and ducks by the thousand lived and propagated along the banks of the lake.

Working as an amateur anthropologist, Walter found the Wafipa to be a quiet people, whose one desire was to be left alone, to eat, drink and enjoy the company of their women. Members of the tribe were anything but untameable savages and there were strong traditions of kinship, albeit laced with a great deal of superstition and utter belief in the power of the witch-doctor. In spite of this, he not only succeeded in getting to the bottom of their marriage and agricultural practices but also made notes on their system of property ownership, religion and the administration of tribal justice. How long it took him, one does not know but in spite of the pains he took to build a relationship with His Majesty's new subjects, a plaintive note enters his account on more than one occasion and at one point, he bemoaned the fact that the tribesmen had forgotten the abuses heaped on them by their past Chiefs and saw little difference between the types of foreign rule enforced on them. As he said ruefully, he doubted whether *the native has ever bothered to compare the present British policy of sympathy-coupled-with-firmness with the arrogant German policy of force and utter disregard for the interests of the natives themselves, or that he sees any difference in the two attitudes towards himself.*

Sympathy-coupled-with-firmness is in fact a coherent statement of British colonial policy at that time and Walter Fryer would have been fully conscious of this during his sojourn in Ufipa and in his subsequent postings. In 1925, he found himself based in Lushoto in the midst of the Usumbara Mountains, that majestic range which lies along the Kenya-Tanganyika border. His administrative duties also took him further north into the Pare (pronounced Paar-ay) Mountains, which lie between the Usumbaras and Moshi, and in May of that year, he penned some notes on Pare Customs and Laws to the Chief Secretary in Dar es Salaam. He was not quite as impressed with the Wapare people as he had been with the Wafipa and noted that they were *backward, intensely superstitious, heavy drinkers with barbarous customs, practiced the most revolting and repulsive rites, and leave one with the general idea that fear of offending the spirits of their ancestors is the one dominating influence of their lives. They were not moral in the European sense of the word, and few opportunities for debauchery, excessive drinking and dances that excite passions are allowed to pass unaccepted.* Later on, he revised this impression and pragmatically suggested they would make a valuable source of labour for the local sisal plantations.

This report on the Wapare tribe was obviously read with interest in Dar es Salaam and stirred up no less a personage than His Excellency the Governor himself, Sir Donald Cameron, who was not a devotee of energetic settlement. Reaching for his pen, the Governor was provoked into writing a minute in response to Walter Fryer's sensible suggestions in which he laid out the philosophy he expected his administration to follow. *Our object,* he wrote, *is not to turn the natives of this country into plantation labourers with as little delay as possible but to give them security of life and property, to eliminate gradually all that is vicious and contrary to natural justice and morality, and to teach the people to administer their own affairs under our guidance in due season.* For 1925, this is an exceptionally well-intentioned statement, though it is heavy with paternalism and lacks concern for economic development. As already noted, however, Cameron was an ardent exponent of indirect rule and considered that the Chiefs of the country should be encouraged to exert as much authority as possible.

This is an argument which can rage in many directions and as will be discussed later, there are several cogent reasons for questioning the wisdom of indirect rule as a method of governance. Ask any elected black politician whether he is keen to share power with a hereditary chief and the answer will be a resounding no—unless, of course, the respondent happens to be a chief himself. Back in 1925, though, the Governor had his way and Walter Fryer applied it to such good effect that the 22 chiefs in the Pare district were formed into a Tribal Council, which dealt with all civil and minor criminal cases. His subsequent report on the chiefs makes good reading and contains gems such as

> *German methods have left indelible marks on natives that today render the obtaining and sifting of reliable information an extremely difficult matter. The native still says just what he thinks you wish to hear and will refrain from saying what he thinks you do not wish to hear.*

More personal comments were made about individuals—for example

> Chambaga (one of the chiefs) *is a competent, cunning old man whom one cannot help liking*

and

> *In Mauya's house are stored all the skulls of the ancestors of the family and it is to him that all the descendants of the family go when in trouble of any kind to invoke the aid of the spirits*

Fryer was later posted to Shinyanga, inland from Lake Victoria, and Singida, situated more or less in the middle of Tanganyika. In both places, he delved deeply into the history and customs of the resident tribes and he became an authority on witch-doctors. In Shinyanga, for example, he found that *mgangas* known as fowl killers were very busy, taking a goat for their fee every time they diagnosed the source of trouble or sickness by studying the intestines of a newly-slain fowl. They could also make a woman pregnant, apparently, by prescribing a certain type of native medicine but the customary fee of a goat was non-refundable if no baby resulted. A more superior type of operator specialised in making it rain and an *mlosi* was another type of practitioner who specialised in poisoning people for a fee, either because the victim was looked on as undesirable or deemed to be exercising evil influence over the life of someone else. Twins, Walter found, were not looked on with favour by the Wasukuma and were disposed of at birth, always being buried in another district to avoid ill-fortune visiting the local Sultan.

In Singida, Walter then encountered the Wanyaturu tribe, who were passionately fond of smoking and drinking beer made from millet or honey. Although they practised agriculture, they were essentially cattle people, and prized their animals so much that they would only kill them on special occasions such as a birth, circumcision or death in the family. Accustomed to walking about naked before the arrival of the white man, the women now wore beads and aprons, the beads sometimes being draped round the body in parallel strings. Unlike the neighbouring Wasukuma, however, the advent of twins was looked on as reason for a great feast—the difference between adjacent tribes being quite remarkable and making the adoption of a unified legal code very tricky.

It is difficult to tear oneself away from Walter Fryer's papers, because he not only had a sharp eye but an equally sharp sense of humour. His description of the Wakwa tribe in the Rukwa Valley who manufactured and wore a garment made from coarse cotton and the Wapimbwe tribe who wore a garment made from the bark of the Milumba tree, are tokens of this and I bid a reluctant farewell to his papers with one last direct quote:-

> *Both these garments,* wrote Walter, *have their disadvantages as the cotton and bark get too heavy and warm in the summer season and in the rainy season, get too heavy and sodden. This leads to the garments being discarded on that account and I have often been amused to see the possessor of such a garment travelling naked and carrying her clothes on her head.*

It must have been fascinating to explore Tanganyika in those early days of British rule and get the country going again after the turmoil of World War One. Much of the exploring had to be done on foot and though the military had established a system of roads during the war, they were actually little more than tracks which quickly became overgrown. As soon as one left the railway line, therefore, it was a largely a matter of walking—a means of travelling which could only be accomplished with the aid of a column of porters bearing all the necessities of life in the way of tents, food, water, clothing, whisky, and medical supplies.

The country was rendered even more colourful during this early period by the discovery of alluvial gold along the Lupa River in the Southern Highlands. This sparked off what was probably the last of the world's major gold rushes and was conducted in the same type of fever which had inflamed California, Alaska, Australia and South Africa in turn. Would-be prospectors came pouring in from all parts of the world and converged on the Lupa, most of them having to walk through the bush in order to get there. Others came by ox-cart, horse or mule, and some by motorcycle or long-suffering car along rudimentary tracks or footpaths. Once on the Lupa, they spread themselves over a considerable area which had as its centre the small town of Chunya—a settlement which would not have been out of place in the Wild West. Very much a mining camp, its focal point was a rambling hotel known as 'The Diggers' Home', an architectural gem featuring a saloon with swing doors in the classic Western pattern. Whisky was a key lubricant of the diggings and Hugh Bailey, who joined the Tanganyika Police Force in 1924 and was stationed in Chunya, records how the miners would bring their pokes of gold to the Manager of the hotel, who would weigh them and extend an appropriate amount of credit in respect of board, lodging and liquor. The miner would then live like a king until his credit was exhausted, at which point he was shown the door and had to go back to his claim to obtain some more gold.

In the initial years of the gold-rush, the nearest town was Tukuyu, some 60 miles away, and essential supplies had to be ferried over to the miners by processions of porters. Naturally, the porters would stop and unload at the closer camps before going on to the ones furthest away, with the result that miners in the former category were not above 'borrowing' items which they fancied or had forgotten to order. The sight of a case of whisky must have been the ultimate temptation and it is related that more than one unhappy miner at the end of the line found his precious case of whisky contained nothing more than a series of IOU chits made out by his friends along the route. There was no hospital in Chunya, either, and any medical help which might be necessary had to come from Tukuyu as well. In this regard, an intrepid nurse known to one and all as Auntie May was known for her work in the goldfields, walking from mine to mine in order to care for sick prospectors.

In papers left to his daughter, Hugh Bailey tells a story about the time that one of the old Lupa die-hards belied this description and actually did die while staying at the Diggers' Home. His friends, suitably stricken, congregated in the bar before the funeral and someone had the idea of putting a bottle of whisky in the coffin to assist the deceased in his journey to the hereafter. This proposal was greeted with acclaim, a bottle was placed in the corpse's hand, and the lid was duly screwed down. The funeral then took place at the little cemetery with great ceremony, and the circle of mourners went off to the nearby camp of one of their number to continue grieving. They did this so assiduously, however, that their supply of liquor ran out while they were still going strong. Yes, you've guessed correctly! It was apparently the work of a moment to go back to the cemetery, re-open the coffin, take the whisky and get back to the party. And in case this doesn't suggest an atmosphere of sobriety, there was apparently another occasion when the mourners went through a complete funeral service without anyone realising they had forgotten to put the body in the coffin—an omission only discovered by the hotel manager when he went into the room where the deceased had been staying and found the body still lying on the bed.

By the time the 1930s arrived, the gold was beginning to run out and the Lupa had become almost respectable. By this time, the town of Mbeya had been established in the foothills, and a viable road system extended throughout the district. Most of the miners were only too glad to join the armed forces when World War Two came along and though some of the old prospectors stayed on and could be seen wandering round the bush in the hope of making one last big strike, the goldfields story was completely over by the 1950s. Auntie May was still a much loved resident of Mbeya when I was stationed there in 1956 but the hills around Chunya contained nothing more than the relics of old workings, and the only profitable activities conducted in that part of the region were centred around Lake Rukwa, where professional hunters like Bert Farren stalked elephants for a living. He was a well-known character and while I met him again in Durban when he was an old man, he was the very picture of the ultimate bush-fundi in Mbeya days as he drove through town in an open and very battered Land Rover, with his gun-bearer and camp cook hanging on for dear life.

Back in Dar es Salaam, life had settled down into a familiar colonial pattern by the time 1930 arrived. White men—all of them automatically falling into the classification of bwanas—were expected to wear a light suit to the office and the social system depended on leaving a calling card at the home of people you wished to meet. Rickshaws were an indispensable part of life and a typical European household would have a retinue of at least four servants—a houseboy, an *mpishi* (cook), a *dhobi* (laundryman), and a *shamba* boy (a gardener). The word 'boy', of course, was in common use for a male person who fell into the description of a native servant or labourer, and if this sounds condescending to modern ears, I think it was more of a convenient label than an expression of superiority. Like the word 'native', it became non-U rather quickly after World War Two but prior to that time, no one seemed to mind very much. Domestic service was a respectable calling in East Africa and strangely enough, it was an exclusively male preserve. The only local females who assisted domestically were *ayahs* (nursemaids), who were hired to look after babies and young children.

By this stage of Dar's development, the Governor (known as HE, aitch-ee, short for His Excellency) had been suitably housed in Government House—a new palace built in white Moorish style that dominated the harbour entrance and exuded a strong sense of Empire. A fully-fledged civil service was also in place and the administration of Tanganyika had been reinforced by a range of technical personnel which included doctors, engineers, vets, policemen, surveyors, railwaymen, judges, agricultural experts, geologists, foresters and so on. Their commercial equivalents were fully ensconced as well, and commercial houses such as Smith Mackenzie, the African Mercantile and Karimjee Jivanjee were household names. As a large and mainly Indian corps of clerical and administrative staff was required to keep this lot going, the overall addition to the population was considerable and its growth was further extended by a number of Germans coming back to Tanganyika to try their luck for a second time.

The recruitment of officials and commercial staff was a complex matter, however, and Bill Johnston's arrival in Tanganyika during the 1920's gives a good picture of the way the Crown Agents went about their business of providing the Empire with the skilled manpower it required. It must have been something like the Army system of posting people to fill gaps wherever they occurred and not necessarily to where they wished to go. In Bill Johnston's case, it was nothing to do with the Empire at all because he actually applied for a job with Argentina Railways, which Britain had helped to build many years previously and with whom the Crown Agents still maintained a working relationship. Arrangements were concluded on this basis and he was about to sail for South America when he was asked out of the blue whether he would mind going to the Indian Railways instead. Since he was an adventurous young man who wanted to see the world, he agreed to this and was told to come back in a week's time to collect his ticket and luggage labels. When he did so, however, he found there had been another change of plan and this time, the Crown Agents asked him if he would be prepared to go to Kenya.

'All right,' he said, and this time he succeeded in boarding a ship and actually travelled to East Africa on it. He was then in the process of disembarking at Mombasa when a man arrived with a telegram from the Crown Agents asking him to stay on board and go to Dar es Salaam instead in order to join the Tanganyika Railways. Again, he agreed and mercifully, no further changes of plan were forthcoming. He stayed on for the next 30 years and became a senior figure in East African Railways and Harbours. As he said later, he was so glad to have found his ultimate place of employment that having to take off his shoes and roll up his trousers in order to get from the Dar harbour launch on to Tanganyika soil was the least of his problems. He had finally arrived!

My own father reached East Africa in 1930, having decided to give up his seagoing career with the Bullard King shipping line, which plied between South Africa and India. He did in fact want to join the Durban Pilot Service and had been provisionally accepted, though it was a question of waiting for dead men's shoes. Needing stopgap employment, therefore, he walked along the wharf and applied to TB Davis for a stevedoring job. Liking his Master's ticket, TB's office was glad to have him—but not in Durban. They wanted him in Mombasa. So he took the job and I still have his letter of appointment, whereby he was engaged as a stevedore foreman on a salary of 600 shillings per month on condition that he found his own passage money to get there. Employers did not believe in spoiling staff in those days and if you wanted a job, you had to like it or lump it.

While Mombasa of that era was certainly more primitive than Durban, I think he must have liked it because he was soon in contact with the girl destined to be my mother with a view to getting married. Bless her, she did agree but by the time she was due to travel to East Africa, he had been transferred to Dar es Salaam and it was a case of joining him in Dar, where they were duly married by the District Commissioner—or would have been if the DC had not been away on safari. In point of fact, one of his District Officers had to officiate, having first looked up his law books to check he was properly authorised to conduct the ceremony. He was, apparently, but the slight uncertainty gave rise to a long-standing family joke about my legitimacy.

Now, it may sound like paradise to modern ears but there was no income tax in Tanganyika at this time. This was not indulgence on the part of the imperial system but more a case of recognising there were too few potential taxpayers to make collection worthwhile. In addition to this, there were precious few services provided and expatriates had to be hardy to survive the constant heat and peril of catching some tropical disease. There was more than a touch of the White Man's Grave about the whole thing, and people were encouraged to retire at the age of 45 or whenever they had completed 20 years service. Malaria, dysentery and blackwater fever were common illnesses, and everybody went around looking yellow from their daily doses of quinine. A range of crops may have been grown up-country but there were no fresh vegetables in Dar apart from the efforts of a Chinese market gardener on the way to Kurasini. The water was heavily chlorinated, and everybody—man, woman and child—wore topees (solar helmets) when they went outside between 8am to 4pm in order to avoid getting sunstroke. Mosquitoes were a problem after dark and most adults wore long sleeves and a pair of soft boots in the evening to protect them from being bitten. The standard of accommodation was not luxurious, either, and though housing for senior personnel was generally provided by the Government and commercial employers at a nominal rental, facilities were basic. Long leave, usually 6 months at a time, was granted after each 4-year stint as an entrenched right on health grounds, and it was believed the tropics would break both mind and body if one stayed too long without a break.

Further danger arose from the conviction of Dar's white inhabitants that dehydration was the worst death of all. There was a consistent amount of drinking, and thanks were given daily for the revival of the German brewery and its famous Indian Pale Ale, known to one and all as 'IPA'. Aside from beer, the staple drinks of the community were probably whisky and gin, the former being drunk with soda and the latter with tonic, lime or orange squash. The 'sundowner' was a social ritual which most people followed and hostesses vied with each other to accompany the evening libations with *toasties,* small fingers of toast spread with something savoury. Culturally, there was only one movie-house in town, predictably named the Empire Cinema, and people would show up there on Saturday night in full evening dress. The late show never started until 9pm in order not to interfere with the conclusion of dinner, and the venue maintained a full bar for the convenience of its patrons. This was well and good, but someone was sure to kick over an empty beer bottle at a particularly dramatic point in the film and it would roll relentlessly down the auditorium floor with loud chinking noises. The only alternatives to a flickering film were occasional productions by the Dramatic Society, choir practice at the Anglican cathedral or a dance at one of the clubs. In spite of the heat, the latter were well supported when they occurred and the 'mess jacket' (colloquially known as a 'bum freezer') was the favoured article of male attire, being regarded as more formal than a white dinner jacket.

So it was a rather primitive way of life compared to living in Europe, made worse by the financial global crash of 1929 and a subsequent tightening of belts. The incumbent Governor—who happened to be Sir Stewart Symes by the time my parents were married in 1932—had to run the country on a shoe string budget and people adjudged non-essential found themselves being made redundant. My parents were blissfully happy, though, in their rented flat above Kassim's grocery shop in Acacia Avenue, and I could not have been conceived in a more central location or a hotter one, bearing in mind that the historic event occurred in February 1933 during the build-up to the long rains. The nearby figure enshrined in the Askari Memorial—a dramatic and very excellent statue of a black soldier in full battle mode erected in honour of the Great War combatants—must have looked down benignly from his vantage point in the round traffic island at the head of Acacia Avenue. Perhaps he even saluted!

Obviously, there were compensations to living in Dar es Salaam, one of them being that working hours were 8am to 12 noon and 2pm to 4pm. Everyone went home to lunch, and the sport-minded sector of the bwana population could be on the first tee or the tennis courts shortly after their offices had closed in the afternoon. Yachting was popular, too, and the Yacht Club moorings were right in the centre of the landlocked harbour, conveniently close to the Dar es Salaam Club. The latter, a white building with a large verandah, was the social pinnacle of town and membership was restricted to senior officials and commercial managers only. A little stiff, perhaps, but the 'Dar Club' was an essential part of the colonial fabric. Its cuisine was pretty good, too, and apart from the open-air court in the grounds of Government House, it boasted the only squash court in the whole country. It was more social than sporting, however, and the main sporting activities of golf and tennis were conducted at the Gymkhana Club, where cricket and even rugby flourished as well. Visits by an occasional British warship were always good for a contest and I remember years later meeting a retired Rear-Admiral at a function in London, who pricked his ears up sharply at the information I was home on leave from Tanganyika. 'I first went to Dar es Salaam as a midshipman on a cruiser in 1924,' he confided nostalgically. 'We played rugger against you chaps and got fearfully pissed at the Club afterwards.'

While these stirring events were in progress, the indigenous population of Tanganyika lived much as they had always done—only far more peaceably.

No longer disturbed by the initial shock of being colonised and now protected against tribal wars, they went on happily with their traditional methods of subsistence agriculture, tending their cattle and making sundry alcoholic beverages from whatever grew in their district. The principle of indirect rule constituted a very light yoke and the whole country, with the exception of urban areas and the ex-German plantations, was regarded as subject to native law and custom. Unlike the German system, it was now impossible for indigenous inhabitants to be forcibly dispossessed of land they customarily occupied and if a prospective expatriate farmer wanted to establish a farm in Tanganyika, the best he could get would be a long lease from the Government, which was only granted if no tribal interests were affected.

Going back to the personal side of this history, my parents had no sooner become used to Dar es Salaam than they were transferred to Mombasa. This was a very different kettle of fish to Dar es Salaam, the main difference being Mombasa's undiluted Britishness and its status as the gateway to Kenya Colony—the jewel of the British Empire. Technically, it may have fallen within a strip of land leased from the Sultan of Zanzibar but no one was too bothered about this and the picturesque island city was completely and undeniably British. Imperial echoes of the past were still visible and I remember well the imposing statue of Sir William Mackinnon, the Chairman of the British East Africa Company, which stood in a dusty park in front of the main Mombasa Post Office in the older part of the town. The public buildings that were erected in the early days had a beautifully Victorian ambience to them and as late as the 1950s, there was still a red letterbox in the old residential area which was erected in Queen Victoria's day and had VR engraved on it. For many years, too, one could see the tram lines that ran up the hill towards town from Fort Jesus and the Mombasa Club. I allude to them as tram lines but trams as such never ran on them—the early bwanas and their memsahibs were conveyed through the blazing heat on little trolley cars propelled by sweating, black manpower. Shades of Empire indeed!

It's always a good thing to have been on the winning side in a war and certainly, in Kenya's case, it had resulted in a new influx of settlers and money. The status of Kenya as a full colony was readily perceived as more inviting than that of its neighbours and it grew apace in the 1920s. The 'Kenya settler' became a specific breed of colonist and its members were a lively lot—ready, willing and able to give the Colonial Office in London a hard time at any perceived lack of consultation. There was, in fact, a glorious occasion on which they resented an edict from Whitehall so much that they kidnapped the Governor and incarcerated him for several days in a rural retreat until they received a satisfactory response from the British Government. It must have been the most good-natured kidnapping imaginable, however, because the ringleaders were all on good social terms with the Governor and took pains to ensure that his temporary prison boasted some excellent trout fishing.

My friend, Christopher Baker—the brother of Geoff Baker who went to Tanganyika—was typical of young British males of good family who went to Kenya during this period. Relishing every step of his outward voyage on the s.s. *Randfontein,* he arrived in 1928 and worked in the Mount Elgon area as a trainee farmer, later moving to a sisal farm in Athi River. After that, he became a coffee planter and followed this by digging wells in Masailand. Adventurous to the core, he then joined a motorised safari which pioneered the overland road route between Nairobi and Johannesburg, driving a small convoy of Buicks over a series of unformed roads and covering a distance of 7000 miles in a matter of five months. Even more adventurously, he married a spirited Kenya girl who was wont to make an entrance to the Muthaiga Club dance floor by turning a series of cartwheels in full evening dress. I'm sure they would have gone on to be a vital part of the Kenya scene but unfortunately, he developed a stomach complaint which was only solved by opening him up at the Maia Carberry Hospital, taking out his innards, washing them and putting them back again. The treatment worked but he was advised to go back to England for the sake of his health.

Meanwhile, back in Mombasa, it had been decided to construct new deep-water quays at Kilindini, a decision that changed the face of the town completely and lifted it to the status of a major port. New development took place all the way along Kilindini Road towards the new harbour, which spawned a complex of warehouses, offices and sheds. Construction work on the quays took a considerable time and I am indebted to my father for the revelation that the engineers and builders employed by Paulings, the well-known contractor, were so enthusiastic in seeking after-hours female company that their temporary quarters became known as *Pauling's Toolbox.*

The rest of Mombasa expanded in all directions as well and Chris Baker took a photograph of the celebrated Nyali Bridge while it was being built across the Tudor creek to the northern coast beyond. At the time, it was the longest pontoon bridge in the world and may still be so. It has been much photographed since but if you have not seen it, try and imagine a bridge made of a number of different sections resting on a series of floating pontoons far below. The sections were jointed together and as their angles to each other kept changing according to the state of the tide, there was always a pronounced jolt as a car moved from one section to the next. It looked in many ways just like a giant Meccano set but it actually worked very well and to travel across it gave one a sense of definite achievement. The bridge was, I remember, sensitive to vibrations because there were big notices at either end advising that troops must break step while marching across it. Whether the notice is still there, I do not know but the spectacle of a whole battalion of the King's African Rifles having to abandon their customary precision must have been a sight to behold.

In those days, Mombasa was an island city, which was only connected to the mainland by the causeway built to accommodate the Kenya-Uganda railway line. The main road leading inland also ran along this causeway and there were no other physical links to the mainland apart from the new Nyali bridge. Access to the southern coast of Kenya was by means of the Likoni ferry, which utilised a series of ramshackle vessels that played ducks and drakes with the incoming and outgoing ships. The ferry operation has since become a major traffic carrier but back in the 1930s, it was pretty quiet on the far side of Kilindini harbour and the vegetation was only broken on the inland edge of the creek system by the Port Reitz Hotel, which was a great place for official and unofficial honeymooners.

My parents settled into the Mombasa scene in early 1933 and set up home in a *banda* (a small house with a palm-thatched roof) in the suburb of Mbaraki, which was the logical place for junior people connected with the harbour to live. It might not have been a palace but they had servants and a lively social life that was only diminished by my impending arrival. This duly occurred at the Mombasa Nursing Home, a pleasant establishment which was situated near the golf course and looked out over the rollers coming in from the Indian Ocean—as fine a place in which to be born as you can imagine.

What Mombasa was like in 1933 can be answered with some accuracy because my mother kept a copy of the *Mombasa Times* in which the announcement of my birth proudly appeared. Ominously, the main story was all about the way that the Reichstag elections had resulted in an overwhelming Nazi victory and there was a picture of Adolf Hitler on the front page. I still have the newspaper—yellowing a little and showing one or two traces of having been nibbled by white ants—and it gives a vivid snapshot of this corner of the Empire at that time. Its full name, incidentally, was the *Mombasa Times and East Coast Herald* and it billed itself as *The Only European-owned Newspaper Published on the Coast of Kenya*. This seems to imply that there were other newspapers around but if there were, God alone knows what they could have been. The date of this particular issue was 14 November 1933 and the price was 20 cents, which was the equivalent of twopence in English coinage.

The front page is almost completely taken up by events in Europe and the headline is HITLER'S GREAT VICTORY, relating not only to the Reichstag elections but to the simultaneous plebiscite which had been put to the German population, asking them whether they approved of Nazi policy. One can only imagine that the question must have been put to the people by a brown-shirted army of Nazi enforcers because the answer was overpoweringly affirmative. According to the official figures, 40 million people out of 43 million were said to have voted yes and the remaining 3 million answers were described as invalid. There is no mention of any dissenting votes at all and it does not seem to have occurred to the Nazis that this may have looked too good to be true.

The newspaper does not dwell on this, however, and there is considerable light relief in the form of the accompanying front-page advertisements. Not only is there an invitation to stay at the Norfolk Hotel in Nairobi, but there is also a notice inserted by Whiteaways, the leading shop in Mombasa for ladies' clothes, which was offering *Brasknicks* to the public for Shs. 9/50—the item in question being defined as the very last word in dainty underwear, combining brassiere and knickers in one garment. Certainly, in the humid heat of Mombasa, underwear would have to be dainty but lady readers must judge for themselves whether knickers fashioned from fine celanese locknit fabric were cool or not. The brassiere part of it, made from the latest ecru shade lace, certainly sounds quite airy and was promoted as adjustable for wear with backless frocks. What more in the way of fun could a young lady want?

This is reinforced by the newspaper's account of the town's social and sporting life. The Manor Hotel, probably the poshest establishment in Mombasa at this time, was advertising a dance and so was the Palace Hotel, music in the latter case being provided by the band of the *ss. Ubena*—a German liner which happened to be in port. Then there was notice of a water polo match to be held against a team from a visiting French cruiser and also an announcement of the date on which the Rowing Club was going to have its next practice. A long list of golfing results shows the Mombasa Golf Club to have been well patronised and the roster for inter-club tennis matches listed fixtures for eight active clubs.

Fascinatingly, Wilson Airways, (the precursor of East African Airways), had an advertisement in the paper informing the public with pride that their new 6-seater passenger aeroplane was now operational and was making weekly flights to Nairobi on Fridays and to Tanga, Zanzibar and Dar es Salaam on Wednesdays. Fares were quite modest, too—the one—way fare to Nairobi, for example, being quoted at Shs.80, which would have been 4 British pounds at the time.

Equally fascinating was the advertisement placed by the Tangana Garage, who put out this irresistible invitation to potential customers:-

> We have in stock a large selection of Reconditioned secondhand cars, which if desired can be repainted in any colour scheme to suit the most fastidious.

As no one in their right mind would have thought of trying conclusions with the Mombasa-Nairobi road at this time, one can only assume that these cars were a lot of old bangers that had been running round the island for years. If Mombasa people wanted to take their cars with them when they went up-country, they certainly didn't drive them but put them on the train.

Up-country cars were a different matter, of course, and the Kenya box-body was emerging as the type of vehicle which was essential to farmers or anyone who lived out of town. You acquired one of these estimable conveyances by buying the chassis and engine of a big V-8 American car and then having a body made for it by a carpenter out of good solid timber, preferably teak or a similar hardwood. The body would typically be in the form of a wooden box containing seats and numerous stowage compartments, with the rear windows closed off with expanding metal—an iron mesh with wide spacing that made for maximum ventilation. If it rained, you could draw green canvas curtains across the windows and lash them to cleats set in the framework. Spare petrol was usually carried in a drum which sat in the back, and if this sounds like the original jalopy, this is not necessarily true. Most of them were carefully made and the woodwork was oiled and polished regularly. My father built one himself on a Chevrolet chassis and though it was a little heavy by the time he had finished with all the carpentry, it served us well and I even learned to drive in it.

Leaving aeroplanes and cars aside, however, the main business of the town comes across very clearly as shipping. Half the newspaper is taken up with advertisements and announcements by the major shipping companies, with dates of sailings and fares to Europe. You could, if you were so inclined, travel to England first class by *Union Castle* for £55 and if you were prepared to go third class, this would cost you £34. Second class as such did not exist and though third class was eventually rechristened tourist class to make it sound more attractive, it was generally located in the stern and its passengers were not allowed to gatecrash the more forward precincts of the vessel, which were dedicated to the higher fare-payers.

Union Castle was very much the major passenger line serving East Africa at this time and you could opt to go to Europe either through the Suez Canal and the Mediterranean or round the Cape via South Africa. The news value of a scheduled sailing was considerable and my newspaper, for example, contains the entire passenger list of the *Dunluce Castle,* which was due to sail a couple of days later. The list takes up a full half page and would not only have been read with interest by intending passengers but by their shore-bound creditors, who kept a wary eye out for chancers about to skip the country without paying their bills. Other forms of financial hanky-panky obviously went on as well and there is a somewhat plaintive footnote to the Union Castle advertisement, notifying potential travellers that up-country cheques could not be accepted unless endorsed by a local bank.

The other big British passenger line was *The British India Steam Navigation Company,* known to all and sundry as *BI.* These black and white vessels conducted a regular service between India, Great Britain, East Africa and South Africa, and were known for serving wicked curries every lunch time. Then, if you didn't insist on travelling under a British flag, there was a wide choice of German, Italian, French and Dutch liners. What a way it was to travel—each ship had a range of stewards to cater for their passengers' wants, four meals a day were served (including a substantial afternoon tea), and drinks were cheap due to no duty being payable outside national waters. There was no rush and bustle, either, and a three-week voyage to Europe via the Med or a five-week voyage via the Cape was guaranteed to be relaxing.

The cargo-handling side of the shipping scene in Mombasa was very important, too. All Kenya's imports and exports passed through Kilindini harbour and there was much business for shipping agencies, stevedoring firms and clearing-and-forwarding companies. Britain's Merchant Marine was still pre-eminent in terms of world trade during this period and the most frequent visitors to Mombasa were those sturdy workhorses of the seas belonging to the Clan Line, the Harrison Line, and the Ellerman-and-Bucknall Line. Sundry foreign and coastal vessels, tramp steamers, colliers and tankers also frequented the harbour and links to the Far East—somewhat ominously in the light of future events—were maintained by the Japanese, who usually had at least two of their vessels in the harbour at any one time.

As a final word on this particular issue of the *Mombasa Times,* mention must be made of the wireless programmes that were advertised. (Unless you were American, nobody used the word *radio*). The choice was fairly basic— you could either listen to the Empire Broadcasting Service from London or to the local service from Nairobi. The former, which required a decent short wave wireless set to cope with the atmospherics that interpolated themselves between London and East Africa, was available for four hours a night and Nairobi for three. Assuming you succeeded in getting London loud and clear, you would then have heard the time signal from Big Ben, followed by the BBC World News and then a succession of musical programmes. And if this wasn't excitement enough, one could switch to Nairobi for a shorter version of the same musical programmes but with the addition of some local news, a weather forecast and a half hour devoted to the Indian community.

So there it is—a snapshot in time of a bustling colonial city on the eastern coast of Africa in 1933. No backwater by any means, the port hummed with activity and business was improving rapidly after the enforced slowdown following the Wall Street crash of 1929. In addition, Mombasa had considerable strategic significance and was regarded as essential to Britain's control of the Indian Ocean. The harbour and its surrounding comforts were well-known to the Royal Navy, and *God Save the King* concluded every movie that was screened at each of Mombasa's two cinemas. The Union Jack flew proudly from Government buildings and the spit and polish of the *King's African Rifles,* known to all and sundry as the KAR, was much admired. People might have joked about the personnel of the KAR having black privates, but they were very proud of their soldierly appearance.

Obviously, I don't remember much about my first few years but the family records show that I was christened in Mombasa's Anglican Cathedral, a very fine example of tropical architecture. It must be remembered in this context that both the Anglican and Roman Catholic churches were major players in East Africa's colonisation and had exerted considerable influence throughout the process. Without their missionary zeal in the early days, matters would have proceeded more slowly and less surely. The development of Swahili into a widely-used tongue, for example, is largely due to the efforts of Bishop Steere, who published his authoritative work on the grammar in 1870. I still have an updated edition in my possession, which was used as a textbook by generations of Government officials who had to pass examinations in the language in order to get a rise in salary.

As most people know, Swahili is the *lingua franca* of East Africa and the Congo, and it is doubtful whether development of the region could ever have been achieved without the use of this elegant language. It wasn't only a matter of the early colonists communicating with the local inhabitants but more a case of the different tribes needing a means of communicating with each other. Though the use of English is now more widespread than it used to be, Swahili is still in common use and in Tanzania particularly, has been developed into an advanced form—so advanced in fact that Tanzania's neighbours have difficulty in understanding it. Without delving into its etymological basis, a very simple definition will tell you that it is a mixture of Bantu and Arabic, pronounced with Italian vowels and English consonants. It's a very logical language, too, though English speakers find it difficult to cope with grammatical changes occurring at the beginning of a word instead of the end. There is also initial confusion with the fact that *m* and *n* occur by themselves as a syllable without any vowel being involved. *Mzima*, (good), is pronounced exactly as written and you simply make a *mmm* sound before going on with the rest of the word.

Many bwanas and their memsahibs only went as far as learning kitchen Swahili and confined themselves to domestic instructions. Certainly, in 1933 the only Europeans in East Africa who spoke good Swahili were Government officials, KAR officers and church functionaries. The rest all spoke the kitchen variety, centred round the office, home and garden. Communication by this means was thus fairly rudimentary, as may be evident from the story about the old days in Mombasa when the banks opened for business in the early 1900s. First on the scene, apparently, was the National Bank of India and while it was the only bank in town, it was a simple matter to tell the office boy to go to the *banki*. Then along came Barclays (Dominion, Colonial and Overseas) and now there were two banks. So the former became known as the *banki kubwa*, (the big bank), and the latter as the *banki ndogo*, (the little bank). This was fine but problems came to a head when the Standard Bank arrived on the scene. The tale goes that one of Mombasa's early businessmen, desiring to send a document to Standard Bank, was having a busy morning and found it difficult to explain where his trusty factotum should go. 'No, not the *banki kubwa*' he is reported to have said. 'No, not the *banki ndogo*. Oh, hell, what do I call it? Go to the *shensi banki.*' Well, this was not very complimentary to poor old Standard because the word *shensi* means a person of low breeding and unreliable behaviour. But, according to my father, the label stuck for some time. (I may be wrong about the order in which the various banks were established and apologies are in order if I have rendered the tale inaccurately. Certainly, no disrespect to the Standard Bank is intended and their role in providing a service to East Africa over the years has been impeccable).

As always happens with languages, the younger generation of bwanas and memsahibs were much better at getting their tongues round Swahili than their parents and most children picked up a fair degree of fluency from their *ayahs*. I still remember the jingle that was taught to me by one of these patient girls, wrapped in her bright *kanga* (a garment fashioned out of a large square of material):-

Moja, mbili, tatu
Simba nakula viatu
Viatu nalia
Simba kimbia
Moja, mbili, tatu.

I taught this to my own children and grandchildren years later and I will never forget the expression on my young grandson's face when he pressed me for a translation and heard the English equivalent. Perhaps it doesn't come through as the most intellectual poem in the world but you must judge for yourself. It goes like this:-

One, two, three
The lion eats the shoes
The shoes cry
The lion runs away
One, two, three.

OK, maybe it's not intellectual but it caused me to fall asleep in my pram—and lots of other children as well.

Looking back from the fullness of time, I think that life in the Mombasa of this era was pleasant and stable for all its inhabitants, which certainly made a change from its previous history of warfare and oppression. The three races who lived there, (officially identified as Europeans, Asians and Africans), co-existed quite happily and lived within their own communities, liaising with the other sectors as and when necessary. I wouldn't have said that there was much racial discrimination as such; any discrimination there may have been was more a reflection of the prevailing social conditions than any feeling of superiority. Today, you might think it shocking that a Samburu tribesman, resident in his own country, could not join the Mombasa Club but at the time, the idea that he might wish to do so was completely inconceivable. It just wasn't a practical proposition and the contingency did not arise. In fact, the class-conscious British of that era probably exercised more discrimination among themselves than was ever exhibited to the two other races. If you were a junior official or a lowly member of the commercial community, you had even less chance of getting into the Mombasa Club than the Samburu tribesman.

As the truly aristocratic black sheep of their families all tended to live up-country, it is probably fair to say that social rank in Mombasa depended on what you did for a living. A husband's occupation was a badge of identity that was worn by their wives in varying states of satisfaction or envy. How much people earned was a great topic of conversation at morning tea parties, and the Government Staff List—which contained details of appointments and salary scales—was a favourite work of reference among civil service wives. Commercial salaries were more confidential but this very fact aroused the most intense curiosity and speculation.

Given that the English class system had transplanted itself to a small community, a certain amount of snobbery was probably inevitable and a story which did the rounds during this period was symptomatic of this. The tale goes that a senior official acquired a young wife and as so often happens in the tropics, made passionate love to her one night. Bathed in perspiration but still obsessed by social status, she was then inspired to question him.

'Tell me, dahling,' she is reputed to have asked, 'do B grade civil servants do this as well?'

'I suppose so,' he replied. 'Why do you ask?'

'Well, it's far too good for them. You must see that they stop doing it immediately.'

Talking of which, there was always a chronic shortage of young women in East Africa, a fact which led the younger men to spend a lot of their leisure time in clubs, playing some vigorous sport until sundown and then drinking freely until it was time to go back to the accommodation they shared with other young men—usually referred to as a *mess* or a *chummery.* Then they would dine on the burnt offerings which their loyal domestic staff had managed to preserve, have a nightcap or two, and retire under the mosquito net until early morning tea signified the advent of another day. This was a fairly standard life style and as can be imagined, a single girl in the East Africa of this era was guaranteed instant popularity. Even the plainest nursing sister was given a good time and had the chance of making an excellent marriage—though not necessarily to a man of her own age. The holy state of matrimony was regarded as fitting for men of relative seniority only and young men were severely discouraged from marrying until they had completed at least one four-year tour of duty.

The trouble with this was that older men tended to become set in their ways by the time they reached marriageable age and found it difficult to relinquish their bachelor habits. My parents had a favourite story about a friend of theirs, who had been a confirmed bachelor for a long time and then suddenly married somebody's widow—probably as the result of a whisky-inspired proposal.

'How do you like married life, Joe?' inquired my father when they met at work a week or two later.

'Oh, all right,' replied the new husband ardently. 'She seems to be quite a good woman.'

In retrospect, it is probably true to say that Mombasa-ites led a life which was quite separate from the rest of the colony, which was referred to as 'up-country'. Nairobi, with its clubs, hotels and racecourse, may have been the social centre of East Africa but aside from occasional visits on 'local leave', Mombasa residents tended to stick to their own tropical world. One can readily understand this because it was not only different scenically but had a much longer history. I will return to it in a later chapter but for the time being, I will close this chapter with a story about Fort Jesus—the incredibly romantic building next to the Mombasa Club near the entrance to the old harbour. As far as I know, the story is true and may even have involved one of my playmates, who returned from Sunday School and told his mother he had been taught a song about Fort Jesus. A little puzzled by this apparent departure from the junior hymnal, she queried him gently.

'How does it go, dear?' she asked.

'I'll sing it for you, shall I?'

'Yes, please.'

'*Stand up, stand up, Fort Jesus,*' he carolled.

CHAPTER 3

THE MIDDLE YEARS

By the mid-1930s, East Africa was more or less settled. The economic crisis and subsequent depression were over and the pioneers who had shaped East Africa's early development had either died or retired. A new breed of settlers, administrators and businessmen took over and a greater degree of sophistication came into vogue. It wasn't just East Africa in which this occurred, either—the whole continent of Africa experienced a decade of stability. This was due to the various parts of the British Empire having become more closely integrated and it was remarked by more than one contemporary writer that you could travel round the world by sea and be greeted at each port by a pilot boat flying a British flag. This was even more noticeable in the air and the story of Imperial Airways, which served Africa, India and the Far East, is a fascinating one. Carrying letters as well as passengers, its fleet of modern aircraft not only revolutionised travel but introduced the concept of 'air mail' as a practical proposition. Tie-ups with Australia and New Zealand through QANTAS (Queensland and Northern Territory Aerial Services Limited) and TEAL (Tasman Empire Airways Limited) extended the Empire link further and the first experimental batch of air mail letters sent from London to Sydney in 1931 arrived in the record time of 26 days.

Famously, Imperial's first long-distance fleet used on the Africa leg consisted of four Handley Page H.P.42 aircraft, which were specially designed for the airline and first took to the air in 1930. These four-engine biplanes flew from Croydon down the length of Africa in a series of hops and passengers were accommodated at night in hotels built specifically for this purpose. In Mbeya, for example, there was a large building next to the grassy landing strip which comprised its airport, and new arrivals in later years could never understand why old timers referred to it as 'the hotel'. But this is what it was in 1932 in the days when aeroplanes were unable to fly long distances without refuelling or resting crews. It may seem a slow way of travelling by today's standards but what a pleasure it must have been to stretch the legs, have a hot bath and a proper dinner at the end of a long day in the air. Not that travelling in the HP 42E, as it was known, was particularly arduous. For one thing, the cruising speed was only 100 miles an hour (160 kph) and you always had a panoramic view of the terrain underneath. It wasn't exactly crowded, either, as the maximum number of passengers was 24 and the accommodation appears from contemporary photographs to have featured a set of comfortable armchairs arranged round the walls of the two cabins. Each aircraft had a name starting with 'H' and the four planes used on Empire journeys were called Hannibal, Horsa, Hanno and Hadrian.

The airline industry was developing rapidly at this time, however, and further advances in aviation soon saw the Short Empire flying boat come into service on Imperial's routes to South Africa and Australia. This graceful bird of the skies made its first flight in 1936, and 42 of them were built at Short's factory in Rochester. The first ones carried 5 crew and 17 passengers at a top speed of 174 knots (320kph) and a through service from Southampton to South Africa was first offered in 1937. This involved stops at Marseille, Rome, Brindisi, Athens, and Alexandria, followed by a series of legs down the Nile to Port Bell and Kisumu on Lake Victoria. Initially, passengers were then transferred to land-based aircraft but later, the flying boat service went on to Lake Naivasha and thence to Mombasa, Dar, Beira, Durban and finally Johannesburg, where it landed on the Vaal Dam. We are told that the worst part of the journey was the 60 mile stretch of road between Vaaldam and Johannesburg, which had more bumps than the flying boats ever experienced.

Naturally, the great talking point of this period was the abdication of King Edward VIII. Distance away from Britain was no bar to the strong feelings engendered by the crisis, and the memsahibs of East Africa followed the situation closely. I was a little young to realise the implications of the affair but the witticism which went around at the time was related to me by my father some years later. Based on the fact of Mrs. Simpson having been married twice before, it was apparently retailed with glee in the clubs and pubs that the lady in question was alleged to have said 'Well, he may be Edward the Eighth to everyone else but he's only John Thomas the Third to me.'

Fortunately, I was immune to scurrilous anecdotes of this type due to my tender years and was more concerned with fitting into the succession of schools to which I was sent. This may result in an autobiographical flavour creeping into this part of the story but having been a child in East Africa during the 1930s and 1940s, it is impossible not to have a young bwana's perspective on that period. While a lot of impressions and news of events did trickle down, they registered on a personal basis and my description of those middle years is obviously coloured by this.

Certainly, the first dozen years of my life were somewhat unsettled because my parents kept moving up and down the East African coast in response to the staffing needs of my father's Company. Though he was primarily based in Mombasa, there was always the need to fill in gaps at the other East African branches caused by someone going on leave, falling ill, resigning or dying. As a result, we moved from Mombasa to Dar es Salaam at least twice and there was also a spell in Tanga, the other main port of Tanganyika, situated south of the Kenya border.

Home in Mombasa was a house in Cliff Avenue, a long tree-lined road that led from the town centre to the eastern part of the island. The large tropical houses in the street went back to the early days of European settlement and the grounds were large in size, typically being about an acre (4000 square metres) in size. This was not solely due to a desire for space but was also prompted by the fact there was no water-borne sewerage and each house had to be served by a septic tank that was liable to overflow, especially in the rainy season. Effective soakage required large grounds and in addition to this, there was also a need to accommodate the various outbuildings deemed necessary for civilised existence. These typically included the servants' quarters, a corrugated iron garage, and an outside kitchen connected to the house by a covered walkway. Aside from keeping smells and flies away from the main residence, the kitchen was sited in this manner in order to accommodate the standard cooking facilities of the time, namely a large wood-burning cast-iron range known as a Dover Stove. It was quite impossible for a white memsahib to manage this monstrous contraption and if she had tried, the heat of the fire in an already stifling climate would have rendered her unconscious in a matter of minutes. Every household therefore had to have an *mpishi* to handle the business of food preparation and within each kitchen of every home, there would be a cheerful black face presiding over a scene which seemed to come straight from *Dante's Inferno*. They did very well, too, and were quite adept at tasks like making bread, which would typically be baked in an old petrol tin or *debi*.

Betty Johnston—who had married Bill Johnston and lived in Dar es Salaam—remembered this dexterity well and had a favourite story about going to a coffee morning at the home of a very proper lady, who was known for serving delicious little sandwiches from bread made by her *mpishi*. 'Oh, come and see how he does it,' said the hostess one day after being complimented on her cook's prowess. Her guests duly followed her into the kitchen and there was the big fat *mpishi* hard at work, stripped to the waste and perspiring profusely in the heat and humidity of the hot season. Nothing particularly untoward, one might say, but what stopped the gaggle of ladies in their tracks and particularly their hostess, was the way he was kneading the dough under his armpit.

As far as I know, we did not have any similar occurrences in our Cliff Avenue home—a comfortable house made of coral blocks which had been plastered over and finished with whitewash. As befitted life in the tropics, the rooms were large with high ceilings, and there was a deep verandah along two full sides of the house which contained an assortment of cane furniture and an array of ferns in pots. The garden was full of *frangipani* trees which grew profusely but there were also some big trees that were suitable for climbing—an invitation that I found irresistible and caused me to do my reading on one particular branch that was especially comfortable. It never struck me that this might be deemed unusual by anyone with a European background but it seemed completely natural to me and I could never understand why my father kept muttering under his breath whenever he passed by.

Like most households at that time, we had a few chickens that wandered around the garden and it was always obvious when my mother had decided that roast chicken was to be on the menu. The cook would single out one of the chickens to be our dinner and I would have a good view from my vantage point of him chasing it round the garden to the accompaniment of much squawking. Once he caught it, he would then despatch the poor thing with one clean stroke of his knife across the windpipe, as befitted a good Mohammedan. It was quite a performance and though I would flinch from the spectacle today, I don't recollect being horrified at all. It was just the way that things were done and it was always intriguing to see how long the bird would keep running round in circles after losing its head.

It was while we were in the Cliff Avenue house that my parents became members of the Mombasa Club, which was situated near the old harbour under the watchful battlements of Fort Jesus. This was absolutely great because it not only gave my mother access to the Club's excellent library but gave me access to the salt water swimming pool at the bottom of the cliff. This was where I learned to swim at an early age and many hours were spent splashing around with other young striplings, while our mothers sat in the shade nearby and gossipped. As one of Mombasa's most enduring and prestigious institutions, there was a strict code of behaviour in the non-pool areas of the Club and I can still recall the utter hush that was insisted upon when I accompanied my mother to the library. It was exactly like going to church and the elderly Goan steward on duty would have been horrified at any utterance louder than a whisper.

In common with most of my swimming pool friends, I attended the Mombasa Junior European School, a pillar of learning which was located at the end of Cliff Avenue. Only tangled recollections of this stay in my mind, though I do remember joining the local Wolf Cub Pack and being proud of my dark green shirt. As traffic was light, one could cycle round the suburbs with impunity and one rather good ride was to follow the coast road round to the Swimming Club, which was situated under the coral cliffs on the channel leading to Kilindini Harbour. A raft was moored there and it was a satisfying challenge to dog-paddle out to it.

At this time, there was no secondary education for white children in Mombasa or Dar es Salaam. There were schools for African and Indian pupils but the needs of the different communities and their cultural backgrounds were deemed to be so dissimilar that integration was never considered. Furthermore, there was a conviction that living at the coast in a tropical environment was bad for white children above the age of eight and that it was held that their health would suffer in consequence. Hence, it was a choice between going to school up-country and being shipped off to Britain. In either case, this meant boarding school and one was made aware at an early age that this was on the horizon. A further complication was a strong belief in the merits of a British education and many children were sent back 'home', where they would be subject to control by their schoolmasters during term time and by any available aunts and uncles during the holidays. Nairobi did in fact have some good primary schools and it was possible at an early stage of Kenya's development to progress from these to good secondary schools in the shape of the Prince of Wales School and the Kenya Girls' High School. A fair proportion of people availed themselves of this option but initially, there was a body of thought that held local schooling to be a bit rough and ready—the attitude to Kenya youth being summed up in the jingle :-

Kenya born and Kenya bred,
Strong in the arm and soft in the head.

This is a little unfounded because the Prince of Wales School for boys was actually modelled on public school lines, and Lord Delamere—supported by Sir Edward Grigg, the Governor of Kenya—was instrumental in getting it established. The buildings were designed by none less than Sir Herbert Baker, the British Empire's best-known architect, and the concept was based on the well-known British public school of Winchester, where Sir Edward Grigg himself had been educated. The first Headmaster, Capt. Nicholson, came to Kenya from the Royal Naval College in Dartmouth and the new school was run along naval lines. The first stage was built in 1929-1930 and there were over 100 boys at the school when it finally opened in 1931.

The Kenya Girls' High School had similar origins and its establishment goes back to 1908, when it was known as the European Girls' School. Irrespective of its official name, however, this estimable establishment was the subject of one of Kenya's oldest jokes and the school was known to one and all as the *Heifer Boma*. Who coined the label, I am not sure but it was surely an act of genius. In case you need any explanation, I would confirm that the term *heifer* has its customary meaning of a young cow and the word *boma* means an enclosure within which cattle are herded for the night. Gallant, was it not? As a result, generations of Kenyan young ladies were collectively known as *heifers* and while this may not sound too flattering, it soon became a verbal badge worn with pride. While it may be true that Kenya's fresh air, sunshine and farm butter produced some fairly hefty specimens capable of clouting an obstreperous young male with some vigour, I'm glad to say the inmates were generally as dainty as you would find anywhere.

Fortunately—or unfortunately—for me, my parents thought that I was still too young to go anywhere before the war broke out and then after it had, it was neither easy nor desirable to go to Britain for a prolonged education. Some of my friends who were shipped off to Europe before 1939 were virtually marooned there and didn't see their mother and father again until after the war was over. It was the same story in Tanganyika—only more so, because the country was even more wild and woolly than Kenya and did not have an up-country capital city situated in the cool highlands. At primary school level, one could either go to the well-known school at Arusha run by Australian missionaries or to the Government Primary School at Mbeya in the Southern Highlands. If we had lived more permanently in Dar es

Salaam, maybe these schools would have featured in my life but as it was, I
went to the Mombasa Junior European School when we were in Mombasa
and to the Dar es Salaam Junior European School when we were in Dar.
The latter, I remember, was situated in a two-story house in Burton Street
and was run by a dynamic headmistress called Mrs. Zimmerman on behalf
of the Tanganyika Education Department.

Living in Dar es Salaam at this time was quite different to Mombasa. It
wasn't as British, for a start, and in addition to the many Germans who had
come back after the First World War, there was a sizable Greek community
as well. We lived in Gymkhana Avenue, next to the golf course and close
to St. Alban's Anglican Church. The road itself was made of white crushed
coral, and Indian funeral processions used to use it on their way to the Hindu
Crematorium, which was situated near the sea front on the other side of the
Gymkhana Club grounds. To this day, I can still recollect the cadence of the
chants they sang as they marched past our house. It was, to coin a phrase,
deadly serious in spite of the jokes that my father used to make about being
able to smell roast pork for the next day or two.

I still have a 1939 school report from Mrs Zimmerman's establishment
and it is apparent from this that we coped with a wide range of subjects. We
not only did the three R's in time-honoured style but also took Scripture,
History, Geography, Nature Lessons and Singing. In addition to this, there
was also Painting and Drawing, and a delightful subject simply called
Plasticene, which was obviously aimed at stimulating the creative impulses.
It sounds quite a lot for a 6-year old child but I remember feeling nothing
but enthusiasm. The school was fun and I wasn't conscious of the shadow
of war which hung over the grown-ups. A kid's life in Dar of that period
was simple and enjoyable; we spent the mornings at school and rested
in the afternoons until it was time to be taken down to the Swimming
Club at Magagoni, situated near the entrance to the harbour opposite the
sunken German dry dock. There we would paddle in the shallows or play
on the sand, often diverting to the unsanitary but attractively forbidden
area underneath the change room building, which was a wooden structure
elevated above the beach by masonry piles. Our parents, meanwhile, would
sit in a row of deck chairs and gossip with each other until the heaven-sent
time of the evening sundowner drew nigh and they could decently round us
up and take us home. Every now and then, a ship would go past on its way
to or from the harbour, the most spectacular departures being provided by
vessels of the Deutsch Ostafrika Line, which went out with the ship's band
playing at full throttle.

The possibility of giving Tanganyika back to Germany has already been mentioned and though no one in authority took this seriously, members of the German community put on armbands emblazoned with swastikas and began drilling and marching in their spare time. Geoff Baker relates that he and his friends laughed heartily at their German colleagues when they saw them goose-stepping on the Iringa sports field, but it was no laughing matter when the latter began bickering among themselves as to who should become the new District Commissioner. This and similar incidents eventually alarmed the Government to the extent of forming a Home Guard, which all local British males were expected to join. In the event, this was just as well because my father told me that when war was finally declared on 3 September 1939, the first job of local force members was to round up their German colleagues, who fortunately gave in without a struggle. It must have been a moment of some drama, though, and I gather it was made worse by having to arrest the German manager of the brewery. This apparently caused great consternation and I have been told the Governor himself issued an instruction to let him out.

My parents at this time were not wealthy—nobody in Dar es Salaam was—but things had started to improve as the world moved out of depression. The house in Gymkhana Avenue, which was leased from a Greek widow, was small but comfortable and the tropical heat was kept out by stout green wooden shutters. There was a patch of sandy garden that supported a fragile *frangipani* and a large mango tree, which was no use as a reading venue because it was infested by ants and was difficult to climb due to its rough bark. There were compensations, however, and I particularly remember a pair of enormous German revolvers in their holsters which we used as doorstops. Left over from the war, they had been spiked and rendered harmless but I would pretend to shoot people with them and in doing so, made a profound impression on the Indian barber who used to cycle round on Sunday mornings to cut my father's hair on the verandah. I then had my first lesson about never pointing a gun at anybody delivered in agitated Hindustani.

The spiritual side of things was not neglected, either, and I went to Sunday School regularly. This was an Anglican affair at the nearby St. Alban's Cathedral which my Greek friend at school also attended because there was no Greek Orthodox Church in Dar at the time. It was run by Archdeacon Hanbury, a senior figure in the diocese, and on Palm Sunday, we would be issued with palm fronds—an accessory of which Dar es Salaam had no shortage. The good Archdeacon often came round to our house for a sundowner and a chat, which greatly pleased my mother who had always been a good churchwoman. She was, however, somewhat critical of a visiting missionary whom the Archdeacon had persuaded to talk to his young charges. Good things happened to people who told the truth, he said, and enlivened the message with several tales of virtue having been rewarded. 'ALWAYS TELL THE TRUTH, IT PAYS,' he concluded eloquently—much to my mother's alarm at this shortcut to morality.

On a completely terrestrial basis, Dar was a beautiful place in which to live and positively exuded tropical atmosphere. The palm-fringed harbour with half a dozen differently coloured ships swinging at anchor, was an incredibly romantic sight and this was even more marked at night time when the lights of ships and shore were reflected off the water. The most prestigious mooring berth, reserved for mail ships and usually occupied by the lavender-coloured vessels of the Union Castle Line, was so close to the shore that a casual stroller wandering down the road which led from Government House towards the seafront could easily think there was a ship parked at the end of the street. Artists and photographers were always unable to resist the harbour's appeal and many are the sketches and water-colours which have been inspired by it.

Needless to say, the East African scene was shattered when war actually did break out. I can clearly remember my parents listening to their crackly wireless set in Dar es Salaam on that fateful day in September 1939 and looking worried beyond belief. There is always a great difference between thinking something is going to happen and actually having it happen, and in spite of the build-up, it was a shock to everyone to hear the announcement. Memories of 1914-1918 were still vivid and no one wanted to go through a war all over again. To take the long arm of coincidence a little further, it struck many people as ironic that Chamberlain should be making the announcement because he had been minded to give Tanganyika back to Germany. My mother was naturally worried that my father might be called up to resume his seafaring life and we lived through a period of uncertainty on this score, which was only settled by the eventual decision of the authorities that stevedoring was an essential occupation and that he should stay with it. This didn't please him particularly but my mother was greatly relieved.

Bill Johnston remembered the outbreak of war in 1939 because he was up-country inspecting the Central Line at the time and happened to be looking round one of the smaller railway stations when he noticed that a considerable crowd of locals was busy assembling on the platform, complete with a small band from the nearby school. A moment later, the

Governor's train—with crossed Union Jacks on the front—pulled in and decanted the Governor and his retinue, fully dressed in the splendour of their white colonial uniforms. They had come to hold an official *baraza* (the equivalent of a pow-wow or indaba) with the tribal elders and unbeknown to Bill Johnston, the date which had been set for this meeting coincided with the day of his inspection. He therefore became an interested spectator and watched the proceedings with fascination, noting that the school band repeatedly played 'When the Red, Red Robin Comes Bob-bob-bobbing Along' on their flutes. This was listened to graciously, however, and the Governor made a speech which was politely acclaimed by his audience. Members of the tribe then made speeches in return, some dancing took place, the Governor was presented with a ceremonial spear, and the gathering broke up with expressions of mutual goodwill.

While the Governor was doing his stuff, though, the possibility of war must obviously have been on his mind because when the crowd dispersed, the Governor's ADC turned to Bill and asked whether there was a functioning wireless set anywhere. Little could he have known it but as luck would have it, he couldn't have asked a better person because Bill Johnston was an amateur radio enthusiast who had a working assembly of wires, condensers and coils in his railway coach which was conveniently parked in a siding. Next thing, Bill found himself playing host to the Governor and his aides as they listened to the news from the BBC. It was certainly an unusual setting in which to hear the course of history being changed but fortunately, Bill had a drop of the right stuff in the cupboard of his caboose and was able to restore his guests with a traditional sundowner.

Mombasa, to which we returned soon after the announcement, was on far more of a war footing than Dar es Salaam. Mussolini was expected to throw his lot in with the Germans at any time and this would mean the adjacent countries of Abyssinia and Italian Somaliland on Kenya's northern border would become hostile territory. In fact, this duly occurred when Italy declared war on the Allies in July 1940 and this put Kenya right into the front line. Italy's colonial army in Abyssinia may have been out on a limb due to Britain's grasp on the Suez Canal but no one appeared to have told the Italians about this, and their army was a formidable force which could be expected to be more than a match for the KAR and the few British units who happened to be in Kenya at the time. It was a case of South Africa to the rescue once again, and so prompt was the response by the Union Government that South African Air Force planes were bombing Italian installations in Ethiopia a day after Mussolini's declaration of war. This did not stop the

Italians from making border raids into Kenya's Northern Frontier District, however, and some very brisk fighting took place in British Somaliland. The British forces were forced to withdraw but this holding action gained precious time for the South African Army to get its act together and despatch the First South African Brigade under the command of General Dan Pienaar to Nairobi in the biggest convoy of trucks the Great North Road had ever seen. A campaign in harsh and inhospitable country then took place and the Italians were rolled back by a series of traditional Boer tactics adapted to modern warfare. Addis Ababa was occupied in April 1941 and a final surrender by the Italians occurred a month later.

Mombasa was very close to these stirring events and though the port was expected to attract the attention of Italian bombers, the air raid sirens only went off on one occasion when an Italian photo-reconnaissance plane flew over the town. As far as one could, though, the progress of the inland fighting was followed closely and the gratifying result was hailed as the first major Allied success of the war. It also saw the award of the first Victoria Cross of the war, which went to a young officer in the Somaliland Camel Corps by the name of Eric Wilson, who gallantly commanded a series of machine gun posts in British Somaliland while badly wounded. He died recently at the age of 96 but I met him during the 1950s when he was the District Commissioner in Mbeya and he taught me a great deal about squash rackets, a game at which he had been a leading pre-war player. If his shooting had been as good as his drop shots, he must indeed have given the Italians serious trouble.

Many years later, I had an interesting reminder of the Abyssinian campaign while I was going about my duties in the Tanganyika Survey Department in Dar es Salaam. Intent on tidying up the plan strongroom, I noticed a steel trunk underneath a filing rack but no one could tell me what was in it. So we opened it up and there were all the survey field books of the East African campaign which had been bundled up, stuffed in a trunk and sent to Dar for safe keeping when the fighting was over. Operating in the desert conditions of the Northern Frontier District of Kenya with scanty maps and few landmarks, the armoured car columns had obviously depended heavily on compass traverses and astronomical fixes. If only I had had the time, it would have been a work of absorbing historical research to go through these yellowing papers. As it was, however, I simply asked the staff to push the trunk back under the rack again. Perhaps it is still there.

Another recollection of the Abyssinian campaign which comes back to me concerns the sexual problems that the Italian troops apparently faced during their brief occupation of Abyssinia and Somalia between 1935 and 1940. It may have been only a story but being born with romance in their blood and given the attractive appearance of females in the Horn of Africa, it is easy to imagine the Italian soldiers wishing to establish closer relations with their new female subjects. According to my informants, however, the big snag in this scenario was the way these same females secreted a razor blade under their thumb nails, waited until their conquerors were fully engaged, so to speak, and then castrated them with one seemingly amorous caress. It is enough to make anyone wince and though I'm not sure whether I understood the details fully at the time, I believed for years that the Italian prisoners of war we saw occasionally in Kenya had to get along without their knackers.

The Ethiopian campaign may have been the first British victory of the war but while it was going on, an even more sinister development was beginning to propel Mombasa further into prominence on the world stage. The new menace had slit eyes, overweening ambition, and bombed Pearl Harbour on 7 December 1941. The British Empire then came under immediate threat, with Hong Kong falling to the Japanese on Christmas Day 1941 and Singapore surrendering in February 1942. The British Navy, or what was left of its Eastern fleet, still had bases in Colombo and Australia but even these were vulnerable and the somewhat safer port of Mombasa, being further away from Japan, became very strategic. Warships and freighters crammed the harbour and the town was full of sailors. Rationing was introduced for the civil population and residents were advised that people who were non-essential to the war effort should leave town. My father found himself up to his ears in it, and my mother took on an essential job in the food distribution office. This made me the only hanger-on and as I was now eight years old, it seemed a good idea to my parents to send me to school up-country and get me out of the potential war zone. It was a turning point in my life for which the Japanese were clearly responsible and to this day, I've never been too sure whether I like sushi or not.

The subsequent problem facing my parents at this point was which school to grace with their son's presence. They didn't know Nairobi very well and eventually decided on St. Mary's School for Boys, which had been established in the suburb of Parklands by the Holy Ghost Order of the Roman Catholic Church in 1939. Neither of my parents were Catholic and the main reason for their choice was that the good Fathers offered both junior and senior education, no change of venue being necessary when the age of 13 was reached. Hence, mid-1942 saw my mother and I travelling up to Nairobi from Mombasa by courtesy of the good old Kenya-Uganda Railway, known to one and all by that time as the KUR.

It's probably still the same timetable but in those days, the mail train left Mombasa at four o'clock in the afternoon and spent the ensuing night steaming through the coastal plateau and intermediate lowlands. The next morning would find the train well into the rolling grasslands of the Athi Plains and a marvellous sight they were, teeming with herds of game as far as the eye could see. There were wildebeest by the thousand, innumerable duiker, hundreds of Tommies (Thompson gazelles), and any number of giraffe, kongoni, zebra, and eland on display and I remember staring out of our carriage window with complete and utter fascination. It was absolutely riveting and must have been one of the most unique spectacles Africa had to offer. I remember being completely wrapped up in it—that is, until the steward started playing his xylophone in the corridor to summon us to breakfast in the restaurant car. The KUR had a well-deserved reputation for never stinting on its catering and its breakfast of paw-paw, eggs, bacon, sausages, grilled tomatoes, toast, marmalade, and good Kenya coffee, was not to be missed—especially in wartime.

I suppose the first few days at any school are an adventure and I remember well the sense of bizarreness engendered by sitting in a grass-roofed classroom and learning to conjugate *mensa.* The playground at break time was adventurous, too, and I remember it being full of large and hairy boys who were liable to stop you and order you to sing a song. As a lot of the new boys didn't know any songs aside from *God Save the King*—every member of my generation was taught the words at the same time as *The Lord's Prayer*—the national anthem was rendered in many piping and tuneless ways. There were always balls of different sizes whizzing about, too, and usually a number of games of marbles going on. The rules of the latter, known as *nyabs,* were localised to Nairobi schools and I never found the same set of rules in England or elsewhere.

The large and dusty school grounds are worth describing. There were large expanses of *murram,* (a reddish Kenya soil that binds well to make a smooth surface), and a whole series of *Christ-thorn* hedges, the latter being a flowering bush full of fierce thorns which are reputed to have featured in the Crucifixion. The original stone building in the centre of the complex was surrounded by a series of thatched classrooms, and there was a boxing ring and a *murram* tennis court. Some big trees ran along the boundary and in the centre, near the tennis court, there was a particularly large and memorable tree which bore edible fruit resembling a chestnut. I never discovered its proper name but it was known to one and all as a *bumstitch tree* due to the

ruins just before Shelborne station

shape of the fruit. It must have been a member of the fig family and though the skin of the fruit was quite tough, the innards had a pleasant taste that I have never sampled since. It was also handy to throw at people.

What possessed the Holy Ghost Order of the Roman Catholic Church to bestow the name *St. Mary's* on the school will never be known. Maybe the incongruity of this didn't occur to an Irish mind steeped in Catholicism, but who else would have decided to call a boys' school after a female saint? Admittedly, one of the most revered and precious names in Christendom but nonetheless, a categorically female name. It led to immediate derision on the part of all non-St Mary's Kenya youth and was responsible for many fights and almost-fights. Rhyming with *fairies,* the name was never easy to live down and even when we had reached man's estate and were out in the wide world, it was still difficult to explain to someone where you went to school. Bar cronies would hoot with laughter, and even personnel officers would raise an eyebrow.

Leaving its name aside, however, St. Mary's was a very proper school and came complete with all the trimmings. There was a school uniform for formal occasions, consisting of a blue blazer and a blue and white striped tie, which were to be worn over grey shorts or long grey trousers depending on the age of the pupil. Following the pre-war belief in headgear being essential, there was also provision for a double thickness *terai* hat, (rather like a soft bush hat), but no one ever took the hat business seriously and the spectacle of Allied troops basking in the sunshine without any ill effects quickly led to the bare-headed look becoming widespread. Otherwise, clothing was casual and ordinary life was conducted in khaki shorts and whatever type of upper garments a boy's mother may have chosen for him. We must have looked a lot of scruffs but at least, we were comfortable.

There was also a school song and a school motto, the latter being incorporated into the badge on the blazer breast pocket. I believe, though authorship was never claimed, that both were composed by Father Cooligan, the tall ascetic priest who acted as the Dean of Studies and taught English and Latin. He was a serious man, whom I discovered years later to have a delightful sense of humour, and maybe the school song was proof of this. The motto, *Bonitas, Disciplina, et Scientia,* ('Goodness, Discipline and Science'), is irreproachable, but the words of the school song, sung to the American Civil War anthem of *Marching through Georgia* make one wonder. I have no idea whether the words are still in use but I remember one of the verses with great clarity. It may have been the opening verse or somewhere in the middle, but it went like this :-

Ours a noble motto, boys, observance is its due
Clean hands, stout hearts and honesty become the white and blue
Goodness is our great hallmark, to discipline we're true
Bonitas, disciplina et scientia.

Certainly, the Fathers, Irish to a man, ran the place in a manly kind of way. Sport was a major part of school life and willing coaches from the outside world were enlisted as and when required. Cricket and soccer were the main sports but there was also a great emphasis on boxing, which was regarded as a manifestation of muscular Christianity. The ethos of learning how to take a punch and shake hands afterwards was deliberately fostered and this was taken to the extent of settling arguments. Within seconds of insults being exchanged, the cry of FIGHT would go up and the two protagonists would be marshalled off to the ring where the gloves would be donned and a prefect would appoint himself as referee. After the fight, both parties were expected to shake hands and the matter was closed.

The warm and hospitable family with whom I boarded during my first year in Nairobi lived close to the school and while it gave me the good feeling of having a second home, it also enabled me to sample the joys of life in a Nairobi suburb at this time. Foremost among these was the way sewage disposal was conducted, and though the same system was to be found in all the British cities of Africa, including Salisbury (now Harare) and Johannesburg, it was certainly memorable. I'm referring here to the sanitary lane system, which called for each row of houses in a block to be separated by a mid-block lane which was negotiable by an ox-cart, whose role was to collect the night soil. While all the houses had running water, there were no loos in any of them and essential functions were performed in a small shed situated at the back of the plot in such a manner that its rear wall bordered the lane. The shed, (known in Rhodesia as the PK or *pikanin kaia*) would typically be furnished with a large bucket underneath a stout wooden seat and there would be a trap-door in the rear wall, through which the bucket could be removed. As part of the daily routine, the disposal cart—attended by a motley crowd of municipal workers and heralded by barking dogs—would then circulate through the suburbs, pausing at the rear of each house to open the trap-door, extract the bucket, empty the contents into the tank on the cart, and then replace the bucket after giving it a quick sluice. It may sound a little primitive and heavy on manpower, but cities were quite small in those days and the system worked well for many years.

The shed in this case was painted dark green and had a cement floor with a wooden door that you could fasten after you. There was a sturdy throne in the middle of the room and this had a hinged seat that could be lifted up if you were a male customer calling on a minor errand. In addition, there was a tap to one side and a nail from which was suspended a wad of torn-up sheets from the Kenya Farmers' Weekly. There was also a small table on which other copies of this estimable publication rested, usually accompanied by some back numbers of the East African Standard. You could either use them or read them, according to choice, but if you dallied too long in the early morning, you ran the risk of the ox-cart showing up while you were enthroned and the bucket being unceremoniously removed by a brawny black hand while you were in residence, so to speak. It certainly spurred one on and cured any tendency to dawdle.

It could well be asked why a simple pit system would not have been preferable but pits fill up quite quickly and new ones would constantly have had to be dug. Septic tanks and French drains may have been an option but their suitability depends very much on the geology and size of property involved. As I've said, the system worked and in the case of Parklands, the lanes were kept in use until the end of the war and it was only round about 1946 or thereabouts that internal toilets were installed in the houses. Up till then, it was a bit tricky if you wanted to go somewhere in the middle of the night and the potty was an essential item of furniture. In consequence, the morning procession would feature a string of people taking their potties to the PK with the intention of emptying them, each person bearing a studiously casual expression. 'Just going for a morning stroll,' the expression would proclaim, 'and my golly goodness, I just happen to be carrying this but it's got nothing to do with me.'

School terms in Kenya during this era consisted of three equal terms of three months each, separated by three holiday periods of one month each. There was no long holiday as occurs in other parts of the world and as most of the pupils were boarders, travelling to and from school usually involved a long journey by train. The only snag in this was that Dar es Salaam was not connected by rail to Nairobi and of course, my parents were transferred back to Dar as soon as I started school. For the first two or three years, this involved flying between Dar and Mombasa and then catching the train, and in 1942, I even had the experience of flying in one of the Short flying boats mentioned earlier. Because it was wartime, the windows were all blacked out, however, and it was nowhere as exciting as I had hoped.

By late 1942, the war was beginning to look up a bit for the Allies. Not only had the Japanese Navy suffered its first major defeat at the hands of the Americans in the Pacific but the Russians were winning the Battle of Stalingrad and the British scored their first major victory over the Germans at El Alamein in North Africa. General Montgomery—'Monty'—became everybody's hero and there was a tangible sense of relief in the air at Egypt and the Suez Canal having been saved, not to mention the imperial links with Kenya and India. It was still very much wartime, however, and I remember that every second adult person in Kenya seemed to be in uniform—women as well as men. There were numerous Italian prisoners-of-war to be seen and also a wave of refugees from various European countries. We even had a young Prince, (I think from Yugoslavia), at St. Mary's with us, and quite a scattering of Poles. The school matron was Polish, too, and was a key figure in my life after I became a full-time boarder in 1943. Ample, motherly and genial, Mrs Alexandrovic (commonly referred to as *Ma Vitch* by her young charges), was expert at enlivening the burnt offerings produced by the Kikuyu cooks in the refectory kitchen and kept a sharp eye on our welfare. 'You have got teeth like a sheep,' she once said to me, 'you must brush them harder.' So I did—and years later, every dentist who looked inside my mouth would immediately comment on the signs of early toothbrush damage.

There was rationing in Kenya during the war but compared to Europe, East Africa was a land of milk and honey. We didn't go hungry as boarders at school, though luxuries such as jam and butter were strictly shared out. Used to this regime, I will never forget spending the weekend at Ngong with a friend whose father was very senior in the Army and had invited a number of fellow officers to make up a house party. We all shared breakfast together and to this day, I remember one elderly staff officer piling his toast high with good Kenya butter and marmalade to an extent that beggared description. My friend and I just gaped at him in a mixture of shocked envy and followed his every bite with open-mouthed fascination.

As often happens, the war also had its positive side. At first, all imported goods were virtually unobtainable in East Africa and basic things like toilet paper or toothpaste were in short supply. This prompted a number of local industries to start up and by the middle of the war, canning factories were turning out large quantities of goods such as jam, tinned fruit and corned beef. Obviously, there were some teething problems due to labour force inexperience but the quality was quite good and the stories which circulated about fingernails finding their way into bully beef cans were probably

I thought this would be a book about subjugation.

apocryphal. The availability of alcoholic stimulants remained a problem, of course, and though local beer was plentiful, Scotch whisky was at a premium and was not easy to get. On one celebrated occasion, my father dropped a precious bottle of Scotch on his way into the house and gave my mother a crash course in nautical language.

By all accounts, however, the Happy Valley set seemed to have had no trouble laying their hands on supplies of alcohol. The high jinks of these young and wealthy aristocrats were renowned far beyond Kenya's borders and the White Highlands had become known as a home for the black sheep of good families. There, one could drink and indulge in as much sex as one liked—in a well-bred sort of way, naturally—and these activities gave rise to that famous question, 'Are you married or do you live in Kenya?' Described as a scene of altitude, alcohol and adultery, all these ingredients must have played a part in generating the eccentricity which many of the participants displayed. The celebrated and much-argued case of Lord Erroll's murder in 1941 probably marked the apogee of the goings-on and there is still a great deal of mystery about his demise. The popular theory is that Erroll was having an affair with the young and beautiful wife of Sir Jock Delves Broughton, who shot Erroll in a fit of jealousy. Sir Jock was then tried in a Nairobi court for the murder but curiously enough, was acquitted on a technicality. A year later, he committed suicide but his guilt has never been proved conclusively and to this day, there are conflicting theories as to exactly what happened. The fact that Erroll was the Assistant Military Secretary of Kenya at the time has even led to bizarre suggestions of Secret Service involvement. It was real, juicy, Kenya stuff and if you have seen the film *White Mischief,* you would have seen an excellent representation of the atmosphere of the period.

By the time 1944 came along, the heat had gone out of the war as far as East Africa was concerned and there was no doubt who was going to win. Italy had surrendered, the Germans were out of North Africa, and the Japanese were being rolled back by the Americans. The D-Day landings in Normandy were imminent and there was no longer a need to maintain substantial forces in Kenya. There was a definite sense of being on the periphery of things and waiting for the war to end so that everybody could get on with their lives. Life in Tanganyika was even more of a holding action and most of the population did not even know there was a war in progress. Having been fought over in the previous war, the vast country literally slumbered through World War Two and though it may have been noticed there weren't so many bwanas around and no new buildings or roads being built, that would have been about the size of it.

As far as I am aware, however, the significant part played in the war by the Tanganyika Navy has never been fully chronicled. Indeed, some people may not even have known that Tanganyika had a navy, but in fact, it did. A coastal steamer named the *Azania* was converted into a man-of-war by the addition of some grey paint and placed under the command of a senior member of the Dar harbour administration, ably assisted by one of his colleagues in the role of Chief Engineer. These two stalwarts were then charged with periodically patrolling the coast and keeping the sea lanes open in this part of the Indian Ocean. It was a fairly uneventful set of duties and all went well, save for the occasion they decided to show the flag in Zanzibar and possibly pick up a little duty free whisky. So off they went, had a long and tiring day, and ended up feeling a bit peckish at dinner time. Fish would be just the dish, they thought, but alas, the steward confirmed there was no fish in the ship's galley. This led to some creative thinking and no doubt aided by their Zanzibar purchases, our heroes reached the conclusion it was time for some depth charge practice. Being rookies, this necessitated reading the manual closely but being intelligent seafarers, this was no problem and they succeeded in dropping a charge over the stern which achieved a very satisfactory explosion. The practice was duly entered in the log, a boat was lowered and many dead fish were collected. A good dinner was then enjoyed and the representatives of British naval power in Tanganyika turned in with a feeling they had put in a good day's work.

Unfortunately, this was not the end of the matter. It was discovered a couple of days later that telegrams could no longer be sent to Zanzibar from the mainland. Yes, you have guessed correctly—with the whole Indian Ocean as its playground, the Tanganyika Navy had succeeded in dropping a depth charge on top of the submarine cable connecting Zanzibar to the rest of East Africa. How long it took to fix, I do not know but apparently, it was the only time the ship's armaments were used during the whole war.

On a personal note, we sampled the sensation of everything having come to a standstill when my father was asked to go to Tanga, the country's second port lying midway between Dar and Mombasa. This was all very well but getting to and from school in Nairobi was still a problem. Admittedly, it was simpler than getting to Dar es Salaam from Nairobi but it still involved two nights of travelling and two lots of trains. Firstly, one took the normal KUR service towards Mombasa but only as far as Voi, where part of the train was shunted off in the small hours and diverted on to the branch line which ran through the dusty Tsavo Plains to Moshi at the foot of Mount Kilimanjaro. There, you changed trains completely—a process that involved killing the rest of the day in the sleepy town of Moshi before catching the Tanganyika Railways train that ran down to Tanga. This was quite different to the KUR and conferred a greater sense of adventure. For one thing, the open-ended carriages had a curiously old-fashioned feel to them and looked as if they had been acquired from the set of a cowboy movie. And for another thing, you only had to look out of the window and there was Kilimanjaro with its snow made rosy by the sunset. When this faded away, you could then watch the Pare and Usambara Mountains, which were also pretty spectacular and made immense dark shapes against the night sky. The Pangani River—supposedly full of crocodiles—was worth more than a glance, too, as were the vast sisal estates revealed by the light of morning, which seemed to go on forever with row after row of green spiky bushes stretching away to the horizon.

Tanga in 1944 was very sleepy. My father used to walk to his office in the port area through fields of maize that were cultivated by the locals—or more specifically, by the *bibi's* (wives) of the local gentry. The focal point of life for the younger generation was the Swimming Club a few miles down the road and most mornings during the holidays were spent on its raft, occasionally diving into the clear warm water or pushing each other into it. It was quite idyllic but one morning, a giant stingray came to join our little games and marooned us on the raft for a couple of hours. Nowadays we know that these creatures are relatively harmless but to our little group at the time, the ray seemed as threatening as a whole platoon of sharks and we were convinced that it wanted us for lunch. Certainly, it didn't go away and swam round and round us in circles with what we thought was a hungry look in its eyes. It was quite scaring at the time and I must confess that we broke several Olympic records in our haste to get back to shore when the monster finally went away.

On 4 May 1945, the war in Europe ended and I still remember how Father Tommy O'Sullivan, the then headmaster, rang for silence during breakfast in the refectory that morning and told us that World War Two was over. I know he told us about the millions of people who had been killed or displaced during it but I'm afraid that we were all too pumped up to pay much attention to the figures. The war was over, that was the great thing, Hitler was dead, and the forces of righteousness had triumphed. 'We won' was the overpowering thought and we felt mighty proud to be British. VE Day, (Victory in Europe Day), on 8 May was a major occasion and we all went to see the marching and the fireworks.

The other racial groups in East Africa had a fairly placid time of it during the war. The Asian community kept their shops and the economy going, while the indigenous tribes went on doing what they were doing when the war started. And if that sounds flippant, it must be remembered that they operated an extensive agricultural system on a subsistence basis and their lives were closely prescribed by tribal law and custom. The colonial administration didn't interfere with them and if go-ahead young black Kenyans wanted to try something different, they could either work on white farms or join the KAR. No need was seen for any social integration of the races and when a clever young Kikuyu by the name of Johnstone Kamau had wanted to play an active part in the affairs of the 1930's, he had been rebuffed by the establishment and subsequently went to Moscow for consolation. His subsequent story is quite complex and you may know him better as Jomo Kenyatta, who became the first President of Kenya after independence in 1964.

Young white Kenyans of this era had fairly straightforward attitudes towards race. Anyone with a black skin was called a *wog* and an Indian would be known as a *jindi,* which was an abbreviation of the full label of *jindi-bhai-singh,* dog-Hindi at his finest. Both these terms sound disrespectful to modern ears but were more a means of identification than any form of slur. At that point in time, the three races were undeniably different in language, appearance and culture, and the three official labels of European, Asian and African were recognition of this. No one was confident enough to step into an alien community, and each race did its own thing within its own subdivisions. White children were taught not to put on any airs and graces, however, and as most of us were used to having the other races in our lives, there was never a feeling of strangeness. Any feelings of superiority would have been quite misplaced, in fact, because the welfare of the country depended directly on its black labour force and it would have been an act of lunacy to alienate it. In addition to this, one would have been really stupid to have cheeked an Indian shopkeeper, who was not only the generous donor of chocolate bars but to whom your father was probably in debt. There was, I think, a genuine atmosphere of mutual respect and the three races seemed happy to preserve their identities.

The word *wog* is interesting in itself. Most dictionaries will tell you that it refers to persons of Middle Eastern origin, particularly from Egypt, and that it may be derived from *gollywog.* But this is absurd, because a gollywog is generally acknowledged to have a black face and bristly hair, which Egyptians and Arabs do not have. Most elderly people of British origin will tell one that it stands for 'wily oriental gentleman' and when you question them, it usually turns out that they are alluding to some smooth-talking merchant who diddled them in a transaction when they went ashore in Port Said on their way through the Suez Canal. This does not stand up either, however, because the inhabitants of Port Said are not oriental. To complicate matters even further, the term is used in Australia for people who are not of Anglo-Saxon descent, which nowadays would include half the continent's population. In Tanganyika during pre-independence days, I was even called a white wog myself, on the grounds that I had not been born in England. In retaliation, Kenya boys and girls referred to their English counterparts as *pongos* and we teased them about having pink knees.

The main effect of the war on East Africa was probably the cessation of development during hostilities. The Colonial Service had been pruned of all available men and expertise to boost the Armed Forces and there was a shortage of money and equipment. Everything was on hold and the construction of new buildings, dams, schools and medical facilities was put on the back burner. Agricultural encouragement was suspended and unless it had a direct bearing on the war effort—like the production of corned beef, for example—industrial or political activity simply did not occur. I don't think there were any major famines or epidemics during this period but it certainly was not a time of expansion and the scene was only stirred up on 15 August 1945 when Japan surrendered. This was celebrated in Mombasa by an enormous firework show on the coral cliffs abutting the golf course and I remember sitting in the car and watching the fireworks against a background of stars shining brightly above the Indian Ocean rollers that crashed into the cliffs. Being young and tied up with the present, I didn't notice that the grown-ups were a bit thoughtful and I certainly didn't realise that a major landmark in time had been reached.

The first sign of the momentous changes which were afoot, however, was my father talking about taking some leave and going back to England to see his mother and brothers. In this regard, though, it wasn't so easy to get to England in the chaos that ensued after peace had broken out. A lot of the world's ships had been sunk, thousands of soldiers wanted to get home, and such passenger liners that had survived hostilities were all doing duty as troopships. Berths to Europe were only available to a limited number of civilians and far from being accommodated in a luxury cabin with eager stewards at the ready, getting back to Europe was more a case of slinging your hammock in a crowded cargo hold which had been converted into a dormitory. He decided to go in spite of these drawbacks, however, and experienced a harrowing time—not least during his stay in England, where wartime cheerfulness had given way to the shortages and drabness of post-war austerity.

My mother and I had much the better time of it while he was away, taking ship for Durban in South Africa. 'Durbs' in 1946 was an established city with a high degree of sophistication compared with Nairobi and Dar es Salaam. Its tall buildings gave one a sense of being in a movie, the Playhouse cinema had stars in its roof and you could buy a bottle of fizzy *Suncrush* from the café for a tickey (sixpence). Zulu rickshaw men in skins, horns and feathers paraded the sea front and the departmental stores sold the most colourful ice cream sundaes, which my grandmother would buy me during pauses in the shopping. Politics may have been hotting up in South Africa generally but Durban was very English and it was a long-lasting joke to talk about Natal being the most British part of the British Empire. For that matter, the rest of South Africa was oriented towards Britain as well and there were few signs at this time of the future pressures that would beset the relationship. Prime Minister 'Jannie' Smuts—beloved by all English-speaking South Africans but not so much by his fellow Afrikaners—had just invited the British Royal Family to take a post-war holiday in South Africa and detailed planning was already under way for the tour, which would take place in 1947.

Back in East Africa, I was somewhat startled to find that St. Mary's had moved, lock, stock, and barrel, to Westlands in the vicinity of Kabete. A new campus had been established around St. Austin's Mission, which had been a combination of church, monastery and coffee farm since the early days of Nairobi. The Loreto Convent—a highly respected academy for young ladies—had been established next to St. Austin's some years previously and now St. Mary's was established on the other side of the church to make a complete Roman Catholic educational centre. The fact we were now in close proximity to a lot of girls was an extra bonus and though our occasional contacts with the Convent inmates were closely supervised, it certainly gave an extra fillip to life and gave us boys some valuable exposure to the female sex.

Life in East Africa certainly loosened up after the war was over. Waves of demobbed servicemen and their families began migrating to Kenya, and even Tanganyika got its share of new blood. The political scene, prodded by well-meaning socialists in the British Government, also started to show rudimentary signs of life, though black advancement as a long-term goal was subordinated to organisational matters. The latter were quite extensive, too, and dealt mainly with the formation of common facilities to be shared by the four East African countries. The two different railway administrations were amalgamated into East African Railways and Harbours, (the EAR&H), and this was accompanied by the formation of East African Airways, the East African Income Tax Department, and the East African Posts and Telegraphs Department. Other supporting services also came under the umbrella and for the first time, there began to be some unity in this British-dominated chunk of Africa. Commercial firms, too, started to expand and generally speaking, there was a buzz of activity.

Naturally, we didn't know too much about this as schoolboys, though we could smell the positive elements in the air like a lot of young animals sniffing the wind. Sport had always played a large part in Kenya's life and now it came into its own. Black soccer was encouraged by the formation of vigorous leagues and the white population pursued its traditional sports of tennis, cricket and rugby with enthusiasm. I became hotly involved in tennis and watched Kenya's new post-war players like Rusty Mayers and Denis Tait with admiration. Both of them were successful in getting through the early rounds at Wimbledon and visiting international stars also dropped in from time to time to play exhibition matches. Geoff Brown of Australia played a match at the Nairobi Club, I remember, and we were all very impressed by his service, which was the fastest in the world at the time.

Boxing was also a prominent sport in Kenya and schoolboy boxing was much encouraged. The Prince of Wales School was dominant in this but St. Mary's did its best to give the 'Prinsoes' some competition and our squad of young pugs were fortunate to come under the guidance of Sid Meehan, a senior and much respected pillar of the Kenya Police. He not only taught us how to box but played a key role in shaping exercise and fitness routines. To this day, I still hear his voice in my ears when it comes to doing the tummy roll. 'Just remember to do this when you sit on the toilet in the morning,' he used to say,' and it will all be over before you know it.'

Travelling to Dar es Salaam from Nairobi now became a routine matter and though it took three days and involved three different trains, it was often made interesting if our travel dates coincided with those of the Heifer Boma. The worst part was the bus journey which connected the two Tanganyika railway lines and ran from Korogwe on the Tanga Line to Morogoro on the Central Line. Devoid of tar, the road contained a myriad number of corrugations and potholes, each of which produced a bump and a rattle. Travelling at an average speed of thirty miles per hour, the day always seemed endless and it was scant consolation to reflect that the very same road had been the scene of fierce fighting only thirty years earlier, as the retreating

Germans under von Lettow made life as difficult as they could for Smuts and his advancing troops. In fact, at a place called Kangata, the latter had run into a German ambush and two hundred South African troops had been machine-gunned from positions which had been expertly hidden in the bush. They were buried there in a military cemetery which is kept up by the Imperial War Graves Commission and I will always recollect how incredulous one of our adult fellow passengers was at seeing the sign leading to it. 'Heavens,' she said, 'what on earth is a cemetery doing in the middle of nowhere?' Well, it was too complicated and noisy at the time to tell her the story but I have never forgotten the remark as an example of how you ignore history at your peril. If you go travelling somewhere without knowing any background, the owners of the bones which lie buried under every stone will surely rise up and smite you.

By 1948, things were on the move everywhere. Harry Truman defied the odds by being re-elected President of the United States, the Berlin airlift thwarted the Soviets in their blockade of Germany's erstwhile capital, and Israel came into official existence. Long-playing records came on to the market and the first post-war Olympic Games were held in London. Closer to Kenya and of major significance to the African continent, the National Party in South Africa came to power and Smuts ended up on the sidelines. Vital to East Africa, though possibly not fully realised at the time, was the appearance of the first Land Rover—a vehicle which may have done more to open up Africa than any other invention, before or since. Fortuitously, its introduction coincided with the beginning of the ill-fated Groundnut Scheme in Tanganyika, but even the Land Rover could not steer this project to success. Arguably the largest project ever seen in East Africa, there is no knowing what impact this scheme would have had on Britain and the African continent if it had worked.

Unfortunately, all it did was to provide another object lesson in the way Africa can break the stoutest heart. As I heard the story, it wasn't all that grandiose in its original conception and simply started from an idea which an agronomist had while looking out of an aeroplane window while flying over southern Tanganyika. 'I bet you could grow peanuts down there,' he thought, and subsequently made mention of this in his report. Surprisingly, the idea generated enormous interest and became a major project proposal with remarkable speed. There was, you must remember, an acute shortage of edible oil in the post-war world and an imperative need to boost margarine production. This coincided with a large number of demobbed servicemen being available and also a large amount of surplus machinery in the way of bulldozers, tractors, trucks and heavy earth-moving equipment. It all fitted together and with commendable speed, the British Labour Government reached a decision to grow peanuts in Tanganyika on a vast scale. By 1948, the project was in full swing and huge areas of ground were being cleared. A high-powered organisation named the Overseas Food Corporation was created to manage the project and a new town called Kongwa was built in the middle of the designated area, together with a new port near the Mozambique border. Mercifully, proposals to name it 'Port Peanut' were not adopted and the local name of *Mtwara* was eventually preferred.

The amount of money and effort which went into the Groundnut Scheme was enormous but regrettably, the waste was also enormous. Much of the ex-Army equipment which was brought in from various theatres of war was not in the best of shape and aside from having rusted up, those machines which did work had a hard time uprooting bush trees and baobabs. The military-style approach was not all that efficient, either, and bulldozers from the Philippines, for example, are reputed to have been lost as soon as they arrived in Tanganyika. You might think it's not easy to lose a bulldozer but apparently, they were landed on remote beaches in LCT's (Landing Craft: Tanks) without exact knowledge of where they were. A couple of abandoned LCT's—relics of American landings in the Pacific—were even discovered years later on a deserted beach to the south of Dar es Salaam by a passing aeroplane.

These factors were not fatal, however. What was completely and utterly terminal was the fact that groundnuts would not grow in the areas that had been selected and cleared. The rainfall there proved to be inadequate and the soil conditions turned out to be unsuitable—possibly a reflection of the haste with which the project had been implemented without any pilot schemes being undertaken. Embarrassingly, the only groundnuts which came out of Tanganyika were grown by local tribesmen and the scheme was finally abandoned in the early 1950's.

In retrospect, the only positive gains to Tanganyika from the Groundnut Scheme were some substantial improvements to infrastructure and the continued presence of skilled people who had decided to stay. On the other hand, there was a definite downside in social perception, arising from the way the rougher element of the work force had conducted themselves—especially after nightfall. The scale of the boozing, womanising and quarrelling was apparently awesome and the indigenous population had goggled at the spectacle of bwanas and memsahibs behaving badly. The locals were used to a gentlemanly form of colonialism and their view of white women had been the cool and decorous wives of District Officers. It was thus a shock for them to see what a working man and his missus were capable of getting up to when they were plonked down in the middle of the African bush with plenty of spare time and liquor.

Like most businessmen in Dar es Salaam, my father's life became very busy due to the Groundnut Scheme and aside from the increased volume of stevedoring in Dar, he was charged with setting up a branch of the Lighterage Company at Mtwara. Admittedly, it wasn't a busy port but great things were expected and the essential thing was to be prepared when the expected surge of activity occurred. So he flew down there repeatedly in a light aeroplane to get things moving and supervise the building of an office. The hardest part of this was to find someone to run it but though he tried various people with seafaring experience, they all came to grief sooner or later due to a mixture of boredom, heat and drink. If they stayed sober and didn't get tired of a diet of stringy chicken and fish, they would start making eyes at an equally bored wife belonging to someone else and the staffing troubles would continue.

As youngsters, however, we knew little about sex and it may now be opportune to reveal how innocent my generation of young Kenya males was. We knew the facts of life in theory, of course, but the idea of putting them into practice seemed utterly bizarre. Girls, we felt, could not possibly be interested in getting physical and any base urges were obviously a male secret. One did not want to offend anyone by behaving improperly and when there was a 'social evening' at the nearby Loreto Convent during term time or a party with dancing during the holidays, it was normal to wear swimming trunks underneath one's trousers as a restraining measure. We talked about sex all the time between ourselves, of course, but it was more to impress each other than leading to any action. A great deal of this talk took place at the Magagoni Swimming Club when we were on holiday in Dar es Salaam and the routine was much the same each day—swim out to the raft, congregate there like a pack of seals, dive off occasionally, bask in the sun, and push anyone rash enough to stand near the edge of the raft into the water. Then we would swim back to the beach, lie in the warm sand, light cigarettes, and discuss life. If nothing else, this built up a good tan and I don't know whether it was because there was no hole in the ozone layer in those days, but we never felt the need for any form of oil or lotion.

As a snapshot of East African youth in Dar es Salaam at the end of the 1940s, you must visualise a circle of sandy bodies lying on the beach, enjoying the sun and exchanging deep thoughts about life and what it had to offer.

As a sample of this, I can still recall one of our more advanced members becoming philosophical and telling us his version of life's meaning. 'Life,' he said, 'is not the eerie wail of a distant violin or the burbling of a stream on the mountainside.' Here he paused for maximum effect and then continued. 'Life is the triumphant twang of a bedspring.' Naturally, this gave rise to a big outburst of laughter, and a couple of the fellows threw a handful of sand at him in appreciation. The only snag was that none of us had the remotest conception of how to get into a situation where the twang of a bedspring might be heard.

In fact, the most daring thing we ever did was to join our philosophic friend in taking any girls who might have been hanging around for a drive in his father's car, which was an old-fashioned model with doors that opened outwards from a central hinge. The girls would be put in the back seat and once we were bowling along Ocean Road at a reasonable speed, our fearless driver would open his door and hold it ajar, thereby creating a sudden gust of wind which could be guaranteed to fill and lift the skirts of the rear seat passengers. The squeals and shrieks from the back were relished beyond description and as an extra bonus, one might even get a glimpse of blue, pink or white knickers.

As you have by now probably formulated an image of gilded youths disporting their golden limbs on a tropical beach lined with rustling palms, you are quite right. You might even ask whether we had any black friends in the circle, to which the answer is no, we didn't. Black Africans of that era might have fished but they didn't swim and they lived in a completely different social environment. We were, however, on very good terms with the two amiable Uzaramo gentlemen who were employed by the Swimming Club, and spent many hours discussing sex and debating various fundamental issues with them. Not only did we acquire a most useful vocabulary of colloquial Swahili, but we also acquired an insight into how the ordinary people of the country lived and thought. They knew a lot about us as well and found the romantic intrigues of our set highly amusing. At the same time, they were sticklers for *desturi* (correct behaviour according to custom) and were genuinely shocked and dismissive if a white person behaved badly or spoke rudely.

Just to round off this picture of male East African youth during this period, I must tell you that no one wore any underpants. Why this was so, I don't know. It wasn't as if the weather was all that hot once you got away from the coastal belt but rather like the Scots, it was just the way that we dressed. As we all wore shorts, you had to watch how you sat so as not to give anyone an eyeful, though regrettably, this did happen from time to time. Even in purely male circles, care was still advisable because if you sat around with carelessly-arranged legs while reading the newspaper, you could bet your boots that some joker would flip his *stompie* (the glowing end of his cigarette) into the open area of your shorts. This was always good for a laugh—unless, of course, you were the victim.

Practically everybody smoked like chimneys in those days and the fighting men of both sides in World War Two relied on cigarettes to keep them going. Nobody realised how smoking might kill you and though there was a vague idea that too many cigarettes weren't good for one's health, the underlying cycle of cause and effect was not clearly understood. At school, nearly all the Fathers smoked—probably to compensate for their celibacy— and boys were allowed to smoke in the senior common-room provided they had turned fifteen and had written permission from their parents. Good 'baccy was grown in the country and the East African Tobacco Company put out a variety of products. *Clipper* was one of the better brands, with *Honeydew, King Stork* and *Crown Bird* further down the chain. You could get all the British brands, too, like *Players* or *Craven A* but they were more expensive and beyond the reach of impecunious schoolboys. We naturally gravitated towards the cheaper type and may God now preserve us, had full-blown smoking habits from the age of fourteen onwards.

If 1948 was a busy year, 1949 went by even more quickly. Aside from having to face our Senior Cambridge School Certificate exams at the end of the year, there were all sorts of new and exciting diversions. Rugby was one of them, and a life-long enthusiasm was sparked by the Fathers deciding that the game should now be played at St. Mary's. The issue had been shirked up till then due to the difficulty of finding a suitable coach but the advent of Father Noonan, barrel-chested and quite capable of donning a jersey and scrumming down with the best of them, saw matters brought to a head. Danny O'Loughlin, an ex-Irish international player, was roped in to help and after a few blackboard lectures, we finally tangled with the oval ball at a succession of practices. Then we played our first match—against Prince of Wales, naturally—in the form of a curtain-raiser at Parklands Sports Club and though we lost, didn't put up too bad a show.

Hockey was a major sport in East Africa, too, and given the number of Indians in the community, Kenya was able to field a very respectable team. Cricket was also very much on the menu and I was elated to get into the Kenya Schools team for its annual fixture against the Nairobi Club. It was a memorable day and though the younger generation lost the game, they certainly won the lunch. The Club's cold buffet was justly famed for providing the best spread Kenya could offer, and there were vast veal-and-ham pies together with mounds of sausages, hams, and cold roast beef. Salads and delicious crusty rolls backed up this spread, with apple pies, sundry tarts and trifles to follow. It was mind-bending stuff and we didn't let the Club's air of tradition restrict our enjoyment of its hospitality.

There is no doubt that the decade of the 1940s finished with a wave of prosperity in East Africa generally. Coffee, tea, tobacco and other crops like pyrethrum were all going well and in Tanganyika's case, sisal had suddenly become king. The world needed rope badly, and while the costs of production in 1946 were unchanged from those of 1939, the market value of sisal went up ten times. Anyone who had been brave enough to buy a sisal plantation in the uncertain pre-war years was now in the pound seats, and the Greek community in particular was rewarded for its earlier enterprise. In addition, post-war shortages became a thing of the past, local businesses entered a new era of efficiency, and the face of East Africa's cities and towns began to change under the onslaught of intensive building construction. New cars appeared on the roads and the technique of driving on a corrugated surface changed to one of going faster rather than slower.

For me, the year finished with having to write the much-heralded Senior Cambridge examinations. We wrote them in the Prince of Wales School hall and it may be of interest to itemise the nine subjects involved, i.e. *English Language, English Literature, History of the British Empire and Commonwealth, Geography, Latin, French (written and oral), Elementary Mathematics, Art,* and *General Science.* This was standard for a colonial student at the time and there was no nonsense about choosing subjects. The ones we took were deemed essential to a rounded education and though the absence of Swahili may be regrettable, I think the inclusion of a third language on the syllabus was felt to be top-heavy. Latin, which one might have thought was dispensable, was regarded as a proven basis for cultivating the mind and knowledge of French was regarded as essential to anyone aspiring to be a world citizen. As for history, the emphasis fell squarely on the British Empire and only general coverage was bestowed on regions which were not coloured pink on the map.

Though we may have been reasonably equipped to face the world, however, what happened to young East Africans after they left school was another matter. There were no facilities for higher education in East Africa at the time and school-leavers either took a job locally or went overseas for further study—mostly to Britain and South Africa. Many of us did both—taking a job and studying on the side by means of correspondence courses and on-the-job training. It was quite feasible to qualify for something in this manner because most of the professional institutions had their own external examination systems and you did not have to go to university in order to become an engineer, accountant, or surveyor. It was tough to go this route, though, and few people actually succeeded in ignoring the distractions of daily life. In the end, most of us found our way to Britain and *East Africa House* in London rapidly became an Old Boys club for the new up-and-coming generation of bwanas. Little did we realise we were on a limited time span and that East Africa was going to change rather quickly. Personally, I don't think anyone else realised it either, right down from the Secretary of State for the Colonies to the various Governors, colonial officials, businessmen, and settlers on the spot. Nor, I suspect, did most of the indigenous population.

CHAPTER 4

THE WATERSHED YEARS

The year 1950 is probably the starting point of East Africa's metamorphosis from pure colonial status into a self-sufficient bloc within the British Commonwealth. Up till then, everybody was trying to get over the effects of World War Two and most of the bwanas who had been around before the war were now middle-aged. This had led to the Colonial Office and the commercial houses recruiting a large number of younger men but they had to be trained before being let loose and it took some time for the new boys to arrive. When they did, a whole new era began and things started to hum. Money, vehicles and equipment became more readily available and new ideas took root. It was very much a watershed situation and though the concept of independence seemed utterly far-fetched to white, black, and brown segments of the population alike, the end of the British Raj in India was followed with considerable interest and its lessons were not lost on the diverse peoples of this part of the Empire. In fact, the very word 'Empire' began to be phased out and acquired an old-fashioned connotation.

As an East African youth who had just finished school, I was faced with the perennial problem of what to do with my life and I was lucky enough to be taken on by the Tanganyika Survey Department in Dar es Salaam as a trainee. As my parents were due for home leave, however, it was agreed I could accompany them and only start work on our return. Accordingly, I was able to board the *Dunottar Castle* in their company and experience at first hand the joys of a typical voyage to Europe in a passenger liner which was full of fellow East Africans. We went the long way round, too, via South Africa, and the trip took the best part of an excellent four weeks.

Looking back, I feel sorry for the modern generation who have never had to travel in this fashion, which was so much a part of life at that time. Air travel was still the realm of the wealthy few and the standard mode of getting from one country to another was to go by train if the countries were joined together or by ship if they weren't. The steamship companies were a major global industry and vied with each other to make the journey as pleasant as possible. Our voyage was particularly lively because there were plenty of young people on board and a complete range of diversions with which to amuse ourselves. The *Union Castle Line* knew their business well and there was never a dull moment. Four meals a day, including afternoon tea, was built into the fare, and both drinks and cigarettes were available at duty-free prices. One could play deck quoits or deck tennis or swim in the canvas-lined pool during the day, and then take part in dances, parties, and housey-housey—the nautical forerunner of Bingo—in the evenings after dinner. There was further action after these festivities, too, and when I say action, this is no misnomer because there is something about sea air that generates romance. Few people are exempt from this effect, as whole generations of shipboard travellers will testify. The ozone may have something to do with it or possibly, the sense of being away from it all in a small secluded world, but it was commonly recognised in the era of sea-borne travel that love would blossom freely on the ocean wave. This was not limited to single people, either, and even respectable married women travelling on their own were vulnerable to the tender passion—possibly inspired by the knowledge they were off the leash, so to speak. As I subsequently learned, it was not uncommon in the days of sea travel to see a young wife weeping copiously as she waved goodbye to her husband on the quayside—only to be involved in a steamy affair with the third mate or a fellow passenger within twenty-four hours of the ship's departure.

Fortunately, everybody seemed to know that shipboard romances were inclined to be transitory and there were generally few repercussions. Fellow passengers would all scatter at the end of a voyage and gossip would stop there and then. Certainly, the phrase 'ships that pass in the night' did long and honourable duty in the Empire's history and there is a ring of rueful acceptance about it. Fortunately—or unfortunately—I was a little too young to get involved in this kind of thing on the *Dunottar Castle* but I did note that the choice of venue for getting together with a member of the opposite sex was limited in Tourist Class by single passengers having to share cabins. My mother and father may have had a two-berth cabin to themselves but I had an upper bunk in a standard four-berth cabin, which

I shared with three other males of varying ages. It didn't do to be shy in those days and everyone accepted having to get along with strangers on an intimate level for a considerable period of time. There were, incidentally, no private toilets in the cabins—only wash hand-basins—and all bathing and lavatorial functions were conducted in a series of bathrooms and same-sex ablution facilities, which were located at strategic points in the labyrinth of corridors below the decks.

This absence of en-suite facilities might seem anathema to modern travellers but it wasn't unusual at the time. Ships were not unique in this, either—ordinary hotels all over the world operated in this way and if one needed to go somewhere in the middle of the night, down the passage you went. It made for a great degree of sociability, too, and people had to have suitable clothing to cope with it. Except for young bucks like me, (who circulated in a pair of rugby shorts and a T-shirt), it was de rigueur to perambulate to the bathroom in dressing gowns and slippers. A sponge bag in which to carry one's toilet requisites was also essential and by the time my father had wound a towel round his neck, found the loofah, and picked up a flannel, a visit to the bathroom had become quite an expedition. Shipboard meal-times were also an occasion and everybody had their own chair allocated to them at a specific table in the large dining room. There, one saw one's fellow passengers four times a day (at breakfast, lunch, tea and dinner), and there were precious few aspects of their appearance and behaviour which remained unfamiliar by the time the voyage had finished.

As the *Dunottar Castle's* function was to provide a passenger service to England from the coastal ports of East and South Africa, the trip was pleasantly broken up by frequent landfalls at which one could disembark and see whatever was worth seeing. Travelling southward from Dar, this involved successive stops at Zanzibar, Beira, Lourenço Marques (now Maputo), Durban, East London, Port Elizabeth and Cape Town. Then, after rounding the Cape and heading northwards towards Europe, the ship stopped at Ascension Island, St. Helena and Las Palmas. So it was quite a geography lesson as well as a journey, and brought the map of Africa to vivid life.

Cape Town was especially memorable for me in 1950 because the one day available for going ashore was not only a Sunday but a cold and wet one, with the wind blowing well as it so often does in that city. However, I had written in advance to an old school friend who was at university there and he picked me up on his motor cycle for a reunion with yet another ex-classmate, whose father had very sportingly donated five pounds for us to lunch together. So, no holds barred, the three of us went off to the Mount

Nelson Hotel, which was and no doubt always will be the most luxurious hotel in Cape Town. We had an excellent lunch there and then my friend ran me back to the ship, where I found my mother in a state of some anxiety about my intake of foodstuffs. She and my father had wandered about the city and the only place they could find which was open had been the Railway Station buffet, where they had consumed a meat pie and a nondescript cup of tea.

'Were you able to get some lunch somewhere?' she asked.

'Oh, yes, thanks, 'I answered.

'But where did you go, dear?

'The Mount Nelson.'

'WHAT? YOU WENT WHERE?'

The episode was talked about for many years afterwards and I cannot recall having had such a feeling of superiority before or since.

South Africa itself was fairly stable in 1950. General Smuts was to die in September of that year but Dr. Malan and his newly-elected Nationalist Government hadn't yet rocked any boats and there was a wave of prosperity. The universities were full of young men qualifying for the professions, Castle beer and Springbok cigarettes were ubiquitous, and the All Blacks had just been whitewashed on the rugby field. The country was still a senior member of the Commonwealth, and the only cloud on the horizon was the onset of the Korean War, which kicked off just as we were leaving Cape Town harbour. 'Is this World War Three starting?' someone asked as we began to heave in the Cape rollers, but no one knew the answer and we settled down to more deck quoits. The rest of the voyage went past very pleasantly and when we finally arrived at Tilbury docks, there was the usual blink of disbelief at seeing everybody dressed in European suits and hats. People one had got to know quite well were unrecognisable and familiar figures suddenly turned into strangers.

It was certainly strange seeing 'England, home and beauty' for the first time. I was utterly amazed at the rows of neat houses in the suburbs and by the signs of bomb damage still visible in many parts of London. I was also astonished at everyone wearing long trousers and I couldn't believe there were so many white people congregated together in one small island. The greenness of the countryside was overpowering, too, and I couldn't get over how fat the cows were—not one little bit like the scrawny Masai beasts with which I was familiar. An even greater surprise occurred when my parents took me to Hampton Court and Blenheim, where I must have gawped like a country cousin at the explicit murals on the ceilings. It was a great eye-opener for a simple Kenya lad, and when we went down to the part of Kent in which the family had roots, I was also impressed by the quality of village life in St. Margaret's Bay—the closest part of England to France and popularly reputed to tell the time by looking across the Channel at the church clock in Calais. There, I revelled in exploring the white cliffs, declaiming the immortal words of *Music, Music, Music* to the seagulls as I made my way along the pebbly beach.

London, of course, was especially thrilling and it was weird to see places that had hitherto merely been names on the Monopoly board, such as Leicester Square, Charing Cross and Regent Street. The Thames and the Tower made a big impact, too, and when we reached Piccadilly Circus, I remember my mother peered emotionally at Eros. 'Do you realise,' she said, 'you are now standing at the hub of the Empire.' And she meant it, too. The Empire wasn't an empty concept to people of her generation—or to me, for that matter—and there was something mystical about it in those days which made you stand a bit straighter.

The trip back to Dar es Salaam was a reversal of the outward journey, only this time on an older and smaller vessel in the shape of the *Llandovery Castle*. It wasn't quite such a fun voyage, though, because there was an RAF contingent on board bound for the Empire Training School in Southern Rhodesia and its members snapped up every single female on the ship in double quick time. The ozone didn't only work on them, either, because I rushed into the cabin one evening to fetch something and found one of my co-inmates passionately engaged on the top bunk with the mother of three children, who was on her way to Nairobi to rejoin her husband. It was particularly startling to me because not only was he middle-aged and obviously past it to my youthful eye but she was a formidable lady who spoke with a la-di-da accent and seemed eminently respectable. Needless to say, I rushed out again but the damage had been done and he chided me for having broken the spell. Later on, we laughed about it and I suppose in a way, it was part of my initiation into the adult world of East Africa.

Further initiation came when I started work in the Lands and Surveys Department in Dar es Salaam, reporting for duty every day in the official uniform of white shirt, white shorts and white stockings—adopted after the war as formal office dress for males in coastal parts of East Africa. As a junior man-about-town, I acquired a 125cc BSA Bantam motor-bike and became an active member of the Dar es Salaam Gymkhana Club. As offices closed at 4pm, this gave ample opportunity for sport of different kinds and I played a different game each day of the working week, alternating between tennis, hockey, soccer, rugby and cricket. The Swimming Club was the place to be at weekends and then there was reasonable surf at Oyster Bay when the monsoon was favourable. It was a hard life and the only fly in the ointment was the realisation that I really should be studying in my spare time if I wanted to take my education further.

Fortunately, the job proved to be interesting and I enjoyed my daily task of checking the calculations carried out by surveyors in the field and reporting on their accuracy. As the Department was not only responsible for mapping the country but also for the layout of plots in urban areas and the demarcation of farms, there was always a lot of work in the pipeline and the land registration system of the country depended on it. To readers not familiar with cadastral surveying, I must explain that it is the form of survey by which land rights are defined and recorded. Every country has a system for doing this and Tanganyika had as sophisticated a system as you would find anywhere, property boundaries being demarcated by permanent marks which had to be surveyed on a mathematical basis before any land titles could be issued. In the pre-computer age, this process generated a mass of figures which had to be checked with the aid of calculating machines and trigonometrical tables. The sting has now been taken out of survey calculations by modern electronics but before the advent of computers, it was painstaking work—only relieved by the knowledge that previous generations had had to use 7-figure logarithms to achieve the required results.

Like most other Government Departments in East Africa at this time, the Lands and Surveys Department in Tanganyika was feeling the watershed effect of the war acutely in the matter of staffing. The post-war wave of new graduates was still emerging and the only new appointments to the Colonial Survey Service during 1945-1949 were men who had qualified before the war or managed to qualify during the war. A severe staff shortage had thus built up and this was made worse by the old-fashioned rule that one could retire at 55 or after 20 years service, whichever came first. Most of the senior people who had been there since the 1930s did in fact leave and were replaced by younger men who were itching to introduce modern techniques and changes in organisation. New methods of doing things thus came quickly into operation and purely by an accident of timing, I had the fascinating experience of working with both the last of the old guard and the first of the new brigade—a situation which called for constant diplomacy.

While it was great to be at the forefront of change, my contacts with the old-time surveyors often made me feel they had lived through the best of it. Large parts of East Africa were virtually unexplored at the time they started, and whether you were a District Officer setting up a new administration or a surveyor carrying out a major triangulation, you were making the first footprints. It was all done under primitive conditions and it is a matter of wonder how a working infrastructure of towns, farms, roads, railways, harbours, and airfields, was gradually established in the harsh environment of a raw tropical country. It was done with considerable style, too, and in this regard, I must tell my favourite story about arriving at Sao Hill in the Southern Highlands of Tanganyika, where I had been sent to survey a block of farms developed in the 1930s by Lord Chesham, the Tanganyika equivalent of Lord Delamere. Featuring a number of farms centred round a clubhouse and an airstrip, it had attracted a rather aristocratic group of people and most of the farmers who settled there were either titled or the holders of high military rank, the latter having moved across from India when the British Raj began to run out of steam.

This particular incident happened one afternoon as I settled into my camp, which the survey boys and I had established in a grove of gum trees near a small stream. The former had their own set of tents and my home at that time consisted of what was officially described as an officer's tent, 14½ x10 ft, with an inner and outer fly, complete with verandah and bathroom sections. There I was, enjoying a cup of tea which Yusuf had efficiently brewed up on the primus stove, when a runner from the Club Manager arrived with a note inviting me to a dinner at the club in honour of the new Queen's birthday to be held a couple of days later. A postscript to his note said 'please dress' and I thanked my lucky stars I had had the foresight to bring my trusty mess jacket and evening trousers with me. Fortunately, they had survived the journey from Dar without getting too creased and Yusuf was able to restore them to respectability by a quick press with the charcoal iron.

So on the appointed night, I had my normal evening bath in brown water which had been brought up from the river and decanted into a galvanised iron tub. Then I donned my finery, successfully tied my bow tie, and drove to the club in a dusty truck. What a scene awaited me there! The entire community was assembled in the bar, the women in long dresses and the men in velvet smoking jackets. They made me welcome as 'the young scamp from Dar es Salaam who had come to survey their farms' and after a prolonged sundowner period, we moved to a long table in the dining room. The stars may have been visible through cracks in the thatched roof but we enjoyed an excellent dinner, at the end of which the Queen's health was proposed and drunk to murmurs of 'Her Majesty, God bless her.' The ladies then left the room, the port circulated, and the conversation dealt largely with the price of maize and tobacco. It was all too Somerset Maugham for words and I wouldn't have missed it for worlds.

To give readers an idea of the way of life led by early post-war colonials in East Africa, I can do no better than to refer to the *Kenya Settlers' Cookery Book and Household Guide*, first published under the auspices of the Church of Scotland Woman's Guild in 1928 and subsequently amended in later editions. The copy I have to hand came out in 1951 and is just as much a social document as a cookery book, giving a wonderful snapshot of attitudes and lifestyle at this time. It is also a testament to the resourceful way the memsahibs of East Africa behaved and must have been of great help to young wives. The preface to the book is worth quoting in full because it sets out the motivation behind its compilation in unequivocal terms:-

> *The first edition of this book, published in 1928, was compiled with the hope that it would prove of some assistance to newcomers to the Colony, to young and inexperienced housekeepers, and to bachelor settlers in Kenya, who must often find themselves obliged to put up with incompetency on the part of untrained native cooks or houseboys.*

Several thoughts are provoked by this, one of them being a serious doubt whether bachelor settlers would really read the book and follow its instructions. To my mind, the book is really a female bible, which not only contains 800 recipes but has sections on what to pack when going on safari, how to manage home and garden, how to make home-made soap, instructions in first aid, and useful phrases in both Swahili and Kikuyu for communicating with servants. It is also, I think, more a description of the way bwanas and memsahibs would have liked to have lived rather than the way they actually did live. In practice, it is unlikely they did themselves as well as the book recommends and it is probably more a case of its authors punting the middle-class standards to which they aspired had they continued to live in Britain. Most of the book's readers did in fact come from middle-class backgrounds but had been forced to adapt to a new life which was both primitive in some regards and more sophisticated in others. The presence of servants alone was inescapable and a wife was always in the situation of having to appear poised and confident even if she didn't feel that way.

To go through the book quickly, one is immediately reminded of the extent to which the British Empire was peopled by Scottish colonists. The first section is simply labelled **Porridge** and the first recipe to be described is 'The Scotch Method' (*sic*), in which the reader is sternly bidden to stir the oatmeal with a wooden spurtle instead of a spoon. This is followed by a somewhat derisory reference to 'Another Method'—presumably English— and a rather useful paragraph on how to do it with mealie meal. It then passes on to the right way of making tea—in a thoroughly heated tea-pot with no modern nonsense about tea bags—and moves on to coffee, where the instructions become quite categorical and reflect a degree of expertise that can only come from someone who grows it. They are worth recounting in full and it is recommended that they be given a trial.

Firstly, the reader should take due note of the statement that acceptable coffee should be freshly ground and roasted. If one has no facilities for this, the book grudgingly accepts that it may be bought already roasted—noting that coffee acquired in this fashion will be improved by being warmed up in a hot oven before infusion. The use of a percolator is recommended but if one is not available, it lays down guidelines for using a saucepan, starting off with the suggestion that a small amount of salt and dry mustard should be put into the saucepan before adding one cup of water and a tablespoon of coffee for each person. The subsequent procedure is then a touch complex because the book says the contents of the pan should be brought to the boil, stirred, taken off the stove for a minute, and boiled up again, repeating this process three times. By this stage, one is told the grounds will have sunk to the bottom and the infusion can be safely transferred to a coffee pot without further straining. Why go to a coffee bar when you could do it at home so easily?

About 50 recipes are then presented under the heading **Breakfast and Light Luncheon Dishes,** starting off, as one might expect, with bacon and eggs—a dish which was surely a morning badge of office throughout the Empire. It was certainly important in Kenya farming circles, where the typical denizen would have risen in the crisp high-altitude air at five o'clock in the morning and only returned to the homestead at nine. You can imagine how keen appetites would have been by then and I remember a school-friend telling me that most guests to their farmhouse at breakfast time would specify at least four eggs as the accompaniment to their platter of bacon plus a sausage or two. After this, one can understand luncheon being a light meal or having been skipped completely in order not to break up a working day. However, it is plain that hunger pains were expected as evening drew nigh and the sundowner hour approached, because there are literally pages of recipes devoted to **First and Second Toasties**—terms which might be unfamiliar to the modern diner but which translate as hors d'oeuvres and savouries. Very tasty, too, and a quick skim of the recipes reveals a list which includes anchovy eggs, canapés of herring roes, cheese éclairs, eggs and caviar, marmite and cheese on fingers of toast, oysters on toast, Scotch woodcock, devils on horseback, and marrow bone savouries. And these goodies were only meant to sharpen the appetite for dinner, which could start with a fruit cocktail or a selection of soups, ranging from Cock-a-Leekie, Scotch broth, mulligatawny, or a sporty game soup, which could be whipped up if one just happened to have a few spare cuts of oribi or bushbuck in the larder.

The book then leads on **Fish Dishes,** where a certain lack of enthusiasm can be detected. It is an up-country book after all, and apart from the odd trout with which most of the high-altitude streams had been stocked at an early stage of colonial development, fresh fish would not have found its way easily from the coast to the highlands. The book picks up steam again, however, on **Sauces,** (including a rather tasty concoction called *Gubbins Sauce*), and then hits the **Entrée** section with enthusiasm, where it talks with approval about frying or grilling meat as averse to merely roasting it. This part, aimed specifically at chops, stews, and offal, has a splendid recipe for home-made haggis and in case you were unclear on the subject, you must remember to let the windpipe hang out of the pot until the dish is fully cooked so that it can be cut off easily when the haggis has cooled down. After this, there's a good section on **Curry,** beloved by all East Africans, which is followed by a lone Swahili recipe for muhogo (cassava) and grated coconut. Then it's a short step to the serious matter of **Poultry, Game and Joints,** which is prefaced by diagrammatic illustrations of the cuts to be derived from cattle, sheep and pigs. There's a tip on the best way to pluck a fowl and a succession of chicken, duck, partridge, guinea fowl, rabbit and turkey variations, followed by recipes for rissoles, sausages, brawn, Shepherd's pie, and boiled tongue. Then the book moves to vegetables, paying particular attention to local produce such as sweet potatoes and mealies, the latter being dealt with in both cob and maize-meal form.

A long section on puddings ensues and this surely contains the ultimate truism about Britain and its Empire. While bacon and eggs in the morning may have been a national symbol, nothing comes close to the affection with which Empire-builders regarded their puddings. My father saw pudding as the most important part of dinner and he was not alone in adoring a variety of steamed puddings with custard. Fierce red-faced Colonels and weather-beaten farmers would tuck into their helpings of pud with utter enthusiasm, and God help anyone who denied them. *The Kenya Settlers' Cookery Book* is perfect evidence of this and the longest section in the book is headed **Puddings** and **Pastries.** It's a remarkable collection of over 200 recipes and one can only think that everyone must have been substantial of figure after loading up daily on Spotted Dick, Queen's Pudding, and Treacle Duff to marmalade pudding, apple pie, bread-and-butter pudding, various kinds of trifle, banana fritters with cream, and even a local dish called Kabete Soufflé—a concoction of milk and eggs, served with cold custard and jam.

Just in case somebody had a couple of empty corners left to fill, the book goes on to two meals which have so far been overlooked—namely, morning tea and afternoon tea. The former may have been a purely female occasion but they were both redoubtable meals. The **Cake** section lists over 70 varieties of cake, including all the old favourites such as sponge cakes, Dundee cakes, Madeira cakes, doughnuts, Eccles cakes, and Bath buns—they are all there. After that, one can browse through the **Cake Fillings and Icings** chapter and top up any gaps by looking under the heading of **Biscuits,** which is pretty sound on the subject of shortbread. The menfolk then come back into the picture because there is a whole chapter entitled **Savoury Sandwiches,** which bwanas could take with them on safari. Written in the era before sliced bread while butter still lorded it over margarine, the authors are full of sound advice on this topic—stipulating the bread should not be more than a day old and advising their readers to cut off the crusts before covering the finished sandwiches with a damp cloth, a piece of lettuce or a banana leaf. Attention is then rightly given to classic egg, ham or cucumber sandwiches, but there are also recipes for *foie gras*, salmon, cheese and date, sardine, minced tongue, and avocado pear fillings plus a rather intriguing nasturtium-and-egg mixture.

That is just about it as far as foodstuffs are concerned, save for sections on making jam, marmalade, chutney, ginger beer, lemonade, jellied sweets, marzipan and toffee. There is a special section, though, on cooking for invalids, which begins with a stern injunction to serve their food in a tempting and dainty manner. Things like beef tea, egg flip, steamed chops and oatmeal gruel are suggested but there is also a recipe for 'toast water', said to be excellent for children and consisting of two thick slices of toast, broken up into pieces over which boiling water is poured. The jug is then covered, allowed to cool and subsequently strained.

After this, the book turns to practical matters such as what to pack when a wife has to get her husband away on safari. It's quite a list and what with chop boxes, tents, camp beds, a camp bath, hurricane lanterns, camp chairs, empty petrol tins, plates, and saucepans, one cannot say that bwanas travelled lightly. As a team of labourers and a cookboy—with their own food and camp equipment—would almost certainly be involved as well, a large vehicle was essential and the standard vehicle for most excursions of this type was a three-ton truck. It was a deadly serious matter to get the packing right, too, because the bwana could easily be away for a couple of weeks or more and the absence of toilet paper could be tricky. The book's advice is very sound in this regard and the authors even remember to recommend *charguls* as a source of cool drinking water. (A *chargul* is a canvas water bag, which is filled with water and slung on the outside of a vehicle in such a way that the wind of passage aids evaporation and ensures the water is cold, even on a hot day).

One can imagine the sigh of relief emitted by a memsahib who has just got her husband away on safari but rather than allow the poor girl a cup of coffee, roasted and strained as instructed, the book remorselessly moves on to a variety of household chores. There is a whole section on cleaning the home and its contents, passing on to the best way of making your own soap and doing the laundry. This is followed by instructions on how to manage a broody hen, and then shifts to the topic of first aid and what to do if someone has been poisoned. The effects of chloral poisoning, opium, strychnine, and toadstools, are all discussed and it is interesting to note the standard treatment of giving the patient an emetic, (salt or mustard in a glass of water), was concluded with a swig of brandy.

Finally, this young wives' bible ends with a section of useful Swahili words and **Orders to Servants** in both Swahili and Kikuyu. It's not good Swahili by any means and even gives a separate list of words in **Ki-Settler,** recognised as a simplified version of Kiswahili. Servants were a significant part of one's domestic existence and as very few indigenous people spoke English in those days, it was essential to be able to communicate with them. It was not a straightforward master/servant relationship, however, and there was usually a bond of affection between domestic servants and their employers, who generally lent their staff money on a regular basis and supported them in any crises that might arise in their personal lives. The practice of referring to any black-skinned male, regardless of his age, as a 'boy' was widespread in the early years but this was already frowned on by 1950 and the practice gradually ceased. It wasn't intended to be arrogant or offensive, however, and was more a question of 'boy' simply being a convenient word.

Truly, *The Kenya Settler's Cookery Book* is an excellent record of the times and makes fascinating reading. As already stated, however, the reader must not think everybody lived according to the precepts of the good Scottish housewives who compiled it. Bachelors were completely at the mercy of their domestic staff and few of them enjoyed the range of good food described in the book. It was even worse for single men who led isolated lives in remote stations, such as District Officers, Game Rangers, and field operatives of different skills. A selection of food was not available to these stalwarts and the height of gastronomic indulgence would be a scrawny chicken roasted by the cook in an old petrol tin over an open fire. This gave rise to the standard joke about the art of carving when two bachelors were dining together. The bird was simply cut in half from the breastbone downwards!

Tinned food was nowhere near as varied and expert as it is today and I formulated the opinion very early in my career as a surveyor that the only tins worth carrying about were corned beef and baked beans. Everything else in a tin—from spaghetti and potato salad to meat balls, sausages, and luncheon meat—tasted funny and even in the fruit line, peaches were the only things which tasted natural. As a result, I found it was much better to stick to the corned beef and beans, supplemented by a bag of rice, onions and some curry powder. If, however, chance took one anywhere near an Indian *duka*, it was heaven to get hold of some of *Uplands'* estimable sausages, hams and bacon, which mercifully found their way all over East Africa from the factory in Kenya.

Having been stuffed with information about food, the reader is now probably curious to know what bwanas and their memsahibs drank. Well, a short answer to that is a hell of a lot. East Africa was a hot, dusty country and though all the hotels had bars, there were no equivalents of the English pub. You could be sure, however, that each small town or community had its own club and this was where—secure from the curious eyes of the local population—one could relax, gossip with one's peers, and get plastered without letting the side down. The most popular drinks were beer, whisky and gin, though there was also a strong market for South African brandy. Ladies tended to favour gin (either with lime juice, tonic water or orange squash) but most men worked on the assumption that you needed a couple of beers to settle the dust before turning to the consumption of spirits, which were usually taken long with water or soda. Whisky was the king in this context but that is not to say that men didn't drink gin as well. They did in some quantity, but according to convention, white spirits were held to be permissible at midday and brown spirits were deemed appropriate to

OXFAM

VAT: 348 4542 08

Volunteer here: Have fun,
meet new people & learn
new skills
Sign up in-store or at
www.oxfam.org.uk/jointheteam

AT	SALES		F6312/POS1
	THURSDAY 17 OCTOBER 2024	15:50 2582566	
1	C10 - HISTORY		£5.99

1 Items

TOTAL **£5.99**

CREDIT CARD £5.99

Oxfam Books & Music Shop: F6312
36, St Mary Stre t., Cardiff
CF10 1AD
02920 222275
oxfam.org.uk/shop

TAG YOUR BAG.
RAISE MORE MONEY.
CHANGE MORE LIVES.

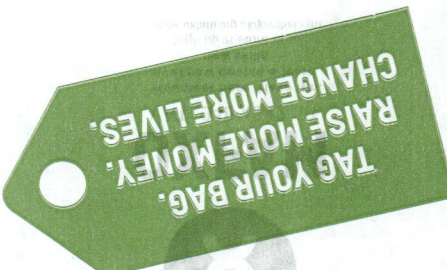

Find out more www.oxfam.org.uk/tagyourbag

THANK YOU

Every item you buy or donate helps beat poverty.

the hours of darkness. Wine was enjoyed but only as an accompaniment to meals; it was not readily available and normally found its way from South Africa in the form of hock or from Europe in the form of Chianti or similar table wines. Aside from its price, Chianti was deservedly popular because it came in an attractive raffia-covered bulbous bottle, which could be converted into a table lamp by the addition of an electric globe and a lampshade.

Regrettably, a lot of people drank far too much and it was not unknown for middle-aged men to polish off at least half a bottle of whisky a day, often more. This was not looked on as excessive and hard-case status was only awarded if the bwana in question needed a snifter to enable him to shave with a steady hand in the morning. Drunkenness as such was frowned upon and holding your liquor was looked on as the sign of a gentleman. Whatever may have happened the previous night, one was expected as a matter of pride and honour to wake early in the morning and be at work at the normal time without showing the ill effects of a hangover. With practice, a lot of bwanas were quite good at this but as one might expect, the fresh early morning feeling would wear off as the day progressed and a hard core of bwanas would start thinking they needed a hair of the leg at eleven o'clock of a morning. Some farmers had their own little shed discreetly tucked away in a corner of the farm where they kept a private supply, while discreet places like the British Legion performed yeoman service in the towns by reviving its regulars on a daily basis.

Naturally, a discussion on alcohol leads to the subject of sex and though people in East Africa were no more promiscuous than people anywhere else, the goings-on of the Happy Valley crowd gave the entire white population a reputation for licentiousness. Unfortunately, being thin on the ground meant that any indiscretions would stick out like a sore thumb and there was no such thing as decent anonymity or hiding oneself in a crowd. For one thing, it was impossible to conceal anything untoward from servants' eyes, and for another, everybody knew which car one drove. Hence, you could bet that news of any little flutter would be round town within twenty-four hours and would be a prime topic of conversation with which to enliven the sundowner hour. Additional strain was put on the situation because the sexes were not evenly balanced and there was a strong predominance of males in the mix. This meant that competition for a presentable female was pretty fierce and there was always someone willing to step into the breach if a husband went off the boil or merely had to go away on safari. Even quite ordinary and respectable people would get caught up in complex situations and a chain reaction was not uncommon. A District Officer, for example, might fall for the wife of the Agricultural Officer, who in his turn might catch the eye of a farmer's wife who fancied a change. Anything too open or scandalous was frowned upon but if it was done with style, people just shrugged and went about their business once the news value had worn off.

As I have already mentioned, young East African males were fairly innocent and though young East African females were delightful, they were generally just as innocent—and also determined not to get pregnant. A few young men were fortunate enough to be initiated into the mysteries by bored or lonely wives, but by and large, most of the fellows I knew had to wait until they reached Europe in order to find out the full story. It's symptomatic of this background that a favourite story of the period deals with a young East African male, newly-arrived in London and highly desirous of coming to terms with a lady of easy virtue.

'Five pounds, dear,' she said, finally and firmly.

'All right,' he said, 'but only if you let me do it the East African way.'

She was intrigued. 'That's a new one on me, ducks,' she said. 'I thought I'd tried everything. How do you do it?'

'Quite easy,' said our hero. 'I give you one pound now and the other four pounds at the end of the month.'

In order to understand this anecdote, you must remember that both he and his parents had probably lived off credit from their local Indian grocer for years and to run an account was looked on as normal. Nobody paid cash on the nail and at the end of each month, you would receive a statement which listed all the purchases you had made. As a result, when salaries arrived in the bank account, they went straight out again, a process that only became onerous if one over-extended oneself or were going on leave. The shopkeepers were pretty smart about this, too—they not only knew how much one earned but also had as good an idea of one's future movements as your employer or Departmental head. They also knew each other, so if one tried going to another shop, no credit would be extended until the first shopkeeper's account had been settled.

Certainly, there was an acceptance of the ephemeral nature of romance in East Africa. A favourite story of the time, which was sworn to me to be true, concerned a young couple in the sisal area of Tanga Province. As one does, they had apparently got into the habit of dropping in every evening at the local Club, where the attractive young wife caught the eye of one of the wealthy planters. Matters quickly became serious and the older man eventually sought out the husband.

'Listen,' he is reputed to have said, 'I must confess that I am in love with your wife and would like to take her away from you. But I cannot expect you to give her up without some form of compensation. I'll make you an offer. Outside, I have a new Mercedes 220SE with only 5000 miles on the clock. If you agree to divorce her without any fuss, the car is yours.'

The husband must have been a car nut because he is reported to have hesitated for no longer than two minutes before agreeing. The deal was done and according to the story-teller, everyone lived happily ever afterwards. Luxury cars had only just begun to arrive in the country and quite a large school of thought felt the husband's decision had been eminently sensible.

Certainly, in 1950, I don't think anyone anticipated the political changes which lay round the corner. The forces of change which did occur were mainly economic and when Tanganyika acquired a new dynamic Governor in the person of Sir Edward Twining, it found itself precipitated into a new era of prosperity. 'Teddy', as he was familiarly known, took over from Sir William Battershill in 1949 just as the Groundnut Scheme came to an untimely end. He didn't let this phase him, though, and one of his first acts was to jack up the Provincial Administration to the highest level of efficiency it had ever known. A large, genial man, he wasn't shy of dressing up in the full paraphernalia of a Colonial Governor, (white uniform and plumed helmet), and having meetings with the various tribes on their home ground. At the same time, he encouraged commercial activity and boosted white settlement in the recognised farming areas. Tanganyika, which had been the Cinderella of the Empire up till then, began to swing—the process being substantially aided by all the Government Departments and commercial organisations being fully staffed at last.

My wife and I met Twining in 1956 when he came to Mbeya on one of his periodic safaris. A cocktail party for important people and senior officials was held by the Provincial Commissioner and somewhat to the chagrin of other wives on the station, my status as the only representative of the Survey Department in the region led to an invitation being extended to us. So there we were, sipping beer, trying to look casual, and watching HE—looking dashing in a palm-beach suit and with a full glass in his hand—circulate round the room and say a few words to everyone there. I didn't think he would notice us, but there was no way that my young and beautiful wife escaped his eye and he was on to us like a flash.

'Hello, my dear,' he said, with a twinkle in his eye. 'Have you got a nice house?'

'Yes, thank you,' said my wife, though our Government quarter wasn't really all that much to write home about.

'Have you got a nice garden?'

'Yes, thank you.'

Twinkle, twinkle. 'Have you got a nice husband?'

He roared with laughter, slapped me on the back, and moved on to talk with another of Her Majesty's loyal subjects, leaving us laughing after him. No pomp or ceremonial stiffness about him, he was absolutely great.

In Kenya, meanwhile, things were also going at a fair lick. Sir Philip Mitchell, whose signature I have on the first passport that was ever issued to me in 1945, was still Governor and was highly regarded—even by the argumentative and somewhat unruly settlers. Kenya was the jewel of the Empire, Hollywood was making movies about it, and the richest people in the world were queuing up to be taken on safari by that most romantic of characters, the Kenya White Hunter. Royalty, too, paid it periodic visits and as widely reported, Princess Elizabeth and the Duke of Edinburgh were actually in Kenya, staying at the Treetops Hotel in Nyeri, when George VI died in February 1952. The royal couple had to rush back to England in order to be there for the funeral, and that particular moment passed into Kenya's history. Maybe, in a co-incidental kind of way, the King's death also heralded the end of an era in Kenya, because only a few months later, its stable world came to a crashing halt with the beginning of the Mau Mau uprising. This came like a bolt out of the blue to the Kenya Government, who had been busy with Sir Philip Mitchell's retirement and the arrival of his replacement, Sir Evelyn Baring. The new Governor had to declare a State of Emergency within two weeks of taking over the reins, and the subsequent history of Africa was changed irreparably.

Much has been said and written about the Mau Mau insurrection from different points of view, but there is no doubt that it hastened the end of the colonial age. Oddly enough, it was not a black-on-white national war of liberation but more of a civil war within the Kikuyu nation, which is only one of Kenya's 70 tribes. Why did it start? There are several reasons but like so many other conflicts which the world has witnessed, it is probably true to say land was at the bottom of it. Not just any old land, either, but a large tract of the best land in Kenya, which had been traditionally occupied by the Kikuyu in pre-colonial days. Naturally, it proved irresistible to the early settlers but to give them credit, they didn't take all of it. Reasoning there was room for everybody, they reserved a substantial portion of it for Kikuyu use according to tribal law and custom—assuming this would not only give the tribe adequate space within which to pursue their normal way of life but would also provide the settlers with farm labour. It must have seemed a win-win solution at the time and worked happily enough for the first twenty years.

Inevitably, like a Greek tragedy, problems slowly arose. In the first place, the methods of subsistence agriculture practised in the Reserve were not very efficient and secondly, the improved health measures which colonial rule brought with it led to a large increase in the Kikuyu population. The Reserve became unable to cope with the demands placed on it and this was made worse by periodic droughts and crop failure. As a result, thousands of Kikuyu migrated to Nairobi to look for non-existent work and ended up eking out an existence in the city. The accuracy of the figure is not known but the population of Nairobi is estimated to have doubled between 1938 and 1952.

At the same time, the urban Kikuyu were fully aware of political trends in the rest of the world and were not immune to the lure of socialism. This led to the formation of trade unions and in common with other developing countries, the growth of unionism resulted in a climate of increasing agitation. Within the Kikuyu sphere of activity, radical elements within the newly-established unions soon broke away and formed a violent and secret society known as the Mau Mau, to which loyalty was pledged by swearing a binding oath in the most sinister manner. A campaign of terror then followed, beginning in October 1952 with the murder of Chief Waruhiu, (a respected figure held in great esteem by the authorities), several white settlers, and a number of Kikuyu loyalists who would not take the oath. This led Sir Evelyn to proclaim the State of Emergency and within days, a battalion of the Lancashire Fusiliers was flown in to reinforce the King's African Rifles and the Kenya Police. Hundreds of Kikuyu leaders were arrested, a Home Guard of loyal Kikuyu was formed, and the Kenya Regiment was mobilised.

Instead of quietening things down, however, these measures persuaded the Mau Mau leadership to embark on an all-out war and the violence continued until well into 1954. At this point, the authorities had had enough and 'Operation Anvil' was launched under the command of General Erskine. Nairobi was declared a military area and the city was cleared of Kikuyu, 17000 of whom were arrested on suspicion of complicity and were either detained or sent back to the Reserve. The exercise was then repeated in other areas and a total of some 80000 people ended up in detention camps by the end of that year. This broke the back of the insurrection and the Mau Mau leaders fled to the Aberdare forests near Mount Kenya. There, they were gradually rounded up and the last of the so-called generals, Dedan Kimathi, was captured and executed in 1956.

This was effectively the end of the matter, though the State of Emergency was only formally lifted in 1960. The number of rebel deaths during the outbreak has been estimated at 11500 but God knows how many of their own kind the terrorists killed in their efforts to broaden their support within the Kikuyu nation. The fact that it was not an all-out war against whites specifically can be seen from the low number of settlers who were killed. The total figure in this regard, (including two of my school-mates), was 32—less than the number killed by traffic accidents in Nairobi during the same period. It was, however, an extremely expensive exercise calling for the deployment of large numbers of troops and police, and there can be no doubt it blunted the enthusiasm of the British Government for continued colonialism. It certainly diminished the influence of the white settlers and curiously enough, it even opened up a chasm between the latter and the British public back in Britain. The popular press became critical of the situation and white Kenyans were accused of living the life of Riley at the expense of the British taxpayer. Despite ties of blood and kinship, an active resentment against the forces of colonial law and order built up and leftist liberals had much to say. Sunshine and servants were in short supply in Britain at this time, too, and ordinary people also became envious of what they perceived as a privileged way of life, resulting in a well-known anecdote of the time about a waitress in a London tea-shop waving a collecting box under customers' noses on behalf of the Mau Mau. When challenged by someone home on leave revealing he came from Kenya, she is alleged to have snapped 'if I'd known that, I'd never 'ave served yer.'

Meanwhile, life for most bwanas and memsahibs went on much as usual, and those of us in Tanganyika and Uganda were not affected at all by the problems which had surfaced in Kenya. Even in Kenya, its problems were limited to the Kikuyu and the major part of its population went on with their normal business. East African Railways and Harbours went on running its network of rail, road and steamer services and East African Airway's fleet of trusty DC3's went on flying between the major towns. Ships of the world came and went on a regular basis, new models of car such as the Peugeot and Mercedes found their way on to the roads, the prices of coffee and sisal boomed, new trunk roads were built, housing estates mushroomed, and modern commercial buildings transformed the city centres of Nairobi, Dar es Salaam, Kampala and Mombasa. Dar even acquired a couple of deep-water berths in the harbour, the new wharf being known as Princess Margaret Quay. (Naturally, when her Royal Highness eventually married Tony Armstrong-Jones, the local wits could not resist the temptation and the new dock area was known to all and sundry as *Maggie Jones' Jetty*).

These new developments mainly affected the major centres, however, and life in a small up-country town in East Africa still had a unique flavour. I can think of no better example of this than Mbeya in the Southern Highlands Province of Tanganyika, where my wife and I were stationed during the latter part of the 1950s. Being a regional centre far away from the beady eye of authority which may have gazed in its direction from Dar es Salaam, the bwanas and memsahibs who lived there constituted a self-contained microcosm of colonial life. It was a plum posting, too, because Mbeya was one of the most scenic towns in the country, being situated at an average altitude of 1700 m (or 5600m ft) above sea level and surrounded by hills. As a result, it enjoyed a cool climate with substantial rainfall and there was never a problem with getting firewood or fresh vegetables. The buildings in the town were not much to look at but due to the fact it was established in the early 1930s before the advent of modern town planning, its layout exhibited a pleasing amateurish quality. As might be expected in a British town, the Mbeya Club with its 9-hole golf course was located at the main intersection of the road system and the rest of town straggled away in all directions. There were two hotels and two banks, several garages, and a respectable number of shops, which included two excellent grocery stores—one owned by a hard-working Goan family and the other by an equally hard-working Greek family. In addition, there was a hospital, an airfield, and a bus terminal. The Mbeya School, a large primary school for European children which had been established in pre-war days, lay on the outskirts of town and there were extensive forestry plantations round it.

It is interesting to run through the different categories of bwana and memsahib in the community because Mbeya was a prime example of a colonial town. To start with the governmental side of the house, there was not only the Provincial Commissioner—who was the Queen's representative and administrative boss of the five Districts comprising the Province—but a whole battery of Provincial Heads of Department in the fields of agriculture, education, engineering, forestry, labour, medical services, police, surveying, veterinary services, and water development. In addition, there were all the people required to run the District, including the District Commissioner, three or four District Officers, the Revenue Officer, and an assortment of specialists and field officers attached to the different Departments. Then there was the Resident Magistrate, a couple of doctors, a dentist, a health inspector, half a dozen nurses, and a whole platoon of teachers, who either taught at the Mbeya School or the African Teachers Training School. Two senior Prison Officers ran the big regional prison and an Aviation Controller looked after the airfield.

The commercial sector included a large number of outlying farmers and miners but in the town itself, there were the bank managers and assistant managers, a brace of lawyers, and sundry representatives of car, truck and farm equipment distributors. The clergy was present in both Anglican and Roman Catholic modes, and there were various representatives who worked for oil, tobacco and liquor companies. In quasi-governmental ranks, there was the Town Clerk of the embryonic Town Council, the manager of the electricity supply company, the Postmaster, and the administrative and technical staff of East African Railways and Harbours. A further number of people were always in evidence, too, in the shape of visiting experts, contracting staff, and people simply passing through on their way to Northern Rhodesia along the Great North Road.

All told, this constituted a fair number of bwanas and memsahibs—about 400 in total—and as a result, the golf course and clubhouse were never empty. There was a lively social scene and the club held regular dances, with a film show every Sunday night which featured an up-to-the-minute movie flown down from Nairobi. Further to these diversions, there was always golf, tennis and squash on the go, plus a keen amateur dramatic company which put on some excellent productions in the Mbeya School hall, including a Christmas pantomime. Cabaret floor shows also occurred at the club periodically and on New Years Eve, most people attended in fancy dress. Very much a gala occasion, the magic hour of midnight gave everyone a perfect excuse to kiss the members of the opposite sex they had been eyeing for the past year, and I will never forget the attractive wife of a senior official draping herself over the bar at 12.30 a.m. on 1st January 1958 and declaring that kissing time was open. A whole queue of bwanas formed up to take advantage of this opportunity and though it was done with due respect and circumspection, it was apparent she was handing out something a little more intensive than a peck on the cheek. Observing this spectacle, the wife of one of the bwanas in the queue came up to him and spoke with emotion.

'If you kiss that woman, I'm going home,' she hissed.

Well, our empire-builder's moustache didn't even twitch. Without looking at his wife and without a word spoken, he simply felt in his pocket, extracted the car keys and gave them to her.

History does not record the conversation—or lack of conversation—which ensued between husband and wife the next morning but the story circulated round the town very quickly. It was a great place for real or imagined scandal, and people knew with unerring accuracy when pregnancies had been initiated. 'You didn't go straight to sleep after that party at the Robinson's place,' someone would say to a blushing wife who was just beginning to develop a bit of a tummy. But it was a wonderful place to actually have babies and the small hospital at the top of the hill was run on very friendly lines. The maternity wing only contained two beds and when our eldest son was born, it was a simple matter to smuggle in a record-player and a supply of Guinness, the latter have been recommended warmly by her doctor—a spirited Irishwoman who had six kids of her own. 'It will do wonders for the milk,' she said, 'but for God's sake don't tell Matron I put you up to it.'

Being a young surveyor in this environment was exhilarating. Whether it involved straightforward bush-whacking or climbing mountains, there was always a challenge about the best way to get a survey done. And what country it was! The job took me into the mountains and tea plantations of Rungwe District, down into the lowlands of the Usangu Flats, into the bush country south of Lake Rukwa, and up to the border of Northern Rhodesia. Before the advent of our son, I was sometimes able to take my wife with me and we had one notable trip to Lake Nyasa, (called Lake Malawi by the people of Malawi on the other side of the lake), where we ended up having dinner and drinks on board the *m.v. Ilala*—the small steamer which went round Lake Nyasa on a regular basis. While we were still in the vicinity, a friendly crocodile hunter—whom I must have trusted—took my wife out in a dugout canoe to help him shoot crocodiles but unfortunately, the latter were in hiding that day and she was never able to say she had shot her own handbag. She did do some good shooting, however, when we went north to see another friend who ran a tobacco farm north of Chunya and he took us hunting in what was prime elephant country. Unfortunately, we didn't see any elephants but my wife bagged a fine Sable antelope, shooting from the back of a truck while six months' pregnant. Not bad for a London girl who used to work in a fashion house! (We still have the horns but she has never shot anything again).

On the last big safari I undertook in that part of the world, I did not take her with me because it was an open-ended safari which involved three weeks of jolting around in a Land Rover along a series of bush tracks through the area of the Great Ruaha River headwaters. Even for surveyors in Tanganyika, the reason for this expedition was somewhat bizarre and stemmed from the fact that a batch of new 1/50000 topographical maps had been compiled for this remote region from aerial photography. They were excellent maps and there were plenty of lines on the paper—but no place names. The only way to turn them into usable maps was for someone to go in there and find out what names for villages, rivers, hills and other features were in local use. It was essential, too, that the names be recorded in the right place and some skill in navigation was obviously necessary. HQ didn't pause in deciding who was to do it—young Dyus was nearest the scene and he was told to get on with it. Hence, in the company of two intrepid survey boys and a driver, I duly sallied forth with a bundle of draft maps, a box of aerial photos, a .22 rifle and a box of provisions which I hoped would last for two weeks. And what a trip it turned out to be! A typical day involved driving through the bush until a group of huts was reached and then asking the inhabitants the name of their village. Getting an answer in tribal dialect and assuming I knew exactly where I was—sometimes a dubious assumption in featureless bush—I would then write the name on the map in what I thought was appropriate Swahili. I am sure in some instances, I must have transcribed words and phrases such as 'I don't know' or 'That's my house' into Swahili-like sounds but how could one do better? To add to the problem, some bush-dwellers were obviously chary of dealing with a government official in case some form of tax would be visited on them, and one group simply ran away because they had never seen a man with a white skin before.

For all the adventure and fun, however, there was a serious downside to being a young colonial civil servant and at the end of our stint in Mbeya, my wife and I took stock of our situation and solemnly swore we would leave the service and lead a civilised life in a developed country. The job might have been fascinating and the way of life fun, but the salary wasn't up to much and we were broke most of the time. In addition, the constant requirement to go on safari made it difficult to lead a normal home life and we felt we were losing ground every year we didn't buy a house, settle down somewhere and start paying back a mortgage. So we went to England on leave in 1959 full of determination to settle there. Ha, ha! As so many other people found out, going back to England cured one of feeling able to settle for a European existence. My wife had been dreaming of seeing Oxford Street again but a day's shopping in London proved to be quite enough and the lure of the English countryside palled before the onset of an English winter. Commuting to work on the Tube no longer seemed an exciting prospect and the High Street proved to be a cramped environment. By early 1960, we were back in Tanganyika—little knowing that the colonial story was about to undergo a few drastic changes.

CHAPTER 5

THE UHURU YEARS

Anybody who remembers the meaning of the word *uhuru* must be at least middle-aged. A Swahili word meaning 'freedom', it was very much a vogue word in the 1960's and even became used as a codeword by African nationalists in other countries which didn't speak Swahili. Aside from its philosophical basis, it was a very useful word at political rallies and could be nicely separated into syllables for crowd participation. First would come the syllable 'u' (pronounced 'oo'), then 'hur' (pronounced 'hoor'), and then the final 'u' (another 'oo'). A skilled orator could get a crowd worked up to fever pitch by repeating this twenty times in succession and after that, the perspiring mob could be trusted to give him a big hand for anything he might say. Though not in Swahili and having to make do with English, this technique was pioneered by Kwame Nkrumah in the Gold Coast a few years earlier when Ghana's independence was heralded with mass shouts of 'Free-dom', 'Free-dom'.

Uhuru became a universal word in the 1960's and a wife in the process of leaving her husband, for example, would say proudly that she had achieved her *uhuru* when the divorce came through. Anything that smacked of a successful defiance of authority was categorised by this word, and it was widely used as a rallying call by any group of people who felt oppressed. It is therefore scurrilous to repeat the theory aired in sundry colonial bars that the word was actually Scottish in origin. This stemmed from the reported case of an irate Glaswegian husband getting annoyed with his wife for having a bit of fun with one of his colleagues and giving her a black eye, meanwhile shouting 'you hoor, you.' Always good for a laugh, the canard was responsible for the subsequent intake of much brown and bubbly fluid.

Certainly, it was never commonly thought—as late as 1959—that any of the East African countries would become independent within the near future. Apart from the activities of a few embryonic Trade Unions, (which in the case of Kenya had gone sideways), there had never been any real political action, and tribal societies still looked to their chiefs for guidance and representation. It was understood that self-government would come into being one day but only when the populace was ready for it. Even the ambitious Julius Nyerere, who had founded the Tanganyika African National Union (TANU) in 1954, was demanding no tighter schedule than a 20-year timetable to independence.

It is probably true to say that most of the bwanas and memsahibs in East Africa failed to recognise the straws in the wind which signalled the passing of the established order. The situation was in fact in a state of flux before the end of the decade with Evelyn Baring stepping down as Governor of Kenya in 1959 and being replaced by Patrick Renison, while Edward Twining had already left Tanganyika and been replaced by Richard Turnbull—previously the Chief Secretary of Kenya. People were used to Governors retiring, however, and in spite of the musical chairs, it was generally assumed the existing state of affairs would go on for a considerable period. If anything was going to change in the fullness of time, it was expected to be limited in the first instance to Uganda, which had always been a Protectorate and did not have as many settlers as Kenya and Tanganyika.

There was also a lack of appreciation of the way in which the attitude of the British Conservative party towards the colonies had begun changing. Having always been faithful to the concept of Empire throughout its history, it had none the less been in power for eight years by the time 1959 dawned and was becoming conscious of its mortality. Both Winston Churchill and Anthony Eden had left the scene and the Suez crisis of 1956 was still fresh in political minds. Suez had been a far greater shock to Britain and French perceptions of the world than most ordinary people realised and Her Majesty's overseas subjects did not know that Harold Macmillan, who started a second term as Prime Minister in 1959, was privately of a mind to shed Britain's colonial possessions at double-quick speed. When he unmasked his convictions during his celebrated 'wind of change' speech to the South African Parliament on 3 February 1960, it was completely unexpected and many people, accustomed to British politicians vociferously supporting human rights for all but not necessarily on an immediate basis, found it difficult to take him too seriously. Certainly, his white audience in South Africa and Rhodesia refused to be impressed and only became a little thoughtful in the aftermath of Sharpeville, which by an odd co-incidence occurred a few weeks later and presented a startled world with the spectacle of white policemen firing into a crowd of blacks, who—depending on the identity of the person telling the story—were either conducting an orderly demonstration or going on the rampage. To make matters worse, the Belgian Congo (now Zaire) blew up a short time afterwards and it seemed Africa was suddenly on the boil. This was cause for serious alarm but again, there was nothing much that interested observers could do—except get on with daily cares and wonder what in the name of God had got into the Belgians to have made them abdicate so rapidly from their prized and well-run colony.

A more detailed look at what was going on within the Conservative Party of Great Britain must now be taken in order to understand subsequent events. The Suez Crisis had occurred only three years previously, forcing Anthony Eden to resign as Prime Minister and causing the British political scene to fall into such a state of chaos that Macmillan, who had stepped up from being Chancellor of the Exchequer to become the new Prime Minister, told the Queen he could not guarantee his government would last more than six weeks. By a mixture of skill and circumstance, however, he managed to stay in power much longer than expected and by the time another General election was due in 1959, had succeeded in turning the economy around. Perhaps he was just plain lucky and the economy was going to turn round anyway or maybe it was because he had packed his government with 35 old Etonians, but the Conservatives won the election decisively. During it, he is credited with having uttered the famous remark 'you've never had it so good' and a favourite story of the time concerned a girl who told the police she had been raped.

'Was he tall, short, dark, fair, or what?' the police demanded.

'I don't know what he looked like,' she sniffed. 'All I know is he was a Conservative.'

'How on earth did you know that?'

'Because he told me that I'd never had it so good,' she replied.

In fact, he never actually said those words. What he apparently said was 'most of our people have never had it so good' but the newspapers preferred the popular paraphrase and that is how it has gone down in history. Why he felt imbued to jettison Britain's imperial past as quickly as possible is a matter on which there is no clarity. A mass of contradictions, Macmillan was certainly no scholar, having left Eton prematurely and never completing the classics degree that he started at Oxford before World War One broke out. Whether or not he was involved in any sexual shenanigans at Eton as has been alleged is also unclear, but it is a matter of public record that his wife indulged in sexy high jinks quite openly for years with Robert Boothby, another Conservative politician with whom Macmillan continued to be friendly. Was his complicity a sign of weakness or a lack of normal morality? One does not know but whatever his motivation, it did not stop him from being a skilled politician. *Supermac*, as he was nicknamed by the press, stayed in office as Prime Minister from 1957 to 1963, and played a major role in shaping world affairs.

Regarded by the media during his middle period as shrewd and unflappable, the contradictions in Macmillan's life set in again towards the end of his term of office. Again, sex was at the bottom of it, so to speak, because his government was beset by a succession of scandals, the best known of which was the Profumo affair. A headline-grabber of the first order, this unedifying story revealed that John Profumo, the Secretary of State for War at the time, had got himself involved in a steamy romp with a couple of call-girls who happened to also be friendly with a Russian diplomat. The risk to security, allied to the salacious details of the case, raised a national storm and the press began comparing the Conservative regime with the last days of Ancient Rome. Eventually, Macmillan had no option but to resign and though the official reason for his sudden departure was put down to severe illness, it is noteworthy that he subsequently lived on until the age of 92.

It wasn't just *Supermac,* however, who wanted to see an end to Empire. There was another major actor in the cast who was even more determined to put an end to it than Macmillan. To make it worse, he was not only recognised as bright but was described by a senior member of the Conservative Party as 'too clever by half'. This, of course, was Iain Macleod, who was Secretary of State for the Colonies in Harold Macmillan's government between 1959 and 1961. A history graduate and subsequently a professional bridge player, he became the Tory whiz kid of the 1950s and held several high political posts, eventually ending up as Chancellor of the Exchequer in Ted Heath's government of 1970. He would have probably gone on to have been Prime Minister, too, if he had not died of a heart attack at the age of 57, leaving behind in his characteristically busy style not only an outline budget but detailed proposals for tax reform.

Macleod's impact was not anticipated and back in 1959, the bwanas and memsahibs of East Africa had no idea the new Secretary of State for the Colonies was bent on decolonisation or that he would be so prompt in achieving his objectives. Unbelievably, however, during Macleod's two years at the colonial helm, he was responsible for independence being granted to

Nigeria, British Somaliland, Tanganyika, Sierra Leone, Kuwait and British Cameroons. He also set the scene for Kenya, Uganda and Zanzibar to get their *uhuru* a short while later and was instrumental in breaking up the Federation of Rhodesia and Nyasaland. Talk about a man in a hurry! He affected the lives of so many million people in virtually one fell swoop and did it without any particular knowledge or experience of their background and readiness. The most charitable view one can take of his actions—and the fact that Macmillan gave him his head—is that they both believed Britain would be financially better off without any colonies. Their exact motivations and the repercussions of their policies will be discussed later but for the time being, the reader is asked to reflect how strange it was for this major change to have come from a Conservative right-wing government and not from the ranks of liberal Socialism.

On a personal note, I have already described why my wife and I—young, ambitious, and broke—chose to go back to East Africa in the hope of pursuing a long-lasting career in Her Majesty's Overseas Civil Service rather than adapt to life in Britain, where I had been offered a job by a private survey firm. Once back in Tanganyika, we then had the good fortune of being posted to Iringa, a thriving town in the Southern Highlands which was the commercial centre for a large farming area. At 1650 metres above sea level, it had a cool climate like Mbeya and the surrounding hills with their outcrops of red rock were remarkably scenic. There was a strong community of farmers and the main crop was tobacco, though tea was grown in the Mufindi area and coffee at Dabaga. The local tribe, the Wahehe, were likeable, and the town had a full range of shops and services, being linked by road with Mbeya to the south, Dodoma to the north and Dar es Salaam to the east. In addition, one of Twining's pet projects had come to fruition there in the shape of a large secondary school, which was intended to become Tanganyika's version of an English public school and had a large complement of sociable teaching staff.

We enjoyed Iringa and it did not take long to get immersed in its social and business scene. Aside from my primary role in carrying out surveys for which instructions were issued by Headquarters in Dar es Salaam, I was not only an honorary Town Councillor but had to represent the Lands and Surveys Department at a local level. The latter role was doubly interesting because it not only involved liaising with the Provincial Administration on land and planning matters but also necessitated attendance at District Team meetings. These were held on a monthly basis under the chairmanship of the District Commissioner and at these meetings, each representative of the

Agriculture, Forestry, Medical, Veterinary, Public Works, Labour and other Departments would report on the state of the district and their activities within it. It was real grass roots government and you could not sit through one of these meetings without getting a full and factual picture of what was going on.

Even more interestingly, I had only been in Iringa for a few months when a United Nations Committee on the Management of Trustee Territories arrived in town and a special District Team meeting was convened in its honour. This was a direct result of Tanganyika being mandated to the British at the end of the First World War and being subsequently defined as a Trust Territory in terms of the United Nations Charter. In pursuance of this, the United Nations had to satisfy itself that the administering powers were performing their duties in a responsible fashion and for this reason, investigating committees were regularly despatched on tours of inspection. I cannot recall who all the members of the committee were on this occasion but at least two of them were South American, two were Asian, and there was possibly an Egyptian. Most of them seemed to have a language problem with English and the questions were mainly asked by a youngish New Zealander, who seemed very competent. (Good though he was, it didn't stop one of my colleagues whispering to me that New Zealand had a bloody cheek—it had only just stopped being a colony itself and here it was, checking up on whether we knew how to run one).

The meeting itself went well and I think our visitors were suitably impressed with British efficiency. The DC was an excellent Chairman, everybody did their stuff, and when it was over, the District Engineer and I went off to the Club as usual to play tennis and drink beer with a feeling of all being right with the world. Little did we realise the United Nations visit was to be the last one of its type and that there would be no future need to check on the way the territory was being prepared for independence. In retrospect, this was naïve because a major player in the game, namely the new Governor, Sir Richard Turnbull, was already working hard to see the Union Jack pulled down in Tanganyika as quickly as possible. Rightly or wrongly, his experience as Chief Secretary in Kenya throughout the Mau Mau troubles had convinced him that the human and financial cost of continued colonial rule was too high and—unbeknown to all but a small inner circle in those early days of his governorship—he had taken the view that it should be brought to a speedy end.

Looking back, one can see clearly how Turnbull's expert opinion on East African conditions was an obvious clincher with both Macmillan and Macleod. The latter were battling with Britain's balance of payments problems at the time and must have been tired of fending off American anti-imperialist sentiment and Soviet attempts at destabilisation. In the circumstances, they must have feared a progressively more expensive involvement and can have taken no heart from the example of Algeria, where the French were having a nightmare of a war. A repetition of Mau Mau was unthinkable, but how the hell did they get rid of Britain's African possessions with honour? The Belgian example in the Congo was too dire for words and I can only speculate on their reaction when Turnbull came along at this point and told them he knew how to do it. 'Richard, my dear chap, this is marvellous,' they must have said. 'For starters, get us out of Tanganyika and hand the bloody place over to the locals. But be sure to do it chop-chop and avoid having to call in the Army.'

So the Governor of Tanganyika set to with a will and sat down with Julius Nyerere, the leader of TANU and the closest thing to a black politician that Tanganyika had yet produced. Up till then, a Legislative Council with local representation through a system of nominated members had been in place for some years and had always worked with an official majority. Now, Nyerere was appointed Chief Minister and the country became self-governing a few months later. A date for independence was set for the end of the following year, and the predominantly expatriate civil service was presented with an elaborate scheme by which the British Government would pay out compensation for loss of office. It was an enormous change of scene when you thought about it but at the time, it was cleverly presented as being a simple change of government, with black faces replacing white faces in positions of authority as was right and proper. Britain's influence would still be strong, we were told, and though its officials would now act in an advisory capacity instead of an executive one, the country was expected to stay firmly within the Western framework. It was also emphasised that this would open the door to investment from the USA and other nations, thereby stimulating commerce and speeding up the pace of development.

Looking back with hindsight fifty years later, one is appalled at the degree of gamble involved in this decision. Obviously, the men in authority believed everything would be all right but like a punter watching the roulette wheel go round, it is difficult to avoid the conclusion that a lot of wishful thinking was involved. If one accepts Macmillan and Macleod acted on financial grounds and that Turnbull was swayed by humanitarian motives, they ignored the important question of whether Africa could handle the independence they were handing out so briskly. Presumably, they thought it could but on the evidence of subsequent developments, this appears to have been either foolishly hopeful or a calculated risk. Was the decision to end colonial rule coldly cynical or was it taken for moral reasons on the basis of a sudden realisation that one people ruling another people was wrong? Who knows? In the case of Tanganyika, there was no war of liberation to be terminated and relationships between all the races in the territory were cordial. Perhaps the motives were mixed but as some critics have pointed out, Macmillan did not withdraw British presence from the Middle East while he was at it. Could this have been due to the influence of that magic three-letter word, OIL? As East and Central African countries didn't have any, the argument runs that they were deemed to be surplus baggage.

Turnbull, incidentally, may have been a humanitarian but he was by no means a softie. He had a reputation for plain speaking and gave out an air of purpose. Subsequently known by the locals as the *uhuru govena,* he made it his business to tour the country and meet as many people as he could. Naturally, East Africa being East Africa, the venue for meeting folks was the club, and my wife and I—along with the rest of the community—had the privilege of shaking his hand at the Iringa Club. Dressed in a business suit, he made brisk work of meeting two hundred people in a short space of time. Our conversation never went past the exchange of how-do-you-do's but I was told a good story about his subsequent visit to the Mbeya Club, where one of the older members became disgruntled with the length of time it took for him to be introduced. Sir Richard kept getting sidetracked and ending up in rival groups of people, thereby irritating my friend who had vainly put on a welcoming smile three times in succession.

'Huh,' he snorted eventually, 'if he doesn't want to meet me, then bugger him.'

His Excellency's hearing must have been very good because he obviously heard the comment above the noise of surrounding conversation.

'And bugger you, too,' said the Governor, turning briskly on his heel.

In retrospect, 1961 certainly was an eventful year. On the face of it, life went on as usual but feelings of unease and uncertainty began to be felt below the surface. In the Iringa area, the farming community began to dwindle and the older type of gentleman farmer vanished. Farms in the Sao Hill area which I had surveyed some years previously now became derelict, and unauthorised squatter housing began to show its face on the boundaries of the town. When a junior TANU politician went to a conference in Cairo and declared that the only enemy left in Africa was the British, this went down very badly with the bwana population with the result that many older officials decided to call it a day and take advantage of the scheme governing compensation for loss of office. 'Lumpers', (as the lump sum compensation for loss of office was affectionately known), became a major talking point in civil service circles and also became the envy of the commercial sector. It was doubly interesting from an actuarial point of view, too, because peak compensation would occur at the age of 41 if one had completed 10 years service or more. There was a table of factors by which one's salary would be multiplied in order to arrive at the lump sum, and many were the discussions as to the optimum way of arranging one's affairs. It was a Catch-22 situation in many ways because a 41-year old senior colonial civil servant could hardly expect to find an equivalent job waiting for him in British private life. On the other hand, the longer he delayed his premature retirement, the older he would be and even less likely to cut the mustard. To complicate matters, the outgoing British administration urged as many officers as possible to stay on to ensure an orderly transition and one had to make up one's mind whether this was lip-service or whether there was a genuine demand for one's services.

In our case, my wife and I decided to start a new life in Australia and I managed to secure the offer of a job with the New South Wales Government. When we learned about the housing shortage for newly-arrived immigrants in Australia, however, we cried off—a decision which was influenced by the fact we didn't really want to leave and genuinely thought the new era would be a progressive step forward in Africa's development. The prospect of increased lumpers was also tempting but aside from this, senior figures in the new Government did seem to want us to stay on and appeared very genuine in saying so. I still have on file a letter from Chief Abdallah Fundikira, who was the Minister of Lands, Surveys and Water in the new government, in which he urged each of us to help in building a new nation and 'play a part in this country where the chances of building a genuine community of goodwill are perhaps stronger than anywhere else in Africa.'

This was very persuasive and I could only feel rueful a couple of years later when I watched Chief Abdallah—one of the most respected figures in Tanganyika—going into the High Court to defend himself against charges of sedition and irregularity which had been brought by the young activists of TANU. He was acquitted but by then, the atmosphere had changed and the initial feel-good factor had been lost. Obviously, no one knew in 1961 how things would turn out and in the absence of a crystal ball, there was indeed a heady feeling that Tanganyika might make a go of it. Though the Congo was going up in smoke, most people looked on the troubles there as a kind of aberration and no one really noticed when South Africa quietly left the Commonwealth and became a Republic. Nor did anyone pay much attention to the unfortunate end of Dag Hammarskjöld, the Secretary-General of the United Nations, which occurred in mysterious circumstances in Northern Rhodesia, now Zambia. In retrospect, this episode was a signpost to the road Africa was doomed to follow for the foreseeable future—a bloodstained path beset by confused politics, brutal conflicts, naked power plays, extortion, corruption and ineffectual government. Like so many warning signs, however, it was simpler to ignore it than to worry about it. The details of his death never surfaced at the time and to this day, there are several versions of what happened.

To start off with, a modern reader may well ask why the most senior diplomat in the world was flying through a highly disturbed part of Africa at night with no flight plan and only three bodyguards for company. But that is what happened and no thriller writer could ever have imagined the scenario. Briefly, the story runs that Mr H, having organised the despatch of a peace-keeping UN force to the Congo, was alarmed to find this force in open conflict with the troops belonging to the breakaway province of Katanga under the leadership of Moise Tshombe—a pro-Western businessman who had split with the Congo's original post-independence government headed by Russian-backed Patrice Lumumba. The latter—variously regarded as a wild revolutionary or a heroic African martyr depending on viewpoint—had then fallen into Katangese hands before being murdered in early 1961 and the situation had steadily got worse from that point onwards. In the ensuing unrest, the country seethed with armed combatants and while the government and anti-government factions of the army fought each other, there were United Nations troops, foreign mercenaries and marauding bands of Simba rebels in the mix as well. Against this background, Hammarskjöld received severe criticism from within the United Nations and with his reputation as a peace-maker at stake, he decided to try and negotiate a cease-fire personally. This led him to fly to Leopoldville in the Congo, from whence he set off in the direction of Katanga in a DC6—having first despatched a decoy plane on an alternative route to foil any would-be assailants. As Ndola in Zambia was the closest town on neutral territory to Katanga, the pilot was instructed to land there but though it was a clear night, something went badly wrong and the plane crashed in the bush. Together with 15 other people, the poor Secretary-General perished and no cause for the crash other than pilot error has ever been officially determined.

In the absence of an official verdict, theories abound that British, American and South African intelligence services were involved and it has been suggested a bomb in the wheel-bay may have been responsible. Naturally, these theories have been rejected by the agencies concerned as Soviet-inspired fiction but what is riveting is the report of an impartial UN officer, who said he found Hammarskjöld's body some yards away from the crash with a hole in his forehead which could have been the result of a bullet. According to him, the Secretary-General had traces of grass and leaves on his hands and must have scrambled clear of the wreckage. If so, something sinister must indeed have happened and strangely enough, this possibility is supported by a conversation I had with an ex-Congo mercenary whom I met by chance in South Africa many years later. My new friend became quite animated at hearing I hailed from East Africa and asked me whether I remembered the Hammarskjöld affair.

'Let me tell you,' he said, 'it's not true what they say about the poor guy having been killed in the crash. He got away from the plane and walked through the bush for quite a long way. A group of us eventually found him, pinned to a tree by a bloody great spear right through his chest.'

Our conversation was unfortunately broken at this point and I never succeeded in getting back to him. Was his story true? It easily could have been because the situation was very fluid at the time, and international tensions were so great that a cover-up would have appealed to both the Western and Soviet blocs. It was, after all, only a few months after the Bay of Pigs fiasco and a year before the Cuban missile crisis, when both sides had their finger on the nuclear button. On the other hand, there may have been no international involvement at all and the spear was simply a present from a local pressure group within the Congolese population who resented United Nations interference in the affairs of Katanga.

Hammarskjöld's death occurred on 18 September 1961 but the ensuing fuss did little to halt the rush to independence by most of the countries in Africa. Jomo Kenyatta was fully released from detention in August of that year and the march to independence in Tanganyika continued apace, the flag of the new republic being officially hoisted on 9 December 1961—less than two years after Macmillan's 'wind of change' speech. Not bad going at all! It seemed quite un-Congo-like in its impact at the time and most people in the country went on with their lives in the same old way. Iringa remained a peaceful spot and the new order was only noticeable due to the large number of political rallies held in the town. These occurred in the rest of the country, too, and TANU spokesmen proved to be very adept when it came to whipping up a crowd with the help of a microphone. Nyerere himself proved to have a completely different manner from his unassuming English method of speaking when he spoke on the radio in Swahili. Then he became very forceful, shouting and yelling with the best of them and given another time and place, you might have thought you were listening to a speech by Hitler at a Nuremburg rally. Some of us were disturbed by this but re-assured ourselves by saying it was the way of Africa and was a necessary means of communication when dealing with an unsophisticated audience.

So what did the bwanas and memsahibs do once the new order had come into force? In general, we went on working as we always had done and even had children in our spare time. Our second son was born in Iringa and this time, the sport-mad Scottish doctor looking after my wife was actually playing tennis with me when she went into labour. I kept asking him whether he shouldn't be off and about his business but he insisted on finishing the set, leaving me to go back home in a state of anxiety. Next thing I knew, he drove excitedly into our driveway and congratulated me on having another son. 'And now,' he said firmly, 'you'll just be in time to come to Scottish dancing.'

It may have been the same night—or possibly another night—that another of my Scots friends dallied at the club a bit too long and had to phone his wife to tell her to come and fetch him. It wasn't the first time this had happened to him, and his long-suffering wife duly got the car out, went to the club, picked him up, and set out for home with her husband lolling in a corner of the back seat. Believe it or not, however, she was only halfway home when she saw a figure reeling along the side of the road and realised that it was her houseboy, drunk as a lord and visibly running out of motive power. So she stopped, put her loyal servitor in the back seat with her husband, and drove home with the two recumbent figures side by side, snoring well and enjoying the sleep of the just. It was a striking testimonial to relations between the races, and the great thing about it was that everyone saw the funny side of it the next day. My Scots friend didn't lose the respect in which the locals held him and his houseboy genuinely appreciated his lift home.

Occurrences of this type seemed to happen frequently in East Africa. Another similar instance concerned our local magistrate who had to take some cases in an outlying court, subsequently sentencing one offender to a lengthy term in prison. Being an old car buff, he had driven himself to the court in his vintage Rolls Royce and was about to drive back again when the police sergeant told him the Police Land Rover had broken down.

'Couldn't you take the prisoner back to town with you and drop him off at the jail?' the sergeant asked.

'Well, yes, I suppose I could,' the magistrate replied, reflecting that the prisoner was neither violent nor threatening. So, off the pair went in the Rolls, with the prisoner reclining in the back seat. As our legal friend said afterwards, where else in the world would you find a prisoner being chauffeur-driven to jail in a Rolls Royce by the very magistrate who had sentenced him?

Uhuru-day in Tanganyika was actually a bit of an anti-climax. There was a full ceremony in Dar es Salaam, of course, and the Duke of Edinburgh made a very genial speech before the flag came down, suggesting that the Tanganyika Government should pay great attention to the preservation of its wildlife. They were wise words and though at the time, I think most of the local population dismissed this as a typical white hang-up and would rather have eaten the wildlife than preserve it, their subsequent reliance on the tourism industry has more than justified the Royal suggestion. Nyerere in reply was suitably modest and placed a great emphasis on self-help—possibly a foretaste of his later doctrine of African socialism. The phrase *uhuru na kazi* (freedom and work) became a catchword and was used freely as a national slogan on every occasion which required a speech or announcement to be made to the populace.

One slightly unforeseen consequence of this surfaced a few days later when I received a letter from the Chairman of a local band requesting a donation to buy musical instruments. It was a worthy cause but instead of ending the letter with the familiar slogan in Swahili, it had been rendered in English and while the writer had obviously meant to say FREEDOM AND TOIL, the wording actually appeared as FREEDOM AND TAIL. My Scots friend, who had happened to drop in at my office, was quite taken with this. 'My God,' he observed in his Scottish burr, 'it's no wonder they were so keen on getting their uhuru. If it comes with a piece of tail, what more could a bloke want?'

In spite of the calm atmosphere, however, a considerable number of white people did decide to call it a day by the time 1962 dawned and the most noticeable group was made up of South African farmers who had lived near Eldoret or West Kilimanjaro. Deciding they didn't fancy life under a black government, they sold their farms and made tracks for 'the Union'—as it was still called in spite of South Africa having become a republic and now being officially the RSA. This group travelled down the Great North Road like a modern version of the Great Trek in reverse, and passed through

Iringa in huge trucks with everything they could carry. As far as I could tell, it wasn't due to racist distaste for black rule, either, but more a realisation that anyone with a South African background might not be looked on as a prized resident by the incoming new order in East Africa, who were not ecstatic about Verwoerd's apartheid policies and tended to take them as a personal affront.

On a personal level, the exodus which occurred during 1962 was brought closer to home when our dear friends, Chris and Peggy Baker, sold their farm and migrated to South Africa as well. Chris Baker, who had been shipped back to England from Kenya for health reasons in 1933, had never been able to get East Africa out of his blood and had come back in 1953, giving up a thriving antique business in Hampshire to do so. He settled in the Iringa district and became a tobacco farmer, turning an old drying barn into a gracious home in the process. A sociable couple, they kept open house on Sundays and served enormous curry lunches—the only snag being that the tobacco didn't do as well as it should have done. Instead of tobacco, he had then developed a dairy herd and battled along until the uncertainty of life in Tanganyika began to be a major worry. Young people, he reasoned, might get by under the new dispensation but to be an elderly white of uncertain means was clearly going to be precarious. This led to us taking them down to Dar es Salaam and seeing them off to Durban on the good ship 'Africa', one of the two Lloyd Triestino vessels that plied the East Coast. My wife gave Peggy a ten-pound note we had left over from our last leave and unbelievably, she used some of it to buy a winning ticket in the Rhodesian Sweep, which was the biggest lottery in Southern Africa at the time.

They were not the only elderly whites to head south by any means and one can only wonder at the way in which Tanganyika had changed in the short space of eight years from being a friendly colony to a newly independent nation. It was remarkably rapid and as an old Africa hand, Chris felt a definite sense of betrayal. If a bookie had offered favourable odds back in 1953 on the country being ready for independence only eight years later, he would have been laughed out of court.

As far as Her Majesty's Overseas Civil Service was concerned, the most obvious casualties occurred within the ranks of the Provincial Administration. They were the one branch of government which had to be replaced by local talent and in consequence, a whole generation of young black District Officers suddenly found themselves promoted beyond their expectations. Provincial and District Commissioners found themselves out of a job and though some of them were switched to management roles, the majority quietly took their lumpers and left. Technical people stayed on longer and in the Survey Department, for example, nothing changed except for a greater emphasis on training and supervision. Other technical Departments followed suit and the ranks of qualified personnel in the field became depleted as more people were pulled into Dar es Salaam—both to fill the vacancies left by senior staff who had taken early retirement and to handle the growing wave of development projects.

After nearly three years, my wife and I were sorry to leave Iringa and we knew we would miss the next blooming of the jacarandas which graced the main street. The Iringa Club, with its tennis courts and golf course, had been very sociable and our involvement in the amateur theatrical society had been a lot of fun. We had made some very good friends, too, and enjoyed some excellent dinner parties. Work had also been a pleasure because the surrounding countryside was so hilly and cried out to be triangulated. I particularly enjoyed visiting primary trig points, which were always at the highest point of the mountain and could only be accessed by a considerable climb along footpaths or game trails. My survey party and I took the message of the theodolite into some remote areas and a week or two could easily go past without speaking English at all, only Swahili. Interestingly, the conversations round the tripod during these safaris were often philosophic and though my companions—technicians and skilled labourers—may not have had much formal education, they were pretty shrewd and aware of contemporary local issues. In addition and in common with Africans of most tribes, they all seemed to have a priceless sense of humour and dearly loved a jest.

One survey safari which brought out the goose bumps occurred when my party and I climbed a prominent hill and found the remains of a German heliograph station on the summit. In case the heliograph is unfamiliar, I must explain they were much used at one time by the military for flashing signals between two inter-visible points. The operator of this device gets the sun to shine into a system of mirrors mounted on a tripod and the resultant signal can be seen up to 40 miles away. Modern communications rendered them obsolete for military purposes a long time ago but surveyors continued to use them and very handy they were, too. Certainly, they were used to great effect by the British Army during the Boer War and in sunny places like India and Egypt. Colonial Germans also had them and back in 1910 or thereabouts, a chain of helio stations was established on prominent hilltops to enable the German Governor in Dar es Salaam to communicate quickly with outlying regions of the country. They were manned the whole time and I am told these stations were able to convey a Morse-code message from the German plantations near Lake Nyasa to Dar es Salaam in a matter of three or four hours—faster than a telegram could subsequently be relayed. Ingenious and efficient as the system was, it was creepy to stand on this particular campsite fifty years after it was last used and I could not stop thinking about the lonely observer who would have spent so much time in his eyrie, ceaselessly scanning the horizon with his binoculars.

Then we found an array of empty beer bottles and I revised my feelings of sympathy. Perhaps things hadn't been so dull after all and I began to feel sorry for the porters who must have carried all those bottles up the hill on their heads while they were still full. The beer bottle, incidentally, played quite a role in the life of the early German surveyors and many a survey mark of their era consisted of an empty beer bottle buried in the ground or embedded in concrete. Obviously, one can only use what is readily available for this purpose and it would seem from the volume of bottles which were used that the Germans were perpetually thirsty. Interestingly enough, the early British surveyors in Tanganyika seem to have been less beery because their standard mark was a cartridge case set in cement. They had plenty of cartridge cases, too, because most surveyors of that generation were keen hunters and were in a unique position to spot game as they roamed from hilltop to hilltop with high-powered telescopes at their disposal. Work, I am told, would sometimes go by the board when a juicy quarry was spotted and the entire survey party would go into hunting mode.

Having to go on leave in 1962 and face the prospect of an English winter was a prospect we viewed with mixed feelings. People would say 'aren't you lucky to get four months leave on full salary with fares paid to Europe?' but to a young couple with two children and not much money, it was a doubtful blessing. As it was our second leave, however, we were considerably better off than the first time and my wife was able to shop on both sides of Oxford Street instead of just one. We were also able to hire a car and managed the obligatory trip to the West End for dinner and the theatre. Otherwise, aside from these highlights and the pleasure of seeing family again, it was not very exciting and we were glad when our leave finally finished in early 1963.

Not that getting back to East Africa was straightforward. Our Comet 4 airliner—the pride and joy of East African Airways—ran off the runway at Benghazi Airport in Libya and got itself stuck in the sand, ending up with one wing perilously close to the ground and the plane in grave danger of catching fire. We had to scramble down emergency chutes and ended up at three o'clock in the morning in the middle of the desert. Eventually taken away in buses, it was dawn by the time we rolled into Benghazi, where we ended up in one of the grand hotels built by Mussolini during the Italian occupation of Libya in the 1930s. It then took two days for a relief aircraft to arrive, and the enforced stay was made worse by everyone's luggage having been strewn over the desert and subsequently vanishing. What an ordeal the journey became! As a group, we became such a bolshy lot of passengers that the airline invited us to order whatever we fancied—an invitation that led to the wholesale consumption of champagne and cigars. We all got to know each other quite well and by the time we left, our sojourn in the hotel had begun to resemble a house party.

Arriving in Dar es Salaam, we found the place awash with a whole new class of diplomats and trade representatives. Various people concerned with foreign aid programmes had homed in as well and the expatriate population had acquired a cosmopolitan flavour. As bwanas and memsahibs in pre-independence days were virtually all British, the new scene required a considerable amount of adaptation and we learned quickly not to keep on referring to the way in which things used to be done. The past was no longer relevant and those of us who had chosen to stay on began to realise that we were a type of mercenary—hired help whose job it was to hold the fort until the locals were ready to take over. It was a bizarre feeling for respectable civil servants who were used to being bwanas but once the penny had dropped, it was fascinating to observe the way in which the proponents of the new order fell into two broad categories—namely, those who gave the money away and those who wanted to spend it for them. There was certainly no shortage of the latter and Dar was crowded with international engineers and project managers, who had hastened to Tanganyika in the search for contracts of one kind or another. The streets were lined with expert advisers and within Government circles, the identification of development projects became the name of the game. Every activity had to be a project and if regular ongoing work could not be classified as a project, it tended to be regarded as unnecessary. It was, after all, far more glamorous for a Scandinavian country to build a new road than to repair an existing one and likewise, the folks back home in Ontario would emote more with a new school building full of smiling black children than the replacement of a lot of rusty old water pipes.

This influx of foreign representatives and advisers was responsible for Dar booming socially. The city's restaurants became more palatable than they had ever been, new cinemas started showing modern films, and the local dramatic society went from strength to strength. The streets were full of luxury cars driven by members of the new autocracy and the local wags devised the slogan of *uhuru na Benz* as a variation on *uhuru na kazi*. It was quite exhilarating in many ways and no one seemed to be worried about Tanganyika having become a Republic in December of the previous year—an event which had occurred while we were away on leave. As Nyerere had explained it, republican status was more compatible with the traditional African way of doing things than the Westminster system and though he personally had no desire to enhance his status, who was he to deny the will of the people? So, lo and behold, Tanganyika had officially become a Republic exactly one year after independence had been conferred and Nyerere was now a President instead of a Prime Minister. As it turned out, he went on being the President for the next twenty-one years but obviously, this was not anticipated at the time and because there was now a strong American interest in Africa, no one dared to suggest that republicanism on the United States pattern was not appropriate.

Julius Kamberage Nyerere was in fact a man of many parts. Selling himself as a man of the people, he was actually the son of a chief and was used to exercising a natural degree of authority. His persona has often been presented as that of a humble man motivated by a desire to lead his people to a better life and while this may be in a large part true, there are many grounds for thinking him not quite so humble. Was he one of Africa's leading statesmen or was he an opinionated idealist who succeeded in bankrupting his country and causing great hardship to its rural population? History must be the judge but while I only met him once and very fleetingly at that, his public utterances during the early days of independence certainly gave the impression of someone out of sympathy with the white advisers he had inherited. He shed them as quickly as possible and made it clear that in his view, Africa was for Africans—black ones. I still recall the astonishment evinced in *The Tanganyika Standard* when Nyerere made a speech decrying the advent of Tshombe in the Congo. 'We've got a foreign policy' ran the headline in some surprise and while it may have been the first time Tanganyika had ever raised its voice in world affairs, it was by no means the last. (He did not like Tshombe, incidentally, whom he suspected of being a business-oriented white man in a black skin).

Obviously, in 1963, no one knew what events were in store or anticipated the socialist polices which Nyerere was to follow throughout the 1970s and 1980s. At that early point in his career, he simply came across as a well-meaning intellectual—an impression which was reinforced by an honorary doctorate and being addressed as *Mwalimu* (teacher). The press made great play of his sojourn at university in Edinburgh and how this had broadened his outlook but it was not realised to what extent he had been exposed to Fabian concepts. He was thus completely different to Jomo Kenyatta who became the first Prime Minister of a self-governing Kenya on 1 June 1963. Imprisoned on suspicion of having been involved with the Mau Mau, (an accusation which has since been claimed to be groundless), one might have expected Kenyatta to have been bent on revenge of some sort but *Mzee* (a respectful term for an old person or elder) was far too wily and experienced to take this route. Staunchly capitalist, he said 'I have no intention of retaliating or looking backwards. We are going to forget the past and look forward to the future.' He also asked white settlers not to leave Kenya and kept many colonial civil servants in their old jobs. Bizarrely, his white critics who had wanted to see him hanged for his alleged role in Mau Mau activities now began to worry whether he might die.

Meanwhile, Uganda had already attained its *uhuru* in October of the previous year and though it amended its constitution a few months later to enable the Kabaka of Buganda to be the titular President of the country, the Uganda Parliament was dominated by the Uganda People's Congress party with Milton Obote as the Prime Minister. The latter—who proved to be a devious politician of considerable staying power—seemed to be in the Nyerere mould and though one would have thought it was a prime requirement for a member of the Bagandan tribe to be Prime Minister in view of its power and numerical strength, the new arrangement seemed to work well and Uganda appeared to be quite stable.

The process of change in East Africa was finally completed in December 1963 when Zanzibar gained independence from Britain and became a constitutional monarchy under the writ of the Sultan. That wrapped up the scene completely and as the assorted collection of bwanas and memsahibs in East Africa began to think about Christmas, there was a feeling of entering a brave new world which was going to be prosperous and multi-racial. Off with the old and on with the new! And, of course, this would take place within the British Commonwealth and result in justice for all. What could be a happier ending to colonialism?

CHAPTER 6

THE SWAN SONG YEARS

Most of the expatriates living in East Africa during 1963 cheerfully accepted the new political order in East Africa as a natural progression of events which would boost development in an atmosphere of easy race relations. After all, the colonial power had stood down in Tanzania and Uganda, and was about to stand down in Kenya. *Uhuru* was no longer a pipe-dream and the machinery of government had been handed over in good working order. What more could any idealistic black politician with the good of his people in mind possibly want? Subsequent events proved the answer to this question to be money and power, but this was quite alien to the atmosphere in which the benevolent conferment of independence had been bestowed and most of the bwanas who stayed on thought life would carry on in its usual vein. Quite a few people left with the intention of making a new start elsewhere but the rest of us played ostrich to any signals which might have indicated a different outcome. The first of these signals was indisputably the Tank Hill party, which took place on the night of 11 December 1963 in Uganda—the same night that saw the Union Jack pulled down at midnight in the neighbouring country of Kenya. The episode is worth recounting in full because it not only set the tone for future race relations in East Africa but heralded a historic shift in the attitude of black politicians to the patterns of thought and conduct which it was hoped they had inherited. The rules of the game were about to be re-written and this time, it was going to be played the African way.

Oddly enough, the incident which provoked this change occurred in Uganda, the part of East Africa which had no history of violent confrontation with a colonial power. It had the least number of settlers, too, since most of the bwanas and memsahibs in the country were either engaged in commercial occupations or were civil servants and quasi-government officials. Centred round Kampala and predominantly British, the efficient running of the economy depended on them and they held down important jobs which carried high degrees of responsibility. Mainly young and vigorous, there was also an active social and sporting side to their lives and much to be enjoyed. The country was scenic, the towns had a full range of amenities, the Kampala Rugby club was active, there was water-skiing to be had on Lake Victoria, and—impossible to imagine East African society without them—there were parties. Not just sedate dinner parties but full-blooded occasions with music, dancing and romantic by-play underneath a tropical moon.

All parties are fun, of course, but they don't just happen by themselves and the Tank Hill saga had its beginning when five young and lively members of the community met together in November 1963 in order to plan a Christmas party. They had all enjoyed hospitality which they were anxious to reciprocate and the Christmas period seemed the ideal time to do this. Upon discussion, however, it turned out that the festive season was already crowded and they decided to throw a party a few days earlier, eventually settling on the same night that Kenya was scheduled to achieve independence. Themed parties were popular in Kampala at this time—a previous party having commemorated Hannibal crossing the Alps—and this time they thought it would be amusing to adopt an end-of-colonialism motif. Kenya's forthcoming independence was a major event, and an appropriate joke seemed to lie in the concept of laying down the white man's burden. Dressing up as an old-time bwana and taking the mickey out of the previous generation was going to be a lot of fun and it did not occur to any of the organisers that it could be deemed offensive to the Uganda Government.

The joke was therefore enshrined in the invitations, which were then printed and sent to a wide selection of likely guests. Specimens of the invitation still exist and a blank one is reproduced below.

Greetings to our right trusty and well-beloved
....
We, the League of Ex-Empire Loyalists
do request and require your presence at a bottle Colonial
Sundown on Wednesday December 11ᵗʰ,
commencing at 9.00 p.m. to celebrate
The End of the White Man's Burden.
Place. The neo-colonial style residence of Mr XXXXX

(by his reluctant consent) on the quarry road, Tank Hill.
RSVP by native bearer in cleft stick or tom-tom to
VVVV, WWWW, XXXX, YYYY, ZZZZ
or send shrunken head to P.O. Box X, Kampala
Dress. 'Sanders of the River'

The venue of the party was in fact a house which had been borrowed from an absent friend of the organisers and there were about 200 guests of various nationalities, many of whom had returned model shrunken heads with their replies to the invitation. No one jibbed at the theme of the party and a large number of the guests turned out in Victorian-style clothing, pith helmets, former Colonial Civil Service uniforms (slightly altered), and explorers' kit. Other guests wore African clothing purchased from the local shops, and one young lady arrived in a Ugandan busuti dress, allowing her partner to lead her in by a rope round the neck to signify that she was a slave about to be set free. The decor, meanwhile, had been enhanced with a Union Jack to give the proper atmosphere, and both Queen Elizabeth and Winston Churchill looked down on the scene with approval from portraits which had been hung on the walls.

By all accounts, the party was a great success and a high time was had by all. It got off to a brisk start with guests being invited to sample a potent punch which was ladled out of a lavatory bowl—a new one straight from the shop, one hastens to say, and without a seat in order to avoid any possible confusion later on. There was much loud music and an enjoyable mix of eating, drinking, conversation, dancing, and the usual aura of potential adultery. I am reliably informed that two of the male guests actually did get lucky in this latter regard, though the occasion was spoiled for one of them later on in the evening when he was confronted by a jealous husband. Naturally, he denied any wrongdoing indignantly—a certain justice being conferred on his denial by the fact he had been trifling with someone else's wife and not the wife of the complainant. His friend was the one who should have been in the firing line but obviously, this was not the time or the place to say so. All good, clean, healthy fun, however, and nothing more than could be expected at any East African party.

In this case, the festivities are reported to have ended at about 5 a.m., the only interruption to the action being the singing of the British National Anthem at midnight after listening to the Kenya independence ceremony on the radio. Again, this was quite spontaneous and though in hindsight, it might not have been the wisest thing to have done, it must have come naturally to the assembled gathering as a kind of emotional reaction to the Union Jack being lowered for the last time. It was certainly not a gesture of defiance as subsequently claimed in the Uganda Parliament and there was no intent to insult or decry the new political order in either Uganda or Kenya.

As parties go, the function is reported to have ended in good order and aside from the odd hangover, there were no untoward effects in the days which immediately followed. Everybody went on with their lives and it came like a bolt out of the blue five days later when the police descended on the offices and houses of the five organisers and various guests, armed with a warrant which enabled them to search for literature and tape-recordings of a subversive and seditious nature. Papers, music tapes and statements were then taken, including a copy of a rugby song about future Kenyan independence which had been sung in humorous vein many years before and which one of the organisers had put away in his possessions and forgotten.

Three days after this, the Youth Wing of the Uganda People's Congress—a typically militant body of young hotheads common to all African political parties at this time—issued a statement calling for the deportation of everybody who had attended the party. As reported in the Uganda Argus of 20 December 1963, Mr. Ally Mukalazi, the Secretary of the Buganda Branch of the UPC Youth Wing claimed that the party was 'an insult to Kenya, and an insult to Kenya is indeed an insult to Uganda.' Startled by this and realising the matter could not be left hanging in the air, the organisers of the party immediately wrote to the Prime Minister, Milton Obote, stating that if any offence had been caused by the party, it was quite unintentional. One of their members also had an audience with Obote but unfortunately, neither the letter nor the interview had any impact. The Prime Minister seemed determined to be offended and far from regarding the issue as a minor incident, proceeded to convene a debate in Parliament on the subject the very next day. In this, he not only accused the guests at the party of having sung a grossly disrespectful song about black rule in Kenya—which they didn't—but also said they had insulted and impersonated East African leaders. Other MP's were quick to join the fray and called for stern action against the organisers because they had trampled on the Uganda flag. One MP even suggested that the guests were associated with the Klu-Klux-Klan, 'which was responsible for the murder of President Kennedy and the negroes in America.'

Naturally, this resulted in more newspaper coverage and the Tank Hill party took up most of the Uganda Argus the next day, which happened to be Saturday 21 December 1963. The front page headline proclaimed PARTY

ANGERS PARLIAMENT and lower down, another headline screamed
THIS IS NO JOKE, SAYS DR. OBOTE. This was then followed by a
faithful account of the debate which went on for three pages, describing
in detail how the Parliamentarians had deemed the League of Ex-Empire
Loyalists to be a subversive group and how some of their more rabid members
had wanted the guests at the party to be flogged at the Independence Arch
before being thrown into jail. The account goes on for a few thousand words
and makes extraordinary reading—so much so, you would think the Editor
would have been warmly thanked by UPC politicians for having given
them such full coverage. Far from it! The UPC Youth Wing became more
infuriated than ever and its members kidnapped the Editor of the Uganda
Argus that same day, forcing him to walk the streets of Kampala with a load
of bananas on his shoulders. Even more alarmingly, the house in which the
party had been held was burned down a night later with one of the owner's
dogs still inside. It was no accident, either, because empty petrol cans were
found nearby and an explosion was heard before the fire broke out.

This sudden wave of anti-white sentiment was a severe shock to
everyone who had thought the granting of independence would result in
a fruitful partnership between the races. Instead of mutual understanding,
all sorts of resentments came to the surface, with one MP accusing the
League of Ex-Empire Loyalists of planning to sabotage independent African
governments and another suggesting the League was capable of murdering
Ugandans on a large scale. Shouts of 'high treason' echoed round the
Parliament chamber and the Youth Wing thugs who kidnapped the Editor
of the Argus said he should be 'tried, given 10 strokes and dumped at the
Congo border.' Great exception was also taken to the words of the song
which the party-goers were alleged to have sung and Obote actually read it
out in Parliament. Apparently composed as an illustration of what would
happen after *uhuru*, the various passages quoted in the newspapers enable
it to be quoted as follows :-

> *The sewage works will soon break down*
> *And the place will stink like mad*
> *But Africans won't mind*
> *Because that's what they've always had.*
> *When the money is finished and the country's on the floor*
> *We'll get the Government printing press to turn us out some more*
> *Chorus*   *Uhuru, uhuru, uhuru, uhuru*
> *Uhuru is good enough for me*

Strangely enough, the song is uncannily prophetic and is an accurate description of what actually did happen in Uganda only a few years later. As no one gets upset more genuinely than someone who is accused of something they haven't yet done, perhaps the song struck a sensitive chord. The populace, however, had never been abused or treated badly and one can only assume that the fuss was due to a presentiment of inadequacy. Certainly, it must have presented the British Government with an embarrassing choice of action. Did they rap the table and tell the Ugandans not to be so bloody silly or did they apologise for having caused offence? In the event, they did the latter. Sir David Hunt, the British High Commissioner, wrote a letter to Milton Obote on 23 December in which he 'deplored the offence caused to the feelings of Ugandans by the party' and expressed the deep regret of his Government at this 'unhappy episode'. It is still a moot question as to whether this was clever diplomacy or not. At the time, the expatriate community of Uganda had no doubt that it wasn't, and rhyming alternatives to Sir David's surname became part of the bitter criticism heaped on the High Commissioner's head.

Thinking about it with the wisdom of hindsight, there are grounds for thinking Sir David's apology may have defused the matter in the speediest and least acrimonious fashion. It may well have been part of a deal with Obote—the details of which we shall never know—but the five organisers and the young lady who had worn the busuti dress were suddenly served with deportation orders requiring them to leave Uganda immediately and were gone the same day. They were then followed shortly afterwards by eight more expatriates and their dependants—mainly Police and Prisons officers who had been at the party in their private capacities—and after that, the affair slowly simmered down.

Much the same thing happened in Britain. The hosts of the party, who had endured a very uncertain time of it in Kampala before finally being flown out to Nairobi and thence to London, were besieged by the Press when they arrived on a freezing Christmas Eve. Interestingly enough, two of the party hosts had Private Pilot's Licences and had planned at one stage to 'borrow' a couple of light aircraft and fly the entire group to the safety of Northern Rhodesia. Fortunately, this turned out not to be necessary and the deportees had an uneventful journey back to London in an almost empty Comet, only relieved by their celebrity status guaranteeing them free drinks throughout the flight. Who paid for the drinks or the airfares is uncertain, though a key member of the group believes it was the British Government. If it was, it shows a considerable understanding of the situation because if anybody ever needed a drink, it must have been the subjects of the deportation order who had been so abruptly bundled off. The drinks must have helped because it was apparently a riotous flight and the participants were only brought back to earth by finding their tropical clothes were quite unsuited to an English December. They also found they had to cope with a battery of television cameras on arrival and when one of the party telephoned his parents to tell them he had been deported, he found they had been watching late television as per their normal practice and had been considerably startled by seeing their son featuring in the newscast.

Despite the initial fuss, though, the affair did not create many waves in Britain. A Labour MP asked a question in the House of Commons and Duncan Sandys, the Commonwealth Relations Secretary, made a brief statement but nothing further transpired and a promised ministerial investigation came to naught. The deportees had no redress of any sort from the British Government and beyond Peter Simple writing a cutting reference to the matter in the Daily Telegraph, the incident gradually faded from public awareness.

Somewhat bizarrely, Milton Obote was reported by the Uganda Argus on 24 December 1963 to have been advised to stay in bed for a few days due to an attack of influenza. This has all the hallmarks of a convenient illness and a cynic would have said he was deliberately lying low in the hope the incident would blow over. Why he chose to fly off the handle in the first place is not entirely clear but various reasons can be identified. Firstly, he was not a member of the dominant Baganda and Busoga sections of Uganda's population and in consequence, was not a popular Prime Minister. Furthermore, his Government was not going well and he was under pressure due to low crop returns and difficulties in the field of national education. His recent marriage was also proving problematic and there had been considerable criticism of the amount of public funding it had incurred.

While these factors must have weighed on his mind, however, it is doubtful whether this was the whole story. Subsequent events show he must have been in the grip of an overwhelming ambition to make his mark in a more emphatic way than being a mere Prime Minister. His friend, Julius Nyerere, had become a President and Obote must have been dying to follow suit. As he succeeded in ousting the Kabaka of Baganda from his position as President of Uganda only three years later, he must have been plotting the transition already and would have seen Tank Hill as a golden chance to create a change in the political climate.

Additionally, though it was not known at the time and only revealed by unfolding developments, Obote was also playing games with a major in the army called Idi Amin, who not only assisted him in getting rid of the Kabaka but played an active role in their joint enterprise of smuggling arms to the Congolese government in exchange for ivory and gold. Amin—the obedient and loyal army officer—must have seemed an ideal ally to Obote but he who sups with the devil must verily do so with a long spoon. Though Amin played a key role in deposing the Kabaka in 1966, the two men grew increasingly disenchanted with each other and Amin ended their friendship in 1971 by deposing Obote.

But that was still to come and at the time of Tank Hill, the Prime Minister must have needed something with which to distract the populace and focus their minds. As Nyerere would no doubt have told him, the essential thing in African politics of the 1960s was to keep discovering plots against the state by imperialists and/or neo-colonials. It was fast becoming a classic tactic in other parts of Africa, too, and Obote must have jumped at a chance of uniting the people behind him and getting them to forget their everyday cares. The Tank Hill affair must have come along at just the right time and he seized it with alacrity.

Being in Dar es Salaam during Christmas 1963, I can well recall how the Tank Hill party was a hot topic of discussion in expatriate circles. Most of us felt considerable sympathy for the party-goers and were startled to realise that a bit of harmless fun had gone down so badly with the new powers-that-be. It could just as easily have happened in Dar and though the affair could be put down to differences in culture and background, it was apparent that the new brand of black politician did not like having bwanas and memsahibs underfoot. Our persistent emphasis on political morality obviously made them feel uneasy and put a brake on their natural tendency to exploit a situation to personal advantage. In African terms, it was crazy not to do so and here we were, preaching about the virtues of humility and self-sacrifice. African logic does not mix easily with western standards of morality and the new wave of politicians were not imitation Europeans in African skins but real Africans in African skins.

Barely had we got over Tank Hill and the subsequent New Year festivities, however, when another weightier signal came crashing into our ken. On 12 January 1964, revolution rocked the spice islands of Zanzibar and Pemba. The African element of the population rose up against the Sultan and declared open season on their fellow islanders who were not of the same ethnic background. Many Arabs and Asians were slaughtered, towed out to sea in lighters, and fed to the sharks. Mob law reigned and gangs of thugs under the sway of 'Field Marshal' John Okello went on the rampage, having successfully broken into and robbed the police armouries. A gentleman named Abeid Karume was installed in place of the Sultan, who managed to escape by air to Dar es Salaam and thence to the United Kingdom. A new Zanzibar Revolutionary Government was proclaimed and the American Consul was held at gunpoint in his hotel before being declared persona non grata and put on another flight out of the island.

By this time, a British frigate and an American destroyer had showed up on the scene but there was no attempt at intervention. As in so many situations of this type, no one knew exactly what was happening and though the headlines in the *Tanganyika Standard* were lurid enough, it was all happening over the horizon and reliable information was not available. I do remember, though, the newspaper report on the first shootings that occurred in the middle of Zanzibar—witnessed by a journalist who happened to look out of the window and saw two young Goan lads about to get on a motorcycle. All quite normal and then suddenly, a couple of armed revolutionaries came round the corner and shot them out of hand. No warning, no presentiment of any danger—just a quiet Sunday morning on a peaceful tropical island.

This triggered off the blood lust, apparently, and the mass killings followed. It was carnage plain and simple but bizarrely, anybody with a white face was exempt. The rebels stayed on good terms with the British High Commissioner and a considerable number of Britons were safely evacuated. Meanwhile, everybody on the mainland—including the Tanganyika Government—watched the scene with a mixture of horror and puzzlement. What on earth had got into the sleepy islanders, who grew cloves, went fishing and watched the coconuts fall? It never occurred to anyone, however, that Zanzibar's troubles could be exported back to the mainland. The islands had always been an oddball part of East Africa and had gone their own way. Also, the forces of law and order in Tanganyika were highly regarded. The police were well-trained and the Tanganyika Rifles—consisting of two battalions of the KAR which had been allocated to Tanganyika at independence—were reckoned to be an elite force. A group of crack British officers had been specially seconded to give them further training and the Colito barracks to the north of Dar es Salaam reassuringly gleamed with spit and polish.

Wrong again! On 20 January 1964, troops of the Tanganyika Rifles battalion stationed near Dar rounded up their British officers, seized the airport, and put their captives on a plane to Nairobi. The battalion in Tabora joined in the mutiny, Nyerere went into hiding, and the key points of Dar es Salaam were taken over by armed soldiers. This was even more bizarre than Zanzibar! In common with most white officials and commercial people, I went to the office that morning without noticing anything untoward going on and found our complex of buildings overlooking the harbour were still locked up. The office cleaners normally arrived there well before us but on this day, there was no sign of them.

'Is it a public holiday?' asked a puzzled colleague, as we paced the verandah outside the Lands and Surveys office. It was a fair question because all the recent political changes in the country had been accompanied by the dispensation of numerous and unexpected holidays.

'I don't think so,' I remember saying.

And just then, there was the sound of boots and a soldier—in full battledress and carrying an automatic weapon in the ready position—walked slowly past, pausing only to give us a dirty look. Mercifully, that was all he did but the sight of him stopped us in our conversational tracks.

'I think there's been a coup,' said my friend.

My God, this only happened in South America. It didn't happen in British territory. But wait a minute, said my brain, the country wasn't British any more.

'Let's all go home,' said someone else.

So we did, noticing as we did so that the streets were now much quieter than usual. When I reached home, I found my wife was already back there with our sons, having found the school also closed. There was only martial music playing on the local radio station but our next-door neighbour had been listening to the BBC and confirmed the news of an armed uprising.

'Go to the shops,' said my wife, 'and buy some food. It may be days before things get back to normal again. Get a bag of rice and whatever tins you can see.'

Well, this idea must have occurred to everyone else at the same time because when I reached Moosa's grocery store at the Oyster Bay shops, there was a crush of people filling shopping bags. The genial proprietors of the shop had given up serving people and were leaning against the counter.

'Just take what you want and write it down here,' said one of them, handing me a piece of paper and a pencil stub. So I helped myself, and was glad to find some rice and some tinned fish. The shelves were emptying fast and there was no point in standing on ceremony. I grabbed what I could, scrawled a list and gave it to my shopkeeper friend.

At home again, all was quiet and we spent the rest of the morning wondering what the harvest would be. Then, during the early afternoon, there was a distant noise of explosions from the direction of town. Later, it transpired that an Arab shopkeeper, mindful of a Zanzibar-type situation erupting, opened fire with his shotgun when he saw armed soldiers in the street. The latter had retaliated and used a couple of hand grenades for good measure. We didn't know this at the time, of course, and assumed that general fighting had broken out. This impression was reinforced later when we heard the noise of heavy vehicles approaching.

By cruel chance, my wife was in the garden with our two sons when the first open truck, filled with soldiers, roared past on its way to the Oyster Bay cliffs. Another truck followed and the inmates, seeing white people in the garden, lifted their guns and pointed them at my precious family. They didn't shoot, though, and the fleeting moment passed as the truck kept moving. Whether they were just trying to be funny, we shall never know but if it was merely a gesture, it was one we remembered.

Again, we didn't know the background at the time but it subsequently turned out that the British frigate, which had been keeping an eye on Zanzibar, had been sighted out at sea and the mutineers were rushing to the coast to repel what they thought might be a waterborne landing. In the event, nothing actually happened and the frigate moved away shortly afterwards, leaving the mutinous troops—in battle order and with shrubbery in their steel helmets—lined up along the coral cliffs with their fingers on the trigger.

After that, the next four days went by in an uneasy calm and we simply stayed at home, moping and exchanging gossip with the neighbours. No one went anywhere and there was little point in listening to the radio, BBC being difficult to get. Our two trusty servants, Simon and Anton, knew nothing more than we did and there was no indication of the government still being in existence. Nyerere had disappeared and though we later learned he had been hidden in the British High Commission, nobody knew whether he was alive or not and the tension perceptibly mounted with each day which passed. Britain had not intervened in Zanzibar and there seemed no guarantee it would do so in Tanganyika. While the evacuation of the expatriate population was on the cards in theory, it would plainly be a hell of an exercise and God alone knew how it might be accomplished. It would, we opined gloomily, probably be limited to diplomatic officials and their families only.

The tension visibly rose day by day and we went to bed on the night of 24 January in the fear of law and order irreversibly breaking down. Next morning, however, we were woken from a fitful sleep by a loud cannonade of bangs and thumps which seemed to be coming from seaward. It was exactly like the sound track of a World War Two movie and I seized my wife in exultation.

'Darling, the navy's here,' I reportedly said. What an immortal line— vintage Noel Coward straight from *In Which We Serve*. Maybe it was a conditioned reflex brought on by reading history when I was young but it simply came to the surface without any conscious thought.

And in fact, the British navy was right there. HMS *Centaur,* a whacking great aircraft carrier normally based in Aden, had anchored offshore opposite the Colito Barracks and was making a fearsome noise, letting off explosive devices and firing blanks out to sea. It sounded the most formidable bombardment but what we didn't know in our Gillman Avenue bedroom was that a task force of Royal Marine Commandos had landed by helicopter on the Colito football field under cover of all the sound and fury. Once there, they had ended resistance by putting an anti-tank rocket through the guardroom roof and the mutineers had then fled to the surrounding bush, whence they were rounded up by helicopter. It was done very quickly and professionally, and when the Marines sent a convoy into town to liberate the airport and the radio station, they were greeted on the streets with a tumultuous welcome. This was followed by a further show of force when a detachment of armoured cars arrived by lighter from the carrier, again provoking a great welcome.

I remember vividly driving into town with a colleague later on that day to see if our office had survived the revolution. As we drove along Ocean Road past the Government Hospital, the carrier came into full view and a procession of helicopters could be seen, going back and forth. One of them passed directly over us and I stuck my head out of the car window in order to exchange thumbs-up signs with the pilot. It was impossible not to feel grateful for the long arm of British power having reached out and saved us—a feeling which was reinforced later in the day when a couple of Sea Vixens from the carrier buzzed the town at low level. Most of Dar's inhabitants had never seen or heard a jet fighter up close and the reaction was one of complete awe.

That night, Nyerere re-appeared and everything reverted to normal. The local radio station went back on the air and the bars in hotels and clubs became peopled again. There was still a loose end in the shape of the other mutinous battalion at Tabora but its members were subdued the next morning by a mixed force of Commandos and the RAF regiment, who were flown into Tabora from Dar and Nairobi respectively. There was no fighting and indeed, the mutineers had to be woken up by bugle, only to be assembled and informed they were surrounded. As with the Colito situation, the ringleaders were promptly arrested and the mutiny in Tanganyika came to an abrupt end.

We didn't know it at the time but the situation had also been quite serious in Kenya and Uganda, where trouble broke out in the ex-KAR units stationed there. As there was still a considerable British military presence in Kenya, however, it had been relatively easy for order to be restored. Neither Kenyatta nor Obote had shown any hesitation in asking for British assistance, and mutinous actions in Nakuru and Jinja were quickly put down. Interestingly, the causes of the mutinies proved to be neither political nor racial but more a case of a growing dissatisfaction with regard to conditions of service and status. The rapid onset of independence had in many ways left the soldiery floundering in its wake and had unsettled its loyalty towards the officer corps, who still bore the marks of the old colonial regime. Obviously, this did not come to light until after the excitement was over and the natural conclusion at the time was that a coup of some sort was under way. No rival political leaders ever appeared, however, and though the threat of an army-backed takeover slowly faded away, I am still convinced that if decisive intervention had not taken place, it would have only been a matter of time before some ambitious private or corporal scented the opportunity to make a name for himself.

In the week following the action at Colito, Dar es Salaam was a strange place. There were more British troops within the city than there had been since 1916 and the locals regarded them with trepidation, fearful the *askari ya wazungu* (soldiers of the white people) were going to put the clock back and terminate Tanganyika's new-found independence. A parade by the Royal Marines' band eased anxieties, however, and the fear of being conquered receded. In some ways, this would not have been too far off the mark because when one thought about it, the Marine Commandos had effortlessly assumed military control over a country larger than France within a 24-hour period and had subdued two battalions of mutinous troops without any casualties. All it needed was a portly figure in a white uniform and plumed helmet to stride into State House, (the new name for Government House), and the colonial show could have been on the road again. Obviously, this was not on anyone's agenda and the conquering forces contented themselves with ferrying naval personnel by helicopter to the first tee of the Gymkhana golf course.

The euphoria of being saved lasted for some time and we all felt proud of the British response. Julius Nyerere sent a personal message of thanks to the British Parliament and I had too much to drink with a friend of mine at the New Africa Hotel. It had been a torrid time for everyone concerned and my wife and I were especially touched by getting telegrams from family and friends outside the country, hoping we were all right and offering us refuge. How they thought we could have got out of Tanganyika and taken advantage of their offers was not clear but it was none the less very reassuring. It also led me to feel it was only civil to reply to their missives and the day after the action was over, I made my way to the main Post Office in town to send some telegrams saying all was well. I duly did this but when I regained the street, I noticed that several pedestrians were looking over their shoulders. So I started looking over my shoulder, too, and we all began walking a little faster. Then one fellow broke into a trot, another followed suit and before we knew it, the whole street was running, myself included. It was a complete false alarm and I felt quite foolish but it shows the jittery state to which everybody had been reduced.

A week later, we were all back in our routine lives—buoyed up and boosted by the visible presence of British troops at key road intersections. One might have thought the East African mutinies, coming as they did on the heels of the Tank Hill episode, were enough to switch any bwana and memsahib off the idea of remaining in East Africa, but most of us chose to regard the disturbances as teething troubles. With hindsight, it is obvious they were nothing of the sort but the penny still didn't drop. If the KAR, a proud regiment with long traditions, had proved unable to adapt to the advent of independence, we should have wondered what still lay in store. The other bone which should have stuck in the throat was Zanzibar. The Sultan may have been living on borrowed time but it had been a very relaxed sultanate and the people of Zanzibar and Pemba were renowned for being easy-going. What turned them into a crazed mob of revolutionaries is still obscure and though Nyerere tamped things down by proclaiming the union of Tanganyika and Zanzibar three months later, it was obviously done to save face and present an orderly image to the world. It certainly made no difference to Karume and his lynch-mob of ruffians, who continued to run the government as they liked. Mainland authority did not extend to the islands in any practical shape or form and even the name, *Tanzania,* adopted for this new country was a subject of controversy as well. Most whites thought it was a play on the word 'Azania'—that mythical kingdom beloved by African historians—and that Tanzania would be pronounced accordingly, i.e. Tan-zayn-ee-a, but Nyerere himself ruled it should be pronounced Tan-zan-ear.

With touching adaptability, therefore, the bwana population settled down again and we all went back to work. Well, not all of us, because my parents coincidentally retired and went back to England. Various factors contributed to this, one of them being the nationalisation of all the stevedoring companies into a new organisation to be called the East African Cargo Handling Services. The East African Lighterage and Stevedoring Company then became history and my father's last business act was to wind it up. They passed through Dar es Salaam for the last time in mid-1964 and that was the end of their East African odyssey. It was indeed the end of an era and there was no more basking in the after-glow of Empire for my poor mother, who had to adapt to being a busy housewife in England. Pausing only to remind us that sticking to East Africa was the best thing we could do—after all, look what it had done for them—they boarded a Union Castle vessel for the last time and my mother gave us her piano as a souvenir of their presence on the African continent. In retrospect, perhaps I should have wondered what tune to play on it.

One of the main reasons which influenced so many bwanas and memsahibs to go happily back to work was the knowledge Britain could reach out with a powerful hand at any time in the event of things going awry. Even though this proved to be a bit of wishful thinking in the face of the Labour Government's subsequent decision not to maintain Britain's military presence east of Suez, the memory of the Marine Commandos' exploits still lingered and gave most of us a sense of reassurance. The post-independence euphoria persisted and we went about our business in a positive frame of mind, encouraged by the way so many other nationalities wanted to play a role in developing the country. Aid programmes became very fashionable and an incredibly mixed bag of people involved with aid programmes centred itself on Dar es Salaam. This led to a considerable demand for after-hours relaxation and the parties which took place on the flat roof of the Gymkhana Club were lively affairs at which the expatriate community let its hair down in a setting of starry tropical nights and rustling palm trees. A large part of the congregation at these gatherings was still British, of course, but there were Americans, Canadians, Germans, Italians, Scandinavians, and members of many other countries as well, including Russia. The Cold War may have been at its height but its local proponents seemed to get along quite well and you would often see the Russian Trade Commissioner playing tennis with his American counterparts.

Obviously, the British troops couldn't stay very long in Dar es Salaam after the mutiny and aside from being needed elsewhere, the ruling hierarchy weren't too comfortable having white-skinned soldiers maintaining law and order. An African solution was sought with some urgency and this resulted in the arrival of a contingent drawn from the Nigerian Army, who seemed very smart and civil. Not speaking Swahili and feeling isolated, they none the less behaved very well and the only criticism of their conduct during their three month stay in Dar arose from their off-duty search for romantic comfort in the back streets of the city, thereby placing a strain on the local hospitality industry.

In the meantime, the Tanzania Rifles was formally disbanded and replaced by the Tanzania People's Defence Force, an umbrella-like organisation made up of men who had not been active in the mutiny. The politicians rightly diagnosed that the Rifles had been too cut off from the mainstream of popular thought and the new Army was placed firmly under civilian control—not quite a commissar system but definitely getting on that way. All the officers were now Tanzanian and political indoctrination became the order of the day. Curiously, however, traces of the Sandhurst tradition still lingered on and I sampled this on several occasions when the Gymkhana Club sent a squash team to the Barracks to play against the TPDF officers. The new boss of the Army, a Brigadier who walked with a swagger stick under his arm and had an Alsatian at his heels, was not only a mean player himself but insisted all his young officers become proficient. The hospitality was good, too, and the after-match beer flowed abundantly.

What a year 1964 was! It may have started with a bang in East Africa but overseas, the Beatles were wowing music-lovers, Cassius Clay (not yet known as Mohammed Ali), became the World Heavyweight champ, the mini-skirt crept ever upwards, the Labour Party won the British General Election in October, and Harold Wilson became the new British Prime Minister. This had little effect on what has been called the retreat from Empire, and Wilson was soon to split decisively with Ian Smith on the subject of independence for Southern Rhodesia after the break-up of the Federation of Rhodesia and Nyasaland. And as if that had not been enough excitement for one year, Kenya chose to follow the pattern which had been set and became a republic as well. Jomo Kenyatta—who else?—became Kenya's first President and though he was 70 years old at the time, remained in this role for the next 14 years until his death at Mombasa in 1978. Generally regarded as the father of the nation, he was plainly a unifying force and not only kept a lid on things but firmly steered Kenya into the western capitalist camp—encouraging investment and urging whites and Asians to stay on. Some Kenyans may say he was too capitalist for comfort but though *chai money* (tea money) became a national euphemism for paying someone a sweetener, matters never reached the Nigerian level where *dash* had to be paid in order to achieve anything at all. To this day, Kenya has done rather better than most of the other countries in Africa, and credit for this must be paid to the foundation laid by Kenyatta.

Back in Tanzania, the dilemma faced by the Government was insoluble. Nyerere and his ministers became increasingly anti-capitalist and kept saying that indigenous Tanzanians were fully capable of running their own country. But the accuracy of this statement depended very much on what standards of evaluation were used and it rapidly proved to be a pipedream. At the date of independence, there were no black doctors, pharmacists, engineers, surveyors, lawyers, town planners and other skilled practitioners in the country, and the few budding professionals coming on stream were immediately catapulted into senior appointments without the benefit of any practical experience. As long as there was a white adviser quietly in the background, this was capable of working but the new setup left a gaping gap in the system as far as support services were concerned. Qualified nursing staff, for example, literally vanished from the hospitals overnight and when my wife needed to have her tonsils out, the surgeon at the Dar es Salaam Government Hospital told us to have it done in Europe. 'I can do the operation with no problem,' he said,' but you'll probably bleed to death afterwards or pick up an infection.' So, in the end, she had it done in a bush hospital run by a Roman Catholic order, which had a nursing staff of wonderful German nuns.

A similar situation existed in the world of commerce. Here, the Government had no power to insist on Africanisation and could only intervene in business if some kind of labour dispute arose. Young black Tanzanians, though full of capitalist instincts, had never been oriented towards business by the colonial education system and the country's commerce was conducted exclusively by whites and Indians. With the influx of foreign diplomats, tourists and aid people that occurred after *uhuru*, it was quite a lively scene, too, and the local shops were as full of luxury goods as anywhere else in the world. Top-line motor cars sold like hot cakes and the social fabric of Dar was given a boost with the opening of several new restaurants, including an exotic Indonesian eatery and a coffee bar which served genuine cappucino. New hotels were built as well, foremost among them being the Italian 'Agip Motel' and the Israeli 'Kilimanjaro'. Aimed at the luxury end of the market, the latter was run in a very businesslike way—an impression which was brought home to me during one of the few occasions we dined there by a conversation I had with the Indian leader of the band which was entertaining the diners. It was in fact Dar's foremost local dance band and I knew him quite well. 'How's it going, Tony?' I asked during an interval between numbers. 'Oh, my God,' he replied, 'These Jewish men are terrible. They argue about our fees and they check our playing time down to the last minute'. He spoke with considerable feeling and I could not help smiling. We had all been brought up to regard our Indian friends as supreme in matters of business negotiation and if the Israelis had succeeded in getting the better of them, they were plainly as tough as their reputations. It would have been fascinating to see their version of aid in operation but unfortunately, they didn't stay very long in the country before falling out with the Tanzania Government, who automatically sided with the Egyptians in the Six Day War that exploded in 1967.

Mercifully, the high drama of 1964 was not repeated in 1965, and this constituted another reason for thinking East Africa's problems had been due to teething. Lulled into a feeling of security, my wife and I decided to take our long leave in rather more style than we had done previously and opted for a voyage up the east coast of Africa on one of the two passenger ships that had been specifically built by the British India Steam Navigation Company in the early 1950's to shuttle bwanas and their memsahibs between East Africa, South Africa, and Europe. These two ships, the s.s. *Kenya* and the s.s. *Uganda,* were fine-looking vessels and had quickly achieved a reputation for speed and comfort. They carried about 300 passengers and, importantly to all young parents, had special facilities for young children. Wonder of wonders, you could take your brats after breakfast to a special playroom and entrust them to the care of a hard-working girl, who would look after them until lunchtime and then do a further shift in the afternoon. To young mothers, this was heaven and though the carers might look a bit frazzled by the end of a voyage, the facility was a great drawcard.

The *Uganda* was the ship that suited our dates and we duly steamed out of Dar es Salaam harbour in her, little realising that the era of passenger ships full of bwanas was shortly to come to an end. The voyage itself was all we hoped it would be and the days passed by in a welter of deck tennis, table tennis, deck quoits, swimming, ice cream, gin-and-tonic, beer, and socialising. Most of the other passengers in Tourist Class were the same age as us and the atmosphere was uniformly cheerful. The catering lived up to its reputation as far as the lunchtime curries were concerned and it was impossible not to sleep the Red Sea afternoons away after sampling them.

Reaching Suez was like a rendezvous with history. One had a sense of treading the same paths which had been followed by generations of empire-builders and colonials on their way to Asia, Australia and Africa. Travelling in naval vessels, *P and O* liners, troopships, whatever steamed and floated—they had all passed through Suez and tasted the pleasures which Egypt had to offer. Some of these were possibly apocryphal but there must have been some truth behind some of the enduring stories which were handed down from generation to generation. The spectacle of a donkey having sex with a woman was one which had been minutely described to me by at least three separate people, and anyone who had been with the Eighth Army during World War Two was guaranteed to be good for an anecdote about the unorthodox way in which nightclub waitresses were wont to pick up their change. (For the record, this anecdote is usually accompanied by a description of the fighting which broke out after Australian soldiers got busy with their cigarette lighters).

Perhaps unenterprisingly, however, we limited ourselves to less libidinous experiences. My wife went off on a tour of Cairo and the pyramids, while I stayed on board with our sons and watched the *gulli-gulli* man go through his repertoire, complete with little fluffy chicks and an impossible-to-read *Find the Lady* card trick. We then enjoyed the taste of travel through the gateway of the British Empire by courtesy of the bum-boat men, who clustered round the ship when it reached Port Said. Not allowed on board, they shouted at passengers hanging over the rail in time-honoured fashion and many were the propositions put forward. Strangely, every adult male with a white face was addressed as Mr. Simpson, a form of address which went back to King Edward VIII's abdication in 1936. Indeed, nothing much seemed to have changed in spite of the Seven Days War with Israel being just round the corner and a fellow-passenger who went ashore for a walk round the town claimed he was targeted by salesmen and pimps in just the same old way. Sex was very much available, apparently, and every proposal hissed at him by these outstanding citizens always involved the traditional sister. 'You like my sister, mister. She give you nice time.' One enthusiastic purveyor of nooky even took it a stage further and his irresistible invitation concluded with the words 'she very nice clean girl. I fuck 'er myself.'

It is, of course, impossible to mention Port Said without being reminded of the old, old Empire joke about the elderly lady who boarded an ocean liner for the first time and asked the steward to direct her to the Ladies' loo.

'Port side, madam,' he is reputed to have said briskly.

'Heavens above, my good man,' she cried. 'I can't possibly wait until we get there.'

Continuing on with our voyage, we ran into a heavy Mediterranean storm after leaving Port Said and all thought of Roman, Greek and Phoenician ghosts gliding around in their galleys became academic. They must have been pretty tough mariners to cope with weather like that and though we had the compensation of seeing Stromboli and Mount Etna at close quarters, we were glad to get off the ship at Marseilles and do the last part of the journey by train. This worked very well but our self-congratulations on avoiding the Bay of Biscay were offset by a very choppy Channel crossing and the white cliffs of Dover were a welcome sight.

On this occasion, we had a wonderful leave and because the days went past so quickly, it was a shock when we realised we had to go back to Tanzania. It shows how blithe we were at the prospect because I had even gone out of my way to address a gathering of student land surveyors with a view to picking up some recruits. 'Come and work in Tanzania,' I remember saying. 'It's the largest, friendliest country in Africa and you'll get some great experience.' No one took me up on this, though, and I have often wondered whether the youngsters I spoke to knew more than I did.

There were some good times on the way back as well. Firstly, we had a highly enjoyable week in Greece and then we flew out of Athens on Ethiopian Airlines, which at the time was one of Africa's best airlines. American influence was very strong in Ethiopia at that stage, and Ethiopian Airlines had a fleet of Boeing 707's which were flown by American pilots seconded from TWA. One of them very capably landed us in Cairo in the middle of a sandstorm and eventually, we reached Nairobi after stopping on the way for a couple of hours in Addis Ababa and wandering round the airport there. It seemed very relaxed and there were pictures of Emperor Haile Selassie on the wall, the last of a long line of monarchs descended from King Solomon. His full title was *His Imperial Majesty, Emperor Haile Selassie I, Conquering Lion of the Tribe of Judah, Elect of God, King of Kings of Ethiopia,* and if this sounds rather splendid, it was actually rather sad because he was in the last few years of his reign. He didn't know it at the time but in the style of emerging Africa which was to become so familiar, he was overthrown by a military coup in 1974 and the feudal aristocracy that had ruled the country in a benign manner for so long was replaced by a Marxist regime of disgruntled Army officers who had neither the common touch nor the ability to run a country.

From Nairobi, it was a short step to Dar es Salaam, where we found the name of the street in which our Government quarter was situated had been changed while we were away from Gillman Avenue to Kaunda Drive in honour of the new President of Zambia. This was another of the many signs we ignored and like so many things in one's life which one does for the last time, we never realised that our leave was the last long leave we would ever take. The whole world was changing, anyway. Britain was into the Swinging Sixties, flower power made its appearance, Winston Churchill died, *Cosmopolitan* magazine was launched, skirts went up even further, and Rhodesia declared its independence. Even the days of the passenger liner came rapidly to a close, the *Uganda* becoming a school cruise vessel only two years later and her sister ship, the *s.s. Kenya,* being scrapped in 1969. (Interestingly, the *Uganda* stuck around for a long time and even saw service during the Falklands War before being finally laid up in 1985).

What we did notice on getting back to Tanzania was a distinct change of atmosphere. To be white, British, and a relic of the colonial period, were now factors which were unpopular in government circles and many an expatriate official found himself precipitately Africanised. It was not uncommon to go to the office in the morning and find a black Tanzanian sitting in your chair and a letter on the desk giving you two weeks to leave the country. Slowly, and sometimes not so slowly, Western influence began to lose its grip, and freedom movements such as FRELIMO (the Mozambique Liberation Front) and SWAPO (the South West African People's Organisation) established themselves in Dar es Salaam. Having tasted the fruits of black rule, Nyerere and his colleagues seemed obsessed with the notion that this happy state should immediately be extended over the whole of Africa, irrespective of economic circumstance or history. A certain amount of belligerence accompanied this view, too, and the resultant atmosphere in Tanzania was not helped by the white Rhodesians unilaterally declaring their independence on 11 November 1965.

Suddenly, a situation of conflict seemed to have come about and instead of a conglomeration of African countries living side by side in harmony and cooperation, the continent was polarised into the Black North and the White-controlled South, the latter comprising the two Portuguese colonies of Angola and Mozambique, Rhodesia (now Zimbabwe), South West Africa (now Namibia), and the biggest player on the continent—South Africa. Support for freedom movements by Tanzania and other newly-independent African countries now became explicit rather than tacit and warlike noises began to be heard in political speeches. At the same time, human rights were declared to be immeasurably precious, instant democracy was demanded for all Africa's inhabitants, and pressure was stepped up in the United Nations to have anything less than universal suffrage declared immoral.

Certainly, by 1966, Western whites were beginning to experience a certain amount of truculence in popular attitudes towards them. Instead of being regarded as kindly experts helping Tanzania along, bwanas and memsahibs now began to be seen as the discredited remnants of imperialism. The new order had lost its shyness, too, and for a country which had never had a foreign policy, there was now no hesitation in advising the United States of failures in its thinking and though most of the population had only a hazy idea where Vietnam was, it didn't stop them demonstrating against American aggression and British involvement. My wife sampled this for herself one morning when she drove round a corner into a street in which the British Council had its Dar es Salaam offices, only to find the road blocked by a crowd engaged in setting fire to the British High Commissioner's Austin Princess motorcar. Fortunately, they were too busy to notice her and she was able to reverse very smartly and get herself out of harm's way. There was not a policeman in sight and God knows what would have become of her if she had gone a few yards further and attracted attention.

A few months later, she did in fact find herself in a sticky situation when she was nosing her way out of a side street and a group of youths suddenly appeared, rocking the car from side to side to the accompaniment of much jeering and banging on the bonnet. Once again, this was in the centre of Dar but there was no one near at hand to help and all she could think of doing was to rev the engine at full throttle. This startled her tormentors sufficiently to stand back for a second, enabling her to slap the car into gear and drive hastily away. It was such a stark contrast with the scene which would have prevailed only two years earlier, when any passer-by who might have been ambling along the sunlit street in a sleepy fashion would have murmured *jambo memsahib* in a courteous fashion and possibly even touched his *kofia*.

What nobody realised was the extent to which Julius Nyerere was imbued with socialist ideals, originally fostered by the Fabians when he was a student in Edinburgh and reinforced by a visit to China. Mao's Cultural Revolution was in full swing at this time and Nyerere had come back full of determination to combine socialism with African communal living. This led to the Arusha Declaration of 1967 and eventually to large-scale nationalisation and the implementation of *ujamaa*, a conceptual word implying togetherness. It wasn't actually put into practice until after we had left Tanzania but as a foretaste of things to come, all freehold land was summarily converted into State leaseholds, a move that rocked the powerful sisal industry to its foundations.

1966 was an uneasy year and by 1967, most of the expatriate businessmen and officials still in Tanzania had started feeling it was time to move on. The writing seemed to be on the wall as far as Tanzania's future was concerned and the rest of black Africa didn't seem to be doing too well, either. Nigeria had blown up in January 1966 and a military coup had seen the Prime Minister, Sir Abubakar Tafawa Balewa, shot and dumped in a ditch—only days after a meeting with the British Prime Minister, Harold Wilson, who had been in Nigeria on an official visit. Regrettably, this prompted some black humour on the verandah of the Gymkhana Club, where it was regretfully said that if only the rebels had acted a couple of days earlier, they could have nailed Wilson as well.

By this stage, we were reduced to making humorous sallies of this sort behind the back of the hand in a surreptitious kind of way. The Tanzania Government had shown itself sensitive to anything that could be construed as an insult and one was careful to whom one spoke. The jokes weren't necessarily anything to do with racism, either, but simply a normal reaction of wanting to make fun of people who took themselves seriously. It would, for example, have been impossible to explain to a black politician what was amusing in the story about Ian Smith, the leader of Rhodesia's breakaway white government, deciding his favourite song was *I'm Dreaming of a White Christmas*. Following the example of Tank Hill, this would plainly have resulted in instant deportation.

Fortunately, the atmosphere in Kenya was far happier. Jomo Kenyatta had proved to be staunchly pro-Western and the Kikuyu became even more dominant than they had been previously, grasping at the fruits of education and independence with considerable energy. Kenya's relative stability encouraged foreign investment and the only visible sign of trouble was the emergence of bribery and corruption on a national scale. With a depth of worldly experience behind him, however, Kenyatta refused to adopt a belligerent attitude towards the white population, and colonial institutions such as the Muthaiga Club and the Nairobi Club continued to flourish. Tourism was actively encouraged and people flew in by the planeload from Germany and other European countries to enjoy game safaris and beach holidays.

Uganda, meanwhile, was in a kind of limbo. In spite of the Tank Hill episode, there were still a fair number of white and Asian commercial people in the country, mainly centred round Kampala and Entebbe. Once described by Churchill as 'the pearl of Africa', the country had a high proportion of Western-educated citizens and was well supplied with hospitals and schools. Its main exports of coffee, tea and cotton were in demand, and Makerere University was well-established. However, the indigenous population was not unified and it has already been described how Milton Obote was plotting to replace the *Kabaka* of Buganda as the country's President. In 1966, he finally succeeded in this aim and this resulted in an uneasy situation which lasted until Idi Amin appeared on the world stage five years later and seized power by a military coup.

Back in Tanzania, the advent of 1967 saw most bwanas and memsahibs wondering what to do with the balance of their lives. By this stage, we all knew we would have to go somewhere and do something new but being used to being a big frog in a small pond, we had an inflated idea of our importance and assumed there was a whole pool of eager employers in Britain and America who were just dying for us to get in touch. As a surveyor involved in the administration of a colonial survey department, I was in close touch with my opposite number in the Survey of Kenya and we put great store on an impending visit from the Director of Overseas Surveys, the boss of the British Department that provided mapping to Commonwealth countries as part of Britain's external aid programme. Obviously, we thought, he would be delighted to know there was so much executive talent available and it was a sobering shock to find that we were of no interest at all. DOS was fully staffed, thank you very much, and if any vacancies arose, they were unlikely to be at a senior level. This experience was shared, I know, by many people in other walks of colonial life—both in government and in commerce—and the sad fact began to dawn that we would all have to start again from scratch and had better get used to the idea.

But where to go? People with British roots automatically thought of going back to the United Kingdom and retraining there in search of a new career. The Aussies, New Zealanders, Canadians and South Africans, of whom there were a surprising number, started planning to return home and many white East Africans began filling out immigration papers to go to these destinations as well. Interestingly, the Asian community, who were the backbone of commerce and the civil service, did not look towards India but more towards Britain. It was an overall diaspora, and one that was wel-comed by the Tanzania Government. The latter were now making no secret of their desire to see the last of the bwanas and it was the end of the trail in Tanzania for most of its non-indigenous inhabitants. Nyerere was itching to get on with his socialisation programme and was more than happy to take the country out of the Western sphere of influence.

Things were different in Kenya, where Kenyatta encouraged whites and Asians to stay on. Quite a few people took the opportunity to move there from Tanzania, a process made easier by the fact that most of the commercial firms in East Africa had always had their head offices in Nairobi. A lot of white people did leave, spurred on by the increasing crime rate and general feelings of uncertainty, but other more adventurous souls saw Kenya as a land of opportunity and actually went there, taking up game management, tourism, farming, and ranching with great energy. I remember travelling on a British Airways flight between London and Johannesburg some years later and being approached by a friendly soul who wandered up the aisle at drinks time and paused next to me. 'I saw a friendly face and thought I'd come and have a sundowner with you,' he announced cheerily in an Irish accent, and indeed, that is what we did with enthusiasm for the next hour or so. It turned out that he was leaving the flight in Nairobi and was then heading for his ranch in order to pursue his cattle business. When I questioned him further, it transpired he had arrived in Kenya at the very time the bwanas were leaving and had literally bought up every bovine animal with four legs and a tail that he could find, thereby ending up as one of Kenya's new meat barons. What a lesson in positive thinking!

For my wife and I, a decision was not easy. My professional qualifications as a land surveyor wouldn't take me very far in England and though we loved the countryside, neither of us fancied life in a semi-detached home in an urban suburb. In addition to this, Harold Wilson's Britain was starting to show signs of strain, with strikes and stoppages becoming the norm. We both loved Africa and it was a natural progression to start thinking of moving to South Africa, a country which seemed to offer an African way of life combined with a booming western-type economy. You had to be very liberal in your outlook back in 1967 to condemn South Africa for its method of government and though one knew there were substantially more black people in the country than whites, this did not strike us as particularly immoral. After all, a small minority of whites had been running East Africa for a long time and it had evolved very well.

So we applied to become immigrants to South Africa and made plans to leave at the end of the year. I gave notice to the Tanzania Government that I wished to retire prematurely—imagine retiring at the ripe old age of 34—and we settled down to our last few months in familiar old Dar es Salaam. It wasn't a bad time, either. We still went on Sunday picnics to Mjimwema on the south side of the ferry and the Gymkhana Club still loomed large in our lives. I even played in my last big tennis tournament and managed to reach the quarter-finals of the Tanzania Open, losing respectably to the Nigerian No. 1 who had been imported by the Department of Sport for the occasion. Our sons did well at the International School and when the mid-year monsoon blew, the surf at Oyster Bay was very passable. Leopards Cove to the north of town also became a popular picnic spot, especially after the Yacht Club was moved there from its traditional part of the main harbour. Its new site wasn't quite as picturesque as the old location had been but someone in authority had considered its presence in the harbour to be a security risk and it was told to move.

For a period, things stayed reassuringly quiet. The troupe of wild monkeys which lived in our street and existed on the seeds and fruits of the tropical trees in the various gardens, continued to do well and often partied on our roof, from whence they tried to throw things at my wife through the window. In her turn, she amassed a wonderful collection of shells and we combed the shops for the best curios to take away as souvenirs. Even the Deputy Minister for Something (I can't remember exactly what) coming to live next door to us wasn't too much of a shock, though his children, attired in grubby shirts ending well above their genitals, used to peer at us through the hedge and shout provocative slogans at our sons. Their father may have owned a Mercedes but their mother was still a simple *kanga*—clad village girl and his chickens persisted in coming through the hedge into our garden. It might have been the new face of Africa, but we used to shoo the chickens back again without compunction.

The feeling of quietly serving out time, however, was shattered by being burgled. It happened in the middle of the night and as all alert husbands are prone to do, I slept soundly throughout the incident and did not hear the faint rustle which woke my wife and made her sense an alien presence in the room. She swiftly switched on the bedside light, and there was a naked black man—clad only in a loincloth and glistening with oil—at the foot of the bed. There was a knife strapped to his waist, too, but mercifully, he didn't use it. The sudden switching-on of the light must have deterred him because he turned swiftly and vanished. 'You were dreaming,' I said when I had been shaken awake and appraised of the situation, but when I went through to the kitchen, there was a jagged hole in the expanding metal over the window and our guest had obviously departed by the same route he had entered. We duly reported it next morning and the Tanzanian police inspector who came to inspect the scene clicked his tongue in alarm. 'You shouldn't have switched on the light,' he said. 'We've had cases like this which have ended violently. You've been very lucky.'

This served as a reality check and we felt confirmed in our decision to leave. Dar itself was beginning to show signs of strain, and squatters' shacks were springing up in all sorts of unlikely places. The world-wide trend of people moving from rural to urban areas was beginning to accelerate and the resources of the Survey Department were increasingly channelled into the provision of housing plots. It was also noticeable that the workload of dealing with Western aid projects was beginning to run down as Tanzania's involvement with China increased. The prime example of this was the Chinese undertaking to build a railway from Dar es Salaam to Zambia, that land-locked country to the west of Tanzania which used to be Northern Rhodesia until it had achieved its independence in 1963. Kenneth Kaunda, its President, was a great friend of Nyerere and while both were prominent in the new wave of black nationalism that was sweeping the continent, KK was especially bitter about Zambia's rail outlets to the sea passing through the Portugese territories of Angola and Mozambique or—horror of horrors—through the white-controlled lands of Rhodesia and South Africa. This was plainly insupportable for good pan-Africans and the Chinese, who had been looking for a juicy project, were only too glad to come forward and offer to build a new railway line that would give Zambia an outlet to the Indian Ocean via Dar es Salaam.

Bizarrely, this project was undertaken without reference to the East African Railways and Harbours Administration, the large and efficient organisation that had been formed in 1948 to coordinate and run the railway system in each of the three component countries on a common basis. This was obviously too colonial for the Chinese and even more remarkably, they wanted nothing to do with survey information such as maps, trig points and bench marks. If their engineers had required this, they would have had to have approached the Survey Department for the necessary records and would have had to see me as keeper of the records. No such approaches were ever made, however, and how they built the line without this information I will never know. No Western contractor would have looked at the project without a massive pre-construction study but somehow the Chinese managed to traverse a long and difficult route full of escarpments and rivers without any of the data generally regarded as essential. Maybe their Chief Engineer simply walked ahead of the rail-laying gang and decided the route as they went; I just don't know. The line had its own rolling stock, a separate railway station in Dar, and was completely separate from the existing infrastructure. Even the gauge used for the rails was different and all aspects of operation, maintenance and administration were jealously shielded from Western-oriented eyes.

Naturally, the Tanzam railway project was known as the Chink Link and though I would have liked to have known more about it, it was still under construction at the time I finally left Tanzania. The only sign of its existence was the occasional sighting of Chinese technicians and labourers in the streets of Dar, typically attired in cotton trousers and singlets. Outwardly quite well-behaved like the Nigerian soldiers, we gathered there were some problems—mainly involving sex—when it came to fraternising with the locals. Whatever their problems, however, they certainly didn't linger on in Tanzania after the line was completed and it was many years before the Chinese set foot in Africa again. One assumes the differences in language and culture were just too vast and not all the goodwill in the world could surmount this.

In the new atmosphere of dislike and distrust, the remaining bwanas and memsahibs in Tanzania unashamedly spent 1967 serving out time. In our case, the plan was for my wife and our two young sons to go to England in early 1968, while I flew to Johannesburg on my own and looked for a job. As the year progressed and the date of departure grew closer, we soon found ourselves involved in a flurry of organisational matters such as booking passages, notifying the Housing Committee we would be vacating our government quarter, and handing over my work in the Survey Department to my replacement—another bwana who wasn't yet due for terminal leave. While we were in the thick of this, the British Government chose to devalue the pound and though Harold Wilson kept reiterating 'the pound in your pocket is still a pound', it was devastating for people like us who were not going back to the United Kingdom. As there was nothing we could do about it, though, we proceeded to combine Christmas and New Year with our farewells—a process that was rendered bizarre by the realisation we might never again see the people who had been part of our lives for so long.

Selling my mother's piano was an interesting experience because it was bought by a well-to-do Indian couple, who enquired politely where we were going. As I wasn't broadcasting our destination due to the sensitivities of the situation, I muttered something about going to South Africa for a spot of holiday before settling down. 'Oh,' said the husband, 'you should go and live there. We've been there and it's streets ahead of this place. Don't you worry about *apartheid* either—everybody lives happily in their own community and the different groups only come together when they have to do business with each other.'

This was certainly re assurance from an unexpected quarter, but I had to admit it accorded with my own observation of multi-racial cocktail parties on the Dar es Salaam diplomatic circuit, several of which we had been invited to attend. For the first hour, everybody made a determined attempt to socialise—excluding black wives who cluttered helplessly together—and the conversation would cover current affairs, cars and sport in the normal way. Then, as a couple of drinks went down the hatch and conversations became animated, the evening would end with a group of white males and their wives at one end of the room and a group of black males at the other. American blacks were in a particularly tricky position, having little in common with locals of the same complexion. I even remember one of them being included in some local bigwig's sweeping statement about 'us Africans', which caused him to turn round and firmly say 'listen, buddy, I'm not African. I'm an American.'

Our departure actually took place during the first few days of January, 1968, by which time we had packed our stuff into boxes and sent them off to the Government Passages Agent for storage until further notice. I sold our car—a Ford Cortina GT, reared in the best traditions of the East African Safari—and did all the obvious things like closing bank accounts, transferring money and buying Travellers' Cheques. There was a great sense of reaching the end of a chapter and though we were young enough to be exhilarated at the prospect of a new future, we still felt sentimental about leaving Dar and all its familiar associations behind. The emotional wrench was considerable, and it was only the check-in farce at the airport when I was seeing off my wife and sons which redeemed our resolution. The immigration official on duty—an indigenous Tanzanian who was lying back in his chair with his feet on the table while he smoked a cigarette—looked through her passport, put a cursory stamp on it, and then flipped it on to the floor near our feet. It was done deliberately and insultingly. The gloves were off and he was plainly hoping to see a white memsahib grovel at his feet. 'He's trying to provoke a scene,' I immediately thought, as I felt my wife's blood pressure rising. 'Pick it up, darling', I hissed in her ear. 'Just pick it up.' And she did, bless her. She picked it up, the official visibly gloated, and off to the plane my loved ones went. And that took care of any sentiment about leaving!

Four days later, I was back at the airport on my own account. It was lunchtime and half a dozen of my remaining friends in Dar had made the journey out there for a farewell drink. We had quite a party in fact and I was full of gin-and-tonic by the time I breezed through immigration. Maybe it was because of the gin or perhaps the same official was off duty, but it went smoothly this time and I was able to board the Blantyre plane labelled 'Air Malawi' without mishap. Naturally, I had to have another gin-and-tonic as soon as we were airborne and while it may be thought this brought on a feeling of nostalgia, I must confess my chief reaction was one of relief at finally getting away. '*Kwa heri*, Dar,' I said under my breath, 'I shall never see you again.'

At Blantyre, I walked round the airport during our stop there and watched with fascination as the maintenance staff peeled off the 'Air Malawi' label which had been tactfully stuck on the aircraft for its trip to Dar es Salaam and substituted 'Air Rhodesia' in its place. Anything to do with the white South would have been anathema to the Tanzanians but it made one wonder whether they knew of the deception and if they did, whether someone had taken a decision to turn a blind eye to it. Certainly, my journey south became whiter and whiter as we progressed and by the time we had landed at Salisbury, (now Harare, the capital city of Zimbabwe), the change in atmosphere was palpable. It was just like being in Nairobi twenty years earlier.

In case a mention of Rhodesia is confusing to the modern reader, a brief history of this troubled country may be of assistance. It wasn't troubled in the days of which I write, however,—it was a very good-looking piece of real estate previously known as Southern Rhodesia, containing vast farms and tobacco plantations. The Matabele and the Mashona lived happily in their tribal areas, sundry animals lived happily in the huge wilderness area along the Zambesi valley, and there were spectacular mountain ranges along the eastern boundary with Mozambique. Cecil Rhodes, (what a name to conjure with or vilify, according to your point of view), had been instrumental in Britain's colonisation of the area through operation of the British South Africa Company from 1889 onwards, and the country had become a self-governing colony in 1923. This lasted until the unilateral declaration of independence in 1965 and at that time, there were approximately 250000 whites in the country—considerably more than Kenya—and some 4.5 million blacks.

The political story is surely familiar and a very simplified version will tell you that the whites controlled the Government and were loath to see the country handed over to black Nationalist rule. When Britain insisted this should be done, the white Rhodesians, led by an ex-fighter pilot and farmer named Ian Smith, refused to go along with the idea and there was an enormous fuss. Liberal opinion saw the intransigence of the whites as a flagrant breach of democracy and most of the members of the United Nations, (some of whom paid very nominal lip-service to the desirability of democracy), were only too glad to join in. Be that as it may, however, the Rhodesians had a small but excellent Army and Air Force, and were prepared to tough things out. Internally, the country was stable and there were plans for increasing participation by the black population in the way the country should be governed.

So there you have it. Rhodesia was a prosperous country in 1968 and I enjoyed the night and day I spent in Salisbury. Then I caught a South African Airways jet in the afternoon and flew down to Johannesburg in company with a hundred or so Portugese emigrants who were also en route to a new life. It seemed prophetic and my consciousness of losing East African individuality was reinforced by the view of tall buildings and mine dumps out of the plane window. Sure as hell, it was going to be different. My East African days were over and I was a bwana no more.

CHAPTER 7

GAME OVER

In retrospect, the episode which finally brought my ex-bwana status home to me occurred shortly after my arrival in South Africa during the early part of 1968. Our dear friends, Christopher and Peggy Baker—whom we had put on a ship to Durban a few years earlier—had succeeded in making a niche for themselves in the thriving business world of Johannesburg and very kindly arranged a small party for me to meet some of their South African friends. Needless to say, they were all white friends because the races didn't mix socially at that stage of the country's history. In fact, the races didn't mix at all and the population consisted of a large number of separate communities, which have since become what is known as the Rainbow Nation. Back in the 1960's, nobody in South Africa mixed with anybody of a different ethnic background—the Zulus didn't mix with the Xhosas, the Vendas didn't mix with the Tswanas, the Indians didn't mix with the Coloureds, and even the white population was split between Afrikaans-speakers and English-speakers with very little social interaction between them.

The episode of which I speak occurred during this party and was set in motion by my bad habit of waving my hands about while talking. True to form, I knocked over a plate of potato chips and the damned things went all over the carpet. This caused a lull in conversation and everybody stopped and stared. Then one of the guests, who turned out to be a prominent newspaperman, peered across the room and gave tongue.

'Once a white kaffir, always a white kaffir,' he observed jovially and the room broke up into laughter.

It was, of course, the use of the word *kaffir* which had set the thought processes working. It had been a word in common usage throughout South

Africa's history for all its black indigenous inhabitants other than Hottentots or Bushmen, and the frontier wars of the nineteenth century were collectively known as the *Kaffir Wars*. There was even a colony at one stage known as British Kaffraria, and South African gold shares on the London Stock Exchange were commonly referred to as *Kaffirs*. An old word derived from Arabic, its original usage was not offensive and merely signified a non-believer. Sometimes rendered as *caffre,* its use would have come naturally to the deeply religious seafarers who sailed past the Cape on their way to the East Indies and had tantalising glimpses of an alien people on the shore. It was only in the middle of the twentieth century that black people began to resent the word and since then, it has achieved ultimate pariah status. It is now regarded as the direst racial epithet and to apply it to any indigenous inhabitant of Africa would cause grave offence.

I must admit that to have been called a white kaffir stopped me in my tracks. It wasn't a case of feeling insulted at the quip because it was very funny and I could share in the joke. What did the mental damage was the final realisation that the bwana stage of my life was irrevocably at an end. Having been born and bred in East Africa, I was now rootless and a strange figure to the outside world—a white man who was perceived to have come from a wild part of the African continent and was now entering civilised society. Even white South Africans found this curious and though many of them were destined to fall into the same mould thirty years later, they were supremely confident at the time of being a western nation in the forefront of progress. The jest was kindly but from that point onwards, it felt curiously old-fashioned to have been a bwana and I felt the need to create a new persona.

Certainly, it could be fairly said by 1970 that colonialism was over as far as Africa was concerned. The only notable exceptions were the two Portuguese colonies of Angola and Mozambique, plus the former German colony of South West Africa which was mandated to South Africa after World War One and eventually became Namibia. Whether Rhodesia was a colony or not was a matter of argument; it certainly had been until its unilateral declaration of independence in 1965 and in the eyes of Britain and the rest of the world was still a colony, albeit one which had enjoyed responsible government for nearly fifty years. South Africa itself, the bastion of white rule, was most emphatically not a colony. It may have had a colonial past during certain periods of its history but had been a fiercely independent dominion within the British Commonwealth since 1910 and had become a republic in 1961.

As already pointed out, the continued existence of these countries in an unchanged form was responsible for the world's media regarding Africa as having been split into the black north and the white south. The concept of a unified 'black north', however, was a gross simplification because its ethnic composition varied from Arab to full-blooded Bantu and exhibited an enormous range of cultures and languages. The only thing that united its politicians, aside from their avidity for power and riches, was their oft-stated desire of freedom for everyone—a cry guaranteed to go down well at United Nations gatherings. The continued government of large tracts of Africa by white people who comprised a minority of the population was presented as a grave affront to human rights by these leaders and was held to be a serious threat to world peace. Colonialism was labelled evil, and the disparity of wealth between indigenous populations and their erstwhile masters was used as evidence of immoral and intensive exploitation. Regrettably, the media, encouraged by the wave of fashionable self-abnegation which had engulfed intellectual opinion in the 1960's, lost no time in jumping on this bandwagon and before you could blink, having been a bwana automatically stamped you as vile and racist oppressor just one notch above a concentration camp guard. The white south being more stable and prosperous than the rest of Africa was deemed to be additional proof of this and a general air of apology towards anyone with a black face was adopted by Western journalists and opinion-makers. The concept of 'empire' which had been so fashionable only a decade earlier was now derided, and the change in outlook was orchestrated so skilfully that few people realised there was a hidden economic motivation behind this sudden onset of humanitarian concern.

Many disconcerting post-*uhuru* developments had in fact already occurred by the time 1970 was reached and had caused the donors of freedom and democracy much anxiety. They had watched helplessly as the Congo slid into a complete and utter mess and though great things had been hoped for the ex-British colonies of West Africa, disillusion had set in when Kwame Nkrumah, the self-proclaimed Messiah of Ghana, (previously the Gold Coast), was deposed by a military coup in 1966. To make matters worse, the Prime Minister of Nigeria, Sir Abubakar Tafawa Balewa, was arrested and shot by dissident Ibo army officers shortly afterwards and the Nigerian situation escalated into the Biafran Civil War, which lasted until 1970 and caused the deaths of nearly a million people.

The same pattern was being followed in the French part of Africa, which comprised a bloc of twelve countries approximately the size of Europe. The

French, who prided themselves on Gallic realism, believed they had the key to successful colonialism and had carefully created an indigenous elite within each country. This had been achieved—in theory at least—by classifying a local person as an *évolué* once he or she was deemed to have achieved the requisite level of manners, language and culture, and thereafter, the person in question was regarded as completely French. As a result, the French colonies appeared relatively sophisticated, French was widely spoken, and crusty *baguettes* could be found in even the smallest villages. Who knows what might have happened if this policy had been rigorously followed but sadly, the effects of World War Two and the loss of Indochina dispirited the advocates of empire and Charles de Gaulle put an end to it in characteristic fashion before it had really caught on.

Students of history will, of course, need no introduction to de Gaulle—a towering figure of the twentieth century. As is well known, *le grand Charles* was not only a military general who played a prominent part in defeating Hitler's armies and restoring France's pride during World War Two, but a consummate politician who returned to public life in 1958 in order to cope with the constitutional crisis which had been sparked off by the volatile situation in Algeria. De Gaulle's handling of this resulted in the creation of the Fifth Republic and as part of the new constitution, a take-it-or-leave-it choice was offered to the French colonies. In terms of this, each country was enabled to choose between complete independence or entering into community with France. If the latter alternative were chosen, it was also made plain that a large measure of autonomy would be conferred on the country concerned and that intensive French aid would be forthcoming.

This offer had considerable appeal to all the parties involved, not least to the French who were keen to shed the colonial baggage they had inherited from the old imperialist days. At the same time, however, they wanted their former colonies to stay within the Francophone tent and made the community option as attractive as possible. Excluding Morocco (which was already independent) and Algeria (which was still regarded as part of France), this resulted in all the colonies bar one accepting the community alternative. Guinea was the only exception and the French made no attempt to hide their displeasure at its decision. The country, which had elected an incipient tyrant by the name of *Sekou Touré* to be its new President, was immediately left to its own devices and the departing French engineers even took the telephone system with them. The Guineans then turned to the Soviet Union for aid but little good came of this and Guinea became increasingly derelict and chaotic.

Though de Gaulle's move may have seemed brilliant to western minds, however, it did not take long for Mother Africa to demolish the concepts on which it was based. Far from the new bloc of French-speaking countries living in peace and harmony, it soon became obvious that expectations for the ex-colonies which had elected to stay in the French community would never be fulfilled. Chad led the way by embroiling itself in an endemic civil war and military coups soon occurred in most of the other new nations. Algeria decided it didn't want to be a part of mainland France and there was some very bitter fighting there until it obtained independence in 1962. Further troubles brewed up in other French Community countries and though most of them only came to a head after the landmark year of 1970, the writing by this time was on the wall. The huge island of Madagascar was the first to go when it was taken over by a military government in 1975, and shortly after this, an ex-NCO in the French Army called Jean-Bedel Bokassa proclaimed himself to be Emperor of the Central African Republic. As he modelled his coronation on that of Napoleon, you could hardly accuse him of disliking France but regrettably, he then went on to become a vicious dictator who instituted such a tyrannical rule that he had to be forcibly deposed by French paratroopers. Only the Côte d'Ivoire under the able management of President Félix Houphet-Boigny has remained relatively stable and even there, the country has experienced its share of social disturbance.

Against this background, East Africa—the home of the bwanas—didn't do too badly at first. In Kenya, Jomo Kenyatta may have become more autocratic by the time 1970 dawned but the country was relatively calm and foreign investment was attracted by his capitalist outlook. Some critics might say he was a bit too capitalist for comfort and it cannot be denied that his programme of land reform not only enriched his relatives and friends but led to him becoming the largest landowner in the nation. Similar accusations were also levelled against the fourth and best-known of his wives, Mama Ngina, who achieved considerable notoriety with her somewhat direct business style of taking a share of whatever was going. Say what one will, however, the economy of Kenya kept turning over and it is still one of the most prosperous countries in Africa. Tanzania, on the other hand, grew more and more socialist as Nyerere began to mount his programme of *ujamaa*—the 'togetherness' concept by means of which he intended to force the rural population into a network of village communities modelled on the Chinese communist system. At the same time, an ultimatum was given to all non-indigenous inhabitants of the country to the effect that they must take out Tanzanian citizenship if they wished to remain. Not unnaturally, this resulted in an exodus of people which the economy could ill afford to lose and Tanzania's position became more and more wobbly.

Uganda, of course, was the scene which really rocked the East African boat with the advent of 'Field Marshal' *Idi Amin*. Much has been written about this colourful character and a number of movies on various aspects of his life have been made, the most recent of which was *The Last King of Scotland* in 2006. If the reader wishes to know more about the way this half-crazed tyrant's mind worked, there is plenty of material on record and possibly a great deal still to be unearthed. In view of his unhinged mentality, one would have assumed him to have been a popular demagogue who rose to power on the shoulders of a rampaging mob but in fact, he was nothing of the sort. He was a product of years of British Army discipline and had come up through the ranks of the KAR. Furthermore, his take-over of Uganda by a military coup against Milton Obote in 1971 was warmly welcomed by the British Government. One would think someone in military or diplomatic circles might have noticed he was off his head but apparently, he was deemed to be a good fellow on the strength of his prowess at regimental sports. The spectacle of Obote and Amin making money by smuggling gold and ivory out of the Congo in 1965 didn't ring any warning bells, either, and when the two subsequently fell out, Amin was believed to be an honest soldier who had only intervened in politics in order to restore good government. The fact that Obote would have nailed Amin's hide to the wall if Amin had not pre-empted him, was not realised and the full implications of the situation only became apparent when Amin declared himself President and appointed his military colleagues to the top jobs in the country.

From that point onwards, one thing led to another. Obote, who had been given refuge in Tanzania by his friend, Julius Nyerere, tried to mount a counter-coup in 1972 but the attempt misfired and Amin retaliated by having thousands of Obote supporters rounded up and killed. It was pure Stalinism at its African best and to compound matters, Amin chose that instant to expel all the Asians from Uganda and expropriate their properties and businesses. The latter were then given to his own supporters—presumably with the intention of strengthening his power base—and just to help things along, he followed this by breaking off diplomatic relations with Britain and expropriating all the British-owned businesses in the country as well. It was a considerable shock to the colonial apologists in Westminster, who not only saw the 'pearl of Africa' going up in smoke but also faced an unexpected influx of immigrants just as Britain was sliding into recession. As it happened, the Ugandan Asians who subsequently arrived in Britain were among the best immigrants Britain had ever had but at the time, their absorption caused more than a little anxiety.

Meanwhile, the Uganda situation went from bad to worse. Civil rights disappeared, and the industries that had been the backbone of Uganda's economy collapsed due to the inexperience and mismanagement of their new owners. Anyone who was perceived as an enemy was imprisoned, tortured and often killed in barbaric fashion. It was literally a reign of terror, and yet in spite of the blood-soaked nature of his regime, Amin stayed in power for another seven years and even enjoyed a term as Chairman of the Organisation of African Unity. He was only deposed in 1979 when he overreached himself and provoked an outbreak of war with Tanzania by attempting to usurp one of its provinces. Though Nyerere had no desire to go to war against a fellow East African nation and Tanzania could certainly not afford to do so, Amin persisted in his folly and kept pushing matters until Nyerere had no option but to order the Tanzania Army into action. Not in the best of shape due to their recent re-organisation, the Tanzanians somehow managed to get it together and eventually achieved victory—mainly due to the Uganda Army being in even worse shape than Tanzania's. Both sides, we are told by witnesses, were more interested in wreaking violence on the civilian population than fighting each other and the fighting went on in a desultory fashion until Kampala was finally 'liberated'. Amin then fled first to Libya and then to Saudi Arabia, leaving behind a scene of chaos and confusion.

By this time, the last vestige of inter-territorial organisation had gone by the board with the demise of the East African Community in 1977 and the cessation of common services that had been painstakingly built up during the preceding 60 years. This was hardly surprising in view of Amin's antics in Uganda but there was also a measure of distrust between Kenya and Tanzania due to their differences in political and economic outlook. Each country wanted to go its own way and the bickering ended with everything which had been 'East African' being put on the scrap heap. The East African Railways and Harbours Corporation was disbanded and all the common services departments that the three countries had shared were split up between them. East African Airways, which was still flying under its own flag, came to a sudden end and the degree of attendant confusion can be gauged from the famous announcement made to his passengers by the pilot of a Super VC10 on 28 January 1977 on an outward flight from Europe. Not a believer in breaking things gently, it is documented that he switched on the microphone and said 'You are on the last flight of East African Airways as the airline has gone bankrupt.' The plane reached Nairobi, apparently, but then that was it.

Prior to this, the East African Currency Board had been disbanded in 1966. This body had been responsible for the joint currency of East Africa since 1919, and its replacement by the newly-formed central banks of each country gave rise to the issue of three different sorts of shilling, namely the Kenya shilling, the Tanzania shilling and the Uganda shilling. Depending how one looked at it, this gave an exciting or ominous new look to the notes and coins with which everybody was familiar. Originally at par with sterling on the basis of 20 shillings to the pound, the passing years have not been kind to the exchange rates of these currencies on the international market and the reader may find it interesting to note that the modern equivalents of the pound, (as for May 2010), are 116 Kenya shillings, 2094 Tanzania shillings and 3230 Uganda shillings. If these numbers are an expression of the world's confidence in the countries concerned, it would seem that the Kenya shilling—which has depreciated against the pound at an average rate of 5% since 1970—is now adjudged to be 18 times stronger than the Tanzania shilling and 27 times more than the Uganda shilling. Could any indication of relative economic performance be clearer?

As for the three Railway Corporations that took over from the good old EAR &H, the story is far from one of success. Despite its awesome history and admirable record, it is understood the Kenya and Uganda railway system reached such a poor state in recent times with regard to maintenance and rolling stock that an independent South African company has had to be brought in to run the operation. Much the same thing has apparently happened in Tanzania, which has turned to an Indian company to sort out the mess and impose some sort of order. The ex-Chinese railway to Zambia from Dar es Salaam is still running, one gathers, but to travel on it has become increasingly adventurous. Alas, the need for maintenance of anything mechanical was not a strong point in the allocation of priorities and the guiding principle which was followed for many years was if it still works, why fix it? Fortunately, this stage now seems to be past and there are welcome signs of cooperation between the East African countries again, not just on railways but in other spheres of activity as well.

Clearly, the exit of the bwanas was marked by a severe breakdown of standards and the only defence which can be made against this conclusion is that many of them were inappropriate to a Third World situation. This may be true but a breakdown in standards automatically leads to an outbreak of chaos and indeed, it would seem this is inevitable if the leadership has no respect for established values. The early days of the Soviet Union in the 1920s and 1930s immediately spring to mind in this regard as the prime example of a system which won the unstinting approval of western intellectuals who were determined to ignore the plight of the peasantry on the ground. To understand this more fully in the East African situation, it is illuminating to consider the composition of the different groups of people who made up the cast in the closing days of colonialism.

Firstly, there were the bwanas and their memsahibs—white, well-educated, hard-working and efficient, kindly but not sentimental as far as the indigenous population was concerned, insistent on maintaining European standards, and not politically-minded unless their interests were directly threatened. Another thing they weren't was rich. The indigenous population was not exploited and though a few bwanas did make money, it was a struggle to reach a comfortable standard of living and there was no social security of any kind whatever. Bwanas didn't have votes, either, and the first time I ever voted in an election was many years later in South Africa. Similarly, though Nairobi did have an embryonic stock exchange, I never knew anyone who bought or sold shares on it and it was long after leaving East Africa that I found out how stock markets operated.

Then there was the Asian community, numerically far superior to the bwanas and permeated by a variety of cultural influences. Grass-roots commerce was exclusively in their hands and so were the administrative echelons of the three East African governments. Though many of them had links with India, they tended to emote more with Britain and as already noted, the exodus of many of them from East Africa gave Britain the benefit of an industrious and talented increment to its population. In the early days, they generally stayed within their own sects but towards the end of the colonial era, the sons and daughters of the professional classes mingled freely with the increasingly cosmopolitan ranks of the bwanas. Most non-Asian people believed them to be uniformly rich but in point of fact, this only applied to Asian businessmen in the top echelons and the salaries paid to Asian staff were generally lower than those paid to expatriates.

The most identifiable group after the Europeans and Asians would have been the broad mass of East Africa's indigenous population, mainly rural at the time of independence and living in villages within their tribal areas. There are many tribes in Africa—120 in Tanzania and 70 in Kenya—and each one has its own customs and language. This makes it difficult to generalise but as a rule of thumb, one could say that a middle-aged male who had settled for village life and resisted the lure of the big city lived pretty well as long as the rains were good. With a couple of hard-working wives, (preferably an old one and a young one), to till the fields, brew *pombe* (maize-beer), and keep him warm at night, he could live like a gentleman. I recall making an early start on a trip from Iringa along a bush road that threaded its way through a succession of Wahehe villages and in each one, there was a gathering of males assembled under the shade of a big tree about to begin a morning of drinking and discussion. It was just like a London club in a different setting and it struck me as not bad going if one could get it. From a woman's point of view, it might not have been so hot but at least, no one was lonely; there would always be other wives to talk to and a whole sisterhood system in the village willing to help with childcare and housework. This is why, I think, Nyerere's *ujamaa* programme came as such a shock to the rural population. They were ticking over very nicely in their own traditional ways—thank you very much—and to be forced into a poorly-administered yet highly-politicised programme of forced labour did not suit them at all.

Fourthly, there was the black urban population—a large and rapidly increasing group who were attracted to the comparative wealth and glamour of the towns. Like so many other less developed parts of the world, this wealth and glamour was perceived rather than actual but this did not allay expectations. There were hardly any squatters to be found in African cities south of the Sahara prior to the early 1960s but the rural-urban drift grew rapidly from this time onward. It was a huge social change and there was no stopping it. Mass communication may have been partly responsible but to a large extent, it was a matter of emerging consciousness and wanting to be part of the mainstream. If you lived in a town, you could get a job, you could earn money, you could socialise with other people, you could get casual sex, you could walk along exciting streets and look at bright lights, cars and shops. Life there was obviously full of opportunity and younger people needed no urging to leave their villages, spurred on by periodic droughts and a breakdown of the rural infrastructure due to increasing population pressure. Wave after wave of urban immigrants started to arrive in African cities and shanty settlements came into being on any ground that was vacant. The process proved to be irreversible and created an enormous hot potato for governments, as it was realised nothing short of military action could hold it back. Even in South Africa, which had strong laws regulating influx control, the authorities proved powerless to prevent the formation of Soweto on the outskirts of Johannesburg. Certainly, in East Africa at the end of the colonial era, there was not much appreciation of the growth of this trend and the newly-independent governments of the region were too busy finding their feet to worry overmuch about it. Even to people with demographic knowledge, it was inconceivable in the late 1960s that the population would grow so quickly and if it had been forecast in 1970 that the existing population of 34 million for all three countries combined would rise to 100 million by 2005, no one would have believed it.

The next and probably the most significant group of people with their fingers in the independence pie were the emergent black politicians. A great deal has been said about their performance—not all of it complimentary—but before judging them by western standards, the nature of African logic and ethical mores must be understood. Their cultural roots go back to pre-colonial times and it is necessary to recall the period when society was organised along tribal lines and the chief of each tribe was a warlord, pure and simple. Any sign of weakness in such a chief could be fatal and power was the ultimate goal—to be obtained and retained at any cost. African logic is quite different to European logic, known as *hakili ya wazungu* in Swahili—a phrase often uttered by members of my survey crew when I wanted them to do something obviously pointless, like taking everything out of the storeroom and putting it back again after being dusted. Everybody knew it would need to be done again in a month's time, so why bother? The fact that I wanted to give them something to do on a rainy day and couldn't bear to see them sitting around was correctly diagnosed as *hakili ya wazungu.*

Certainly, the European concept of human rights was a strange thing to the practical African mind, evolved through generations of trying to survive in adverse conditions. If disease, animals, hostile warriors, drought, floods or famine didn't get you, you were doing pretty well and if you found yourself in an advantageous situation, you made the most of it because you didn't know how long it would last. It must have seemed crazy to the embryonic politicians of Africa to voluntarily stand down after a tour of office or to call an election in which there was a good chance of being defeated. Furthermore, aspiring African politicians in the late 1950s did not fail to notice the United Nations was full of countries which did not embrace American and European versions of democracy, and it must have been obvious to them that the path to power lay in playing a waiting game during which they would make all the right noises required by their colonial masters to prove their readiness to take over. The prospects were glittering and more than enough to make them keep a lid on the real agenda—namely, to get power and then to keep it. Once in power, the gloves could be taken off and constitutions could be amended. The need for a healthy opposition to ensure good government could then be dispensed with and the one-party route could be adopted as the only one that made any sense. Cynical or not, it is fair to say that the unspoken credo of 'one election, once' was behind the outward show of support for western-style democracy.

Politicians of this sort were bad enough but fortunately for Kenya and Tanzania, they were exempt from the second and more sinister wave of African politicians which came later in the form of restless soldiers who saw no need to pay lip service to democracy at all. Usually given high rank at the time of independence, it was anathema to these Army officers to have to subordinate themselves to the wishes of civilian office-bearers. What was the use of all that training and authority if one didn't use it to promote one's own interests? Simple logic decreed that if you and your followers had guns and were prepared to use them, people who didn't have guns were likely to do what you told them. Uganda caught the full force of this reasoning by courtesy of Idi Amin and other countries in Africa were unlucky enough to end up with such fine examples as Joseph Mobutu in the Congo, Jean Bokassa in the Central African Republic, Jerry Rawlings in Ghana, and God knows how many power-seeking Generals in Nigeria and Ethiopia. They were all ruthless and corrupt, and none of them had the slightest regard for human rights and the rule of law.

Other political groups involved in the death of colonialism—not just in East Africa but generally all over the world—were diverse and curiously enough, didn't live in the colonies at all. Americans, singularly uninformed about any countries outside America, had always been averse to the idea of Empire and could not imagine any greater boon than the immediate conferment of American-style democracy. The communist bloc, on the other hand, saw the most wonderful opportunity to undermine the West and draw the erstwhile colonies into their own sphere of influence as part of their plan for world domination. Anything the Soviet Union and its allies could do to de-stabilise the existing setup became part of their strategy, and shipments of arms and essential supplies were made readily available to committed or potential Marxist movements.

However, both the Americans and the Russians were novices at dealing with the dark continent—the latter even sent a consignment of snow ploughs to West Africa—and their respective pressures could easily have been withstood if the central figures of the British and French Governments in the persons of Macmillan, de Gaulle, and their ministers, had not been hell-bent on getting rid of the load they perceived their African colonies had become. This was where the ultimate authority lay and there seems little doubt that the leaders of Britain and France deliberately orchestrated the anti-colony chorus. Naturally, the leftist intellectuals of the West were only too glad to join in and their eloquence gave the process a moral impetus. Well-intentioned but generally without much knowledge of local conditions, this group deemed all colonials to be guilty of racism and exploitation. The Kipling ethos of responsibility was derided and the fashionable scene was rent by the voices of shrill actresses and pop stars campaigning for universal liberty. This coincided with the revolutionary spirit which characterised the 1960s and led to deep antagonism being felt by activist members of the younger generation towards anyone in authority. Colonial governments clearly fell into this category and one now had the strange spectacle of home-based Europeans decrying their own kith and kin, whose only sin happened to be the fact of living overseas and not being paid-up members of the 'Hampstead Thinkers', as the brigade of fashionable intellectuals in London came to be called.

Regrettably, the media was only too keen to jump on this bandwagon and the British tabloid newspapers of the early 1960s became almost hysterical about perceived injustice and police brutality in the colonies. In Nyasaland (Malawi), for example, there was an enormous fuss about a black girl who had her toe trodden on during a protest rally in the middle of Blantyre. Impartial witnesses say the demonstration was actually quite peaceable and it was established later that the young lady in question had not only been trodden on by someone in the crowd but had been helped to her feet by a white police inspector. Observed by several experienced journalists, however, the episode was written up as police brutality of the worst sort and the police were accused of handing out wholesale beatings at the encouragement of hysterical white settlers. The row found its way into the House of Commons and it took a judicial enquiry to find that there was no substance whatever in the stories. In retrospect, of course, one can see this episode as the forerunner of modern journalistic attitudes that have prevailed since the end of World War Two—a sort of knee-jerk reaction against the very people representing your own country. A stranger to the planet during the recent Iraq War, for example, might have easily assumed from the volume of criticism directed at Coalition forces that the British Broadcasting Corporation was supporting the opposition. But there again, if the enemy doesn't speak the same language and won't let journalists travel behind their lines, it is not easy to work up a balanced story and the only alternative is to concentrate on the deficiencies of your own side.

If the reader can now imagine these diverse groups being thrown into the melting pot, the resulting history of East Africa can hardly be a surprise.

It was an incendiary mixture and it is a tribute to human endurance that the three countries are no worse off than they are. In this regard, it is illuminating to consider how the different groups have fared in modern times—nearly fifty years after *uhuru* was conferred on the component countries of East Africa.

Well, the bwanas—the group this book is all about—can be deemed to have ceased existing as a species as from about 1980 onwards and though there are some surviving specimens still in East Africa or otherwise scattered round the world, a state of complete extinction is rapidly being approached. Most of them, particularly those who were not born in East Africa, went back to Britain and were re-absorbed into the British way of life. A large number moved southwards, firstly to Rhodesia and then to South Africa, where Swahili greetings can still be heard in some retirement villages—especially at sundowner time.

As for the indigenous population, the rural peasantry are most certainly still there and in vaster numbers than ever in spite of successive droughts caused by de-forestation and a shrinking of the ozone layer. Their governments obviously keep an eye on them but no one in the outside world knows much about them any more and one suspects they jog along at a bare subsistence level, living a hand-to-mouth existence which is occasionally boosted by Western external aid programmes.

The black urban population is plainly where the action is. For the most part, it is painfully poor and the people occupy vast slums in which the crime rate is horrific. Essential services such as clean water, sewage disposal and electricity are conspicuously lacking and health problems arising from AIDS and other diseases are acute. In spite of this, however, there seems to be an undercurrent of vigorous life and even a sense of identity that manifests itself in music and a new language called *Sheng,* which is a mixture of English and Swahili. A small black middle class has finally come into being, too, and has made its mark in business and academic circles—particularly in Kenya. Its athletes are famous on the long distance running circuit and the country not only puts a respectable cricket side into the international arena but fields a popular rugby team on the World Sevens circuit. There is a circle of intellectuals and the arts are well represented.

What can one say about the politicians? Aside from the Amin era in Uganda, each of the three East African countries has managed to maintain a functioning Parliament in spite of the one-party philosophy. Julius Nyerere in Tanzania was particularly eloquent in justifying the validity of one-party government and produced long and tortuous arguments which conclusively proved it was not detrimental to democracy. Jomo Kenyatta went along with this, too, but being older and having lived in Europe, was more subtle in his approach and stayed out of philosophical debate, though he certainly knew a trick or two about staying in power. Nyerere knew no such inhibitions, however, and for a time, was regarded as the idealistic voice of Africa until it became clear he had succeeded in making Tanzania one of the poorest nations on the continent. After that, overseas people took no notice of him and the last time I saw him in public before he died in 1999 was on television in South Africa after Nelson Mandela's inauguration. Once an autocratic statesman, he appeared as a slight old man who seemed rather forlorn and out of touch with the modern scene. Faced with a glamorous and self-possessed black female interviewer, (quite different to the respectful type of kikoi-clad female he was used to), he squirmed visibly under her barbed questioning. Eventually, she asked him how it was that African socialism had managed to bankrupt Tanzania and suggested he must have been personally responsible. Stung by this, Julius blamed it all on colonialism. 'When the British left, they left us nothing,' he said, the emphasis of this statement only being matched by its inaccuracy. However, she would have none of it. 'The British left thirty years ago,' she said firmly. 'You've had plenty of time to build up the country since then.' She then dismissed him and he shuffled off in confusion, a veritable shadow of his old domineering self.

As for the elderly Western statesmen who decided to shed their colonial inheritance so precipitately, it is interesting to note that death or resignation occurred to all of them within a short space of time. It would be nice to think they worried about the countless lives their actions had affected, but getting rid of the colonies was only a minor pre-occupation and it is unlikely they suffered from any remorse. The roll call is interesting because it is so encompassing. De Gaulle resigned as President of France in 1969 and died a year later while writing his memoirs. Harold Macmillan retired from politics in 1964 in a manner which many people regard as a forced resignation. Iain Macleod died on the job, as it were, in 1970 while he was the Chancellor of the Exchequer and Harold Wilson resigned unexpectedly as British Prime Minister in 1976. The men who had been Governors of the East African countries also had mixed fortunes—Edward Twining, ex-Tanganyika, died in 1967; Andrew Cohen, ex-Uganda, died in 1968; Evelyn Baring in 1973. They were all youngish men, none of whom got past 70, and it makes one wonder whether being a Colonial Governor was a good insurance risk. Patrick Renison, for example, who had the distinction of getting fired from his post in Kenya because he wasn't getting on with independence quickly enough, died even younger and only Richard Turnbull lived to a ripe old age.

The other two groups concerned with the end of colonialism—the leftist intellectual set and the media—obviously survive but it will be recalled how students of the late 1960s nearly brought Western governments to their knees and how anti-establishment rallies had to be broken up by mounted police and tear gas. It was not a time for concise thought and when domestic pressures eventually eased up, it was a simple matter for indignation to be focussed on Rhodesian and South African racial policies. All sorts of mayhem was occurring in various other parts of Africa but no one cared about these particularly and it was generally felt that African countries could fall off the planet once they had attained majority rule. The fact that the West's economic policies were causing widespread difficulties to agricultural production in ex-colonial countries was conveniently ignored and when South Africa finally became a multi-racial society, the whole continent of Africa ceased to be of any interest at all. A newspaper reader or television viewer has to look very hard to find mention in the media of countries like Zambia and Tanzania, and most western people would be hard put to it to explain where Burkina Faso or Eritrea are.

To complete the picture, I must recount what happened to the southern part of Africa which was still under white rule in 1970. Firmly entrenched at that point in time and seemingly impregnable, it actually crumbled quite quickly. The catalyst for this, however, didn't occur in Africa—it took place in Portugal. To understand this strange trick of history, you must remember that this romantic but often hard-pressed land had been ruled since 1932 by Antonio Salazar, an able and authoritative man who was often called a dictator by his opponents. Far from wanting to shed Portugal's colonies, Salazar—an ardent Roman Catholic—was a firm believer in the need for Portugal to maintain its overseas empire. He had no intention of granting independence to Mozambique or Angola and though freedom movements had started operating within these countries, the Portuguese Army had little difficulty in containing them. Portuguese rule thus looked set to continue without let or hindrance and when Salazar died in 1970, his successor—Marcelo Caetano—was quick to pick up the reins and pursue the same policy. He ruled without the same charisma or authority, however, and was suddenly ousted by a leftist military coup in 1974. This coup—marked in true Portuguese romantic tradition by the exchange of red carnations instead of bullets—was not violent but the new administration lost no time in getting rid of the colonies and before anyone could blink, the two countries had been handed over to the independence movements which had been ineffectually campaigning on their borders. Army control was summarily removed, law and order broke down overnight, and the Portuguese inhabitants fled as best they could. I won't attempt to describe their subsequent history but as most people know, Angola has been wracked by civil war ever since those days and Mozambique has become one of the poorest countries on the continent.

This sudden cessation of Portuguese control over its former colonies left Rhodesia surrounded on three sides by states which had black governments who were in complete sympathy with the nationalist groups who aspired to take over the country. Minor armed incursions by the latter grew in scale until they became a fully-fledged guerrilla war, and though the Rhodesian security forces showed themselves to be tough bush fighters, their lack of numbers and the drain on resources eventually began to tell. Naturally, the black nationalists styled themselves as 'freedom fighters', while the white population alluded to them as 'terrs' (an abbreviation of terrorist). Whatever the terminology, however, virtually every able-bodied white man in the country found himself in uniform and the effect of this on the economy, allied to the cumulative effect of sanctions, finally led Ian Smith to consider some form of political settlement. In the event, Dr. Henry Kissinger, (the gravelly-voiced American Secretary of State who remains an enigma), gave Smith an outright ultimatum of 'negotiate or else'. Britain then came back into the picture and for four months, Rhodesia became a colony again while preparations were made for an election. The white population reconciled itself to the advent of black rule and it was widely believed that the moderate alliance that had been struck between Bishop Abel Muzerewa and Joshua Nkomo would sweep the board. It did no such thing, however, and a previously discounted Marxist named Robert Mugabe scooped the pool on the back of wholesale intimidation carried out by his followers in rural districts during the run-up. What was the West to do? It couldn't say it wouldn't recognise the result because it didn't like the winning candidate, and it would have taken an enormous effort to clear matters up on the ground. So on 17 April 1980, the Union Jack was duly pulled down and the Republic of Zimbabwe was born.

Following this, the last colony in Africa to reach independence was the territory known as South West Africa, which is now Namibia. Previously German and mandated to South Africa after the First World War, this large and sparsely-inhabited land was the target of a freedom organisation known as SWAPO (the South-West Africa People's Organisation) who had set themselves up in Angola after the Portuguese had pulled out. The South African Government had other ideas, however, and the SADF (South African Defence Force) was deployed along the Angolan border to keep the would-be invaders out. This they did at first without too much trouble but then the pressure began to build up as the civil war which had been raging in Angola assumed international proportions and became a Marxist-Capitalist conflict. The Soviet Union, which had always had its beady eye on the goldmines and harbours of Southern Africa, called in the favours owed to it by Cuba and in a sudden move which took everyone unawares, the Marxist-backed forces in Angola were suddenly reinforced by thirty thousand Cuban troops. This put Western nations into a tailspin because they did not wish to be seen siding openly with South Africa in view of its apartheid policies. They therefore did nothing to help and some very major battles took place between the South Africans and the Cubans on Angolan soil, complete with all the mobility and firepower of modern warfare. The SADF was victorious in most of these encounters but the ongoing strain on manpower and resources was so great that the South African Government eventually agreed to a peace plan sponsored by the United Nations in 1988. Elections were then held and not surprisingly, the SWAPO movement won in a canter. Independence came in 1990 and the somewhat inarticulate Sam Nujoma became the first President of the new Republic. Namibia has been a very quiet country since those times and now jogs along on the proceeds of tourism and diamond mining.

After this, the end of white rule in Africa came without any undue fuss in the very country in which one might have expected the mother and father of a battle—namely, South Africa. But strangely enough, matters never came to this type of head, mainly because the whites were too powerful and the African National Congress too ineffectual for any serious hostilities to take off. Incredibly enough, it all happened by negotiation and South Africa turned itself into a multi-cultural nation with a minimum amount of violence. It is far too complex a story to attempt to summarise in a few words but basically, it boiled down to the realisation that separate development simply would not work—either economically or morally. The predominantly Afrikaner Nationalist Government may have foreseen a far greater power-sharing role for itself than it actually achieved but at the end of the day, it lost an open election in 1994 and had to hand over administration of the country to the African National Congress. Nelson Mandela was inaugurated President on 11 May 1994 and what has since become known as the rainbow nation has been in existence ever since. Whether South Africa's subsequent progress has been an unqualified success is a matter of opinion but importantly, it has remained stable and the varied ethnic strains which inhabit it seem to co-exist in reasonable if precarious harmony.

Before leaving the topic of South Africa, however, I must tell you with some pride of the important role played by a Kenyan in ensuring the orderly transition of power. The process wasn't quite as smooth as commonly made out and in the early part of 1994, it looked as if the Zulus, under the leadership of Chief Gasha Buthelezi, were going to become physical in their opposition to an ANC government. In fact, they declared they would take no part in the forthcoming election and started sharpening their *assegai's* in preparation for massive protest marches in the central area of Johannesburg. The security forces—still mainly white at this stage—were fully mobilised in consequence and it looked as if South Africa was about to begin its own civil war. It was a very tense moment and there was a run on the food shops as people stocked up in anticipation of major trouble. Who saved the day by outstanding shuttle diplomacy? None other than Professor Washington Okumu of Kenya—an ex-Kissinger associate and a long-standing friend of Buthulezi, who went back and forth between Johannesburg and Zululand like a homing pigeon. Three days later, the crisis was over. Okumu had spelled out the facts of life to Buthulezi and persuaded him to accept a deal with the ANC by which certain constitutional changes were guaranteed. It really was diplomacy at its finest and probably saved South Africa from imploding.

What remains to be said about Africa and the end of colonialism? Rather like a suspicious death or the termination of a game of bridge, an inquest is clearly merited. The present state of Africa in 2010 is hardly re-assuring and the end of colonialism was categorically not a passport to peace and prosperity on the continent. Look at the present state of Africa now. After 50 years of continuous strife, the fighting in the Congo is still going on and even intensifying. The population of Zimbabwe is starving under Mugabe's 30-year rule, and the people of Darfur have fared so badly for so long that the President of the Sudan was recently declared an international criminal. Somalia hasn't had a government of any sort for the last 20 years and the only form of income it can generate is from the proceeds of piracy—an ongoing activity which requires the world's navies to protect ships rash enough to go round the Horn of Africa. Ethiopia has been stalked by massive famines, Nigeria and Chad are busy inventing new levels of corruption, Angola and Mozambique are in ruins, Rwanda is notorious for past genocides, Sierra Leone went through an incredibly vicious time that required the services of

British troops to restore order, the Ivory Coast had a long period of anarchy, the Algerians are busy cutting each other's throats, Liberia literally blew up in the 1990s, Niger and Mauritania both changed their governments as the result of coups, the President of Guinea-Bissau was assassinated—the list goes on and on.

As it has turned out, the leading countries of the continent are indisputably South Africa and Kenya, though each of these has major problems and has had its share of misfortunes. Egypt manages to stay afloat but can't make up its mind whether it is Arab, African or European. It is currently trying to re-invent itself after deposing its President, while the neighbouring country of Libya will need to recover from the intensive civil war aimed at ousting Colonel Gaddafi. Namibia is too sparsely populated to have much significance and Botswana, which has done very well in comparison to other African countries, is sorely beset by an abnormally high incidence of AIDS. Otherwise, the rest of the continent is in dire straits and it is impossible to escape the conclusion that the end of colonialism came thirty years too soon. If orderly rule and hi-tech development had proceeded under colonial auspices, they would very probably be better off today and would have politicians more capable of governing responsibly. Only an elderly idealist, living in the heart of Hampstead, would not admit that the conferment of instant democracy in the 1960s was a mixed blessing for the countries concerned. Many commentators, including black intellectuals, freely acknowledge it and the subject is only avoided by Western politicians for fear of giving offence to the current rulers of the states in question. As Lord Deedes, that well-known doyen of British journalism, said in one of the last articles he wrote before his death in 2005, independence was conferred far too hastily and Macmillan had bamboozled everyone with his wind of change.

As a talking point on the virtue of extended colonialism, one only has to look at the success achieved by Hong Kong, where British colonial status was only terminated in 1997. Critics may throw their hands up in horror at this comparison and assert there is no similarity between Asian and African situations but this is ignoring the central point. The process worked because the colonial yoke became lighter and more sophisticated as the years went past and by the time the flag was pulled down, the local populace was fully capable of controlling its destiny—both economically and administratively. By 1997, in fact, the city-state had become one of the showpieces of Asia, with wonderful commercial buildings, excellent housing developments and a transport system which put Britain itself to shame. A lot of tradition inherited from Hong Kong's past has survived and while its residents are as fiercely independent as they can be under Beijing's shadow, there is still a British feel to many of its institutions and methods of conducting local politics.

It is surely not stretching the case too far to suggest that African nations would be in immeasurably better shape if independence had only come when there was a multi-racial middle class in place, from which the leaders of commerce, industry and politics would naturally emerge. The hard-headed men who turned the colonies loose must surely have known this and though Britain and France had been severely weakened by World War Two, recovery during the growth period of the 1950s was strong and if the will had been present, the means would have been found. De Gaulle may have had problems in trying to get the Fifth Republic off the ground and the Macmillan/Macleod duo may have been obsessed with Britain's economy, but the decisions they took bear all the marks of indecent haste and have ended badly.

It is interesting to reflect that Rhodesia, the last colony in Africa, was scuttled thirty years ago in similar fashion by men who were neither idealistic lefties nor Communist fellow-travellers. On the contrary, Henry Kissinger and Lord Carrington were outstanding exponents of American and British pragmatism. The fact that their efforts resulted in handing over the country to Robert Mugabe is ironic. Obviously, they didn't mean things to turn out the way they did but the facts are unassailable. Zimbabwe was a stable, prosperous country in the 1970s and could not only feed itself but the surrounding parts of Africa as well. Black political participation was slowly increasing and the black middle-class was growing rapidly. Why this was regarded as undesirable is a mystery—the country was self-supporting and wouldn't have cost Britain anything if it had continued its course without interference.

History is full of wrong turnings, however, and life goes on in spite of them. People keep working, eating, loving, and sleeping as part of the daily struggle for survival, and only pause occasionally to wonder how things got the way they are. As the parties responsible for any problems which may have been bothering them are usually dead by the time they start asking questions, they then have to fall back on history for an intelligible answer. Assuming this to be the case with the endemic poverty and strife experienced in East Africa and many other African countries, the plain answer would seem to be that colonialism ended too soon. The abrupt termination of support condemned millions of people to a lifetime of hardship, and it is one of history's major ironies that the step was taken by conservative Western politicians—descendants of the very same men who had started the Imperial rush eighty years earlier. Was it short-term self-interest or the sudden development of a social conscience? Take your pick.

CHAPTER 8

REFLECTIONS

Looking back is always a luxury because one's views on events are not clouded by the present. Immediate pressures are out of the way and what people said they were going to do has long since been overtaken by what they actually did. Like the valiant men and women who fought in World War Two, the bwanas and their memsahibs are fast fading into history and movie producers are hard put to it to re-create plausible characters for the Africa-oriented entertainments they occasionally set before us. Unfortunately, the tale seldom gets past the adventures of a beautiful countess and a dashing 'White Hunter' up to their tricks in the foothills of Mount Kilimanjaro. In truth, there were many such adventures in real life but movies or books about them are inclined to suffer from a shortage of information on the way the bwana tribe worked, ate and lived. Above all, there is scant reference anywhere to the way they thought.

In this regard, there are several fundamental issues at stake and some pre-conceptions on the part of non-bwanas which need to be discussed. Contemporary thinking seems to be divided between those who believe the era of colonialism in East Africa was something to be proud of and those who look on it as exploitive and even shameful. Naturally, the last person likely to be consulted by the latter group is someone who was part of the colonial scene and they would hold—with some justice—that there is nothing like personal involvement to destroy objectivity. Relying on the media and the opinions of other people is no more scientific, however, and the court of so-called world opinion is an esoteric forum. As every primitive tribesman well knows, the truth behind any situation depends entirely on who is telling the story.

Firstly, there is the perennial question of whether the colonial system in East Africa was oppressive. A short answer to this is that it wasn't, but this is hardly enough for a concerned reader with opinions to the contrary. Most people in this category were weaned on stories of exploitation and though I believe this to be a hangover from the 1960s-type media attack to which the system was subjected, there seems to be a willingness to believe the worst. Whether this arises entirely from a burning concern for human rights is not clear but there also seems to be a tinge of envy due to the perception that bwanas and memsahibs enjoyed a privileged lifestyle without necessarily deserving it. I have met many people who immediately go po-faced when the subject of my background comes up and I tell them I used to live in East Africa and South Africa. They take one look at my white skin and you can see them thinking 'my God, he's one of those'. All it would need to complete the thought is for me to be reeking of gin and slapping a *sjambok* against my boot. (In point of fact, I have never owned a *sjambok* but my wife possesses a splendid one which was presented to her with great merriment by a Zulu friend as an aid to keeping me in order).

This immediate assumption that bwanas and memsahibs were superannuated racists is quite common and does no justice to the hard-working, kindly people who made up their ranks. Most of them were fully engaged in trying to make a living and battled away in an environment which called for frequent improvisation. There was emphatically no such thing as forced labour during the British administration of colonial East Africa and though the wages which were paid to manual workers were low, so were the salaries and profits of their employers. It is absurd to say that everyone should have lived in a mud hut in order to make things more equal—one might as well say that the wealthier inhabitants of Britain should all join the ranks of the homeless and sleep on the Embankment to show solidarity with the disadvantaged. The indigenous population of East Africa came off a very low economic base in the early days of colonisation and those members of it who chose to join the work force were quite unskilled in the occupations required by a modern economy. Productive work had to be coaxed out of them for many years and this period of learning and adaptation probably took the first half of the twentieth century. It is not natural to like work and the locals not only had to be convinced of its virtue but also had to get used to a money economy.

There was no alternative to a slow start on the educational front, either, because there were no schools in existence when the colonial regime started and no history of an established academic culture. The educational system had to start from scratch and though the missionaries played a valuable role in this regard, it took a long time before indigenous secondary school leavers appeared on the scene. A scholastic tradition cannot be created overnight and in the circumstances, it was a very enlightened move to have established Makerere College in Uganda as early as 1922. It functioned well as a technical and teacher training school for many years and its absorption into the University of East Africa in the 1960s was the culmination of years of patient effort. From academic zero to degree standard in forty years is not bad going and local graduates have since proved their worth in many ways, though handicapped in two vital aspects—namely, a lack of experience brought about by ultra-rapid promotion and an abnormally low representation of females among the graduate tally. Both these deficiencies are changing with time but they still remain very real problems. The need for more female emancipation and education is probably the biggest key to the transformation of Africa into modern society and the only plausible way of keeping birth rates down to a sustainable level. It is an uphill struggle and even now, traditional practices such as female circumcision have still to be abandoned.

Another reproach frequently levelled at bwanas and memsahibs stems from the question of servants. Hampstead philosophers may have Filippina maids or subscribe to a char service without any brickbats being cast at them but East African memsahibs are usually portrayed as being indolent and spoilt. I don't think they were at all and even if they didn't work at a job—which most of them did—they were pretty busy running their homes, bringing up their children, and keeping cultural values alive. As anybody who has ever had servants will testify, it does not follow that households manage themselves and a high degree of organisation and supervision is required. Domestic service was a major source of employment in East Africa from the earliest times and it would have been nonsensical not to have been part of the system. A large sector of the community comprised of full-time male workers depended on domestic service as a regular source of income and there was a whole tradition of *desturi* (respected custom) behind it.

Life with servants of a different cultural background is, of course, liable to be tricky as illustrated by a true story about the occasion a Dutch couple in Tanganyika decided to have a celebratory dinner party at which the main dish would be a roast sucking pig. Keen to do justice to this ambitious project, the wife was keen to have the pig served up in style and instructed her houseboy in her broken Swahili to put an apple in the mouth and parsley behind the ears. To her distress, however, and to the intense amusement of her guests, the honest fellow did exactly what he thought he had been told and came into the dining room proudly bearing the roast pig on a salver—with an apple in his own mouth and a couple of sprigs of parsley behind each of his ears.

One cannot help but smile in sympathy and it is no secret that the servants of East Africa were firmly convinced that all Europeans were off their heads. I have heard them compare notes and shrug their shoulders at some of the strange customs they were asked to observe. A bank manager who lived in Lindi, for example, tells a story about having had a serving hatch cut into the wall between the kitchen and the dining room in order to avoid the need to carry food down a long passage. When the building alteration had been completed, his wife proudly told their houseboy to use the hatch when serving dinner. She thought he looked at her a bit strangely but thought no more about it and was completely unprepared for the scene which eventuated when they were sitting at the table and she rang her little bell to indicate they were ready. First, there was a whole series of grunts and groans betokening extreme exertion and then a big black foot appeared in the hatch as the houseboy battled to get through it with two plates of soup in his hands.

It is not recorded whether any soup was spilled but no doubt, all the participants—including the houseboy—dined out on the story for years to come. Again, this is nothing more than a valid comment on cultural perception. Unthinking Europeans might laugh at the misunderstanding but this is judging the instance by Western standards. The same people would have had no idea how to behave at a Masai feast and would have caused an equal amount of merriment to their hosts.

As for the colour bar which is often cited as a characteristic trait of colonialism, it is quite true that certain places and institutions were designated for use by different race groups. This was more an expression of cultural identity, though, and was not based on a sense of racial superiority. Skin colour was more a convenient badge, giving out an immediate clue as to its owner's cultural and economic status. It would tell you what language he or she spoke, whether they had any money, whether they used a knife and fork, how they were likely to behave, and—quite importantly—what sort of toilet manners they had and whether they preferred to sit or squat. It was, if you like, an early warning sign as to whether the fellow human being you were with would be socially compatible. Given a uniform culture in a country, there is no need for this type of assessment but East Africa contained the most diverse groups of people imaginable and there was a constant need to adapt to one's audience. There is nothing more artificial on this earth than a conversation between two people of different backgrounds who are attempting to socialise because they feel constrained to do so and it would be far better if they simply exchanged greetings and went about their business.

The club—an institution which is an integral part of the social fabric in most westernised countries—is a good demonstration of this. One applies to join a club because one wishes to mingle with other people who enjoy the same things, whether it be some form of sport or business. The club, on the other hand, has to make up its mind whether the applicant is suitable and bars its doors to anyone who tries to walk in and use its facilities. Is this a curtailment of human rights? Possibly, but how else can human relationships work. The Greek farmers of Iringa had a club, for example, where they could get together, talk Greek to each other, drink their special brand of coffee, arrange marriages for their children, and discuss farm prices. How would I have fitted in if I had insisted on joining? I'm sure they would have been very courteous but nothing could change the fact that I wasn't Greek, didn't know Greece and wasn't a farmer. The British, of course, have always been very keen on clubs and it has been said that the Empire itself functioned like a large club. It has also been said that the Empire only came about because the English wanted some decent cricket opponents but this may be stretching things a little.

The concept of a club demanding a certain standard of behaviour was in fact mirrored in colonial administration. There was a sort of muscular Christianity about it as well, which demanded allegiance to certain codes of conduct. Kipling talked about 'sending forth the best ye breed' and certainly, when you were in an outpost of Empire, you were expected to comport yourself in the manner befitting an officer and a gentleman. The similarity between this and military custom was not accidental, because one was expected as a matter of routine to supervise the activities of numbers of people and get them to do things. Members of the Colonial Civil Service were actually alluded to as 'officers' in General Orders, which was the bible that regulated conduct. Heaven help a junior officer who kicked over the traces because the book would literally be thrown at him and he would either find himself posted to an unpopular station or have his next increment stopped until he made good. Racist attitudes were severely frowned upon in this regard and respect for people of different ethnic backgrounds was part of the general ethos.

If colonialism in East Africa hadn't finished at the time it did, I believe a whole generation of bright young locals would have started coming through and would have effortlessly joined the system. Local girls would have started to catch up and once inter-marriage started occurring, you would have had a vigorous class of managers and administrators capable of running the economy efficiently. Ethnic backgrounds would not have featured in this and indeed, the schools of East Africa were already multi-racial before *uhuru*. The Prince of Wales in Kenya, for example, opened its doors in 1962 and Tanzania's secondary school at Iringa had been that way since its inception. Unfortunately, however, the creation of a mixed middle class never occurred to any significant degree because the requisite evolutionary process ended too soon. As the bwanas began leaving, the first wave of local graduates went straight to the top without the benefit of any experience or understanding of the traditions they had inherited. Regrettably, too, many of the brighter locals who followed up this initial wave saw fit to migrate to other countries in search of a better life and a more tangible appreciation of their worth. It is a shame their talents were not utilised in their country of birth but one can clearly see the dilemma. Why would a young professional Kikuyu girl, for example, opt to take her chances in crime-stricken Nairobi when she could lead a dynamic life in Australia, free from political and other pressures?

If the colonial system in East Africa had such a proud record, what were its failures? Discussion on this point is subjective but one of the main causes for regret in my opinion is that not enough money was spent on development. The collapse of the groundnut scheme in Tanganyika put paid to truly large scale schemes and though the limited funds which were made available were spent to good advantage, the projects involved were relatively small in scale. Furthermore, it was firm policy not to intrude into established patterns of tribal life and large areas of country were deemed to be subject to 'traditional law and custom'. Within these areas, there was no co-ordinated agricultural development on a major scale and no individual land ownership save for the dispositions made by the local chief. Government experts gave advisory help only and the Provincial Administration concerned itself primarily with preserving stability. As a result, progress was painfully slow and the ecology suffered badly from over-grazing and tree-felling on a large scale. Wood was and still is the only fuel available for cooking in most parts of East Africa and as the population has increased, so has the demand for firewood. Vast areas of land have been denuded of trees for this reason and the de-forestation has resulted in increased soil erosion and a reduction in rainfall.

Whether this state of affairs can be attributed to the Lugard doctrine of indirect rule is open to argument. Certainly, it was an excellent way to run a country without too much expense and there was minimum interference with the traditional way in which people lived. The incoming British administration in Tanganyika after the First World War was only too glad to adopt the German *jumbe* system of village chiefs, and the Kenya Government relied heavily on men such as Chief Waruhiu of the Kikuyu nation. The Kabaka of Buganda, who was a hereditary king, played an active role in the administration of Uganda, and the Sultan of Zanzibar retained a great deal of authority in the way the islands were governed. The system worked well for a long time but in hindsight, one can see that large portions of the population were left behind in the march of progress. It may be very laudable not to interfere with the noble savage in the wilderness but if this policy is adopted, one mustn't expect him or her to simultaneously be a modern citizen up to all the tricks of production and marketing. The conundrum is familiar to many societies. Is it more satisfactory to have the indigenous citizens of a country looking picturesque in skins than to see them wearing jeans and eating hamburgers? It is fair comment, I think, to say that colonial settlers and administrators preferred their Masai warriors to look the part and would have been horrified at the idea of them wearing trousers and licking ice cream cones.

The land tenure question is also arguable. It was conventional wisdom at one time to believe that a class of small landowners was essential to a state of healthy husbandry in a nation and in furtherance of this aim, various programmes were set up in selected areas to provide for individual ownership of parcels of land. Aside from anything else, it was felt this would enable people to borrow money on the strength of their land titles, which in turn would encourage agricultural production. This was, however, more honoured in the breach rather than acceptance, and the embryonic financial system was not geared to making small mortgages available. Was this a failure? Modern experience has taught us that small farms are uneconomic and incapable of making a major contribution to a country's agricultural production. Certainly, in South Africa after the war, the experiment of creating smallholdings in low income areas did nothing more than create a series of rural slums. Nowadays, it seems to be accepted that efficient food production comes from large scale mechanised farming and it may be just as well the East African landscape was not turned into a patchwork quilt of small plots.

The other area which is often cited as a failure of the colonial regime in East Africa was the form of education which was handed out to the indigenous population. 'We've done nothing but produce a race of clerks' some horny-handed old settler would grumble, but one can hardly blame someone who has just learned to read and write from wanting to use his new accomplishments. This often had unintended results and one of the most delightful examples of this comes from the papers of Jack Hill, who was a District Commissioner in Tanganyika during World War Two and subsequently became the Member for Communications, Works and Development Planning in the last years of the pre-independence Government. While still a DC, he had run out of patience with one of his clerks and been forced to fire him for laziness. This provoked the letter quoted below, which was written in the early 1940s and shows clear evidence of its author's classical education:-

Kind Sir,

> *On opening this epistle, you will behold the words of a dejobbed person and a very bewifed and much childrenized gentleman who was violently dejobbed in a twinkling by your good self.*
>
> *For heavens sake, sir, consider this catastrophe as falling on your own head and remind yourself on walking home at the moon's end to five savage wives and sixteen veracious children with your pocket filled with non-existent shillings and a solitary sixpence, pity my horrible state when being dejobbed and proceeding with a heart and intestines filled with misery in this den of gloom, myself did contemplate greedily culpable homicide, but him who protected Daniel safe through the lions' den will protect his servant in the home of evil. As to the reason given by yourself, esquire, for my dejob, the incrimination was laziness. No, sir, it was impossible that myself who has pitched sixteen infant children into this vale of tears can have a lazy atom in his mortal frame and the sad departure of many shillings has left me on the verge of destitution and despair. I hope this vision of horror will enrich your dreams this night and pulverise your heart of nether milestone so that you will awaken with such alacrity as may be compatible with your personal safety and will hasten to rejobulate your servant. So note it be,*

> *Yours despairfully*
> *AKUKA SABASH*

This is not bad going at all for the 1940s and must rank as one of the most persuasive letters an employer ever received from an employee about to be dismissed. As one might suspect, it did the trick and melted the DC's heart so much that he rejobulated Sabash to his old position. Jack Hill's sense of humour would not let him part with the letter, however, and he made a copy on which he could not resist adding the following footnote :-

Gentle reader, do not sob
Akuka Sabash got his job

There is indeed something irresistible about Sabash's use of English but rather like India where babu-English became famous during the Raj, a grounding in classical literature often had unintended effects. This in itself was no problem but what made it worse was the enduring African perception that a secondary education was a passport to wearing a clean shirt and preserving clean hands. Even today, young black up-and-comers see how bosses conduct themselves and yearn to sit behind a desk and use the telephone. The need for this activity to be economically fruitful is not necessarily appreciated and a mind unused to business finds it easy to believe that going to the office every day will automatically generate a salary cheque. Young indigenous graduates in Africa are well-known for this attitude and though budding engineers and lawyers fill out their time sheets conscientiously, it doesn't seem to occur to them that their recorded times may well be over the level for which a reasonable charge can be made.

This characteristic is curious in some ways because most Africans are natural capitalists and can be very sharp when it comes to a matter of trading. Sadly, they also make world-class criminals. The conmen of Nigeria, for example, are famous all over the world for their scam techniques and the strong-arm *tsotsis* of Johannesburg are eminently successful in the car hi-jacking business. The latter is a very highly organised affair and matters have reached the stage where more cars are stolen in South Africa every day than are manufactured or imported. By all accounts, too, Nairobi is not far behind in the crime stakes and though it can be argued this is due to desperate poverty, there seems to be a growing acceptance of crime being a perfectly reasonable occupation. If a young hi-jack operative can make more money in one day by stealing cars than he can get from a month's employment in a normal job, he is plainly not going to switch. Again, it's a question of African logic and one must admit there is some validity to it.

In general terms, the reproach to ex-colonials is always the same. At some point in a discussion, the western liberal with whom one has been talking will adopt an expression of the utmost reason, lean forward judicially in his chair and ask why more was not done for the local population in terms of financial support. Reference will be made to the immorality of a society in which there are vast disparities of income. 'Surely,' your liberal friend will say, 'there was something badly skewed about the white inhabitants of the country earning an average income so many times greater than the average income of the black inhabitants.' This sounds indefensible at first but how in the world does one achieve equality of income in a country where the population is not homogenous? It doesn't even occur in leading economies, where bankers, pop stars, top sportsmen and fashion models earn vast amounts compared to the poor widow scraping along on a pension? It's sad, it's unfair, but that's the way it is. Certainly, the white population of East Africa tended to live at a higher standard than the black population but they didn't live at a more luxurious level than they would have done in their countries of origin and often in a far more primitive way. As the indigenous locals were coming off a very low base, the gulf in incomes was not only inevitable but impossible to correct overnight. The trickle-down effect may seem incredibly long-winded if one is at its receiving end but unfortunately, economic history has not identified any other way to achieve upward mobility. If one really wants to see ostentatious luxury, one should look at the style in which many of Africa's new rulers and merchant princes conduct themselves. Robert Mugabe's palace in Zimbabwe is perhaps the prime example but he is not alone by any means.

A further question which often arises is whether bwanas and memsahibs should have socialised more with the local population and done more to create an integrated society? Given the disparate cultures between the races at the time, however, I believe this would not only have been impossible but would have come across as artificial and unacceptable. The races lived in separate worlds and the bwanas had no time to set themselves up as amateur social workers. Aside from anything else, the business and professional scene was as competitive in East Africa as anywhere else and the bwanas were all pretty busy trying to make things grow or fighting each other in the jungle of business. With increasing levels of education and urbanisation, however, more indigenous people would have joined the rat race and social interaction would have increased—especially between members of different races who had been at school together. This is already occurring in South Africa and the old *apartheid* days are fast becoming a memory in the more affluent sectors of its society.

One can hardly call it a failure of colonialism because it didn't surface until after independence, but looming over all other problems to face East Africa is the question of population growth. Obviously, this is not unique to East Africa and the effects of over-rapid population growth are common to most developing regions of the world. Governments and politicians don't know what to do about it and the problem keeps intensifying. Put simply, there are too many countries which cannot cope with an ever-increasing number of mouths to feed or bodies to house. In East Africa, the growth rate of its population has been 3.1% per year since 1970 and though this doesn't sound too alarming when said quickly, it is responsible for the population of East Africa having grown from 34 million in 1970 to a reported population of 100 million in 2005. A further 12 million souls would have been added to this by 2009 and if the same rate is maintained, the population will reach 135 million by 2015. This will obviously put an enormous strain on resources and short of sterilising each male inhabitant, it is difficult to escape the conclusion that the outcome will be increasing poverty. Family planning is not popular in Africa and the lack of social security in the form of an old age pension leads to people having large families in the hope their children will provide some form of support in their old age. Additionally, the population likes sex. Maybe this is due to the climate being exceptionally fecund or there is something in the soil or maybe they are just born that way. It is not just popular superstition but a documented fact that the good Lord blessed Africa's male children with the biggest working parts you will ever see on this planet. If you take a drive along any river where there is some bathing going on, you will see for yourself. The parts in question are not ornaments, either, and their owners use them freely.

Whether birth rates will ever decrease in the fullness of time remains to be seen but developed nations have found this only happens when there is a rise in the general standard of living. Some countries—such as Australia—seem to have lived through this stage and are actually seeing family size increase again but this can only happen where there is a strong system of social security and maternal benefits in place. In Africa as a whole, this is an unaffordable dream and the population continues to rise to unsustainable levels. The only conceivable hope for the future appears to lie with female emancipation and some form of really easy contraception which does not rely on male co-operation. African males are very inclined to help themselves and unless local girls reject the idea of having babies every year, there seems little hope of a wholesale reduction in birth rates. Failing this, it looks as if the charitable organisations of the world will stay in business for a long, long time.

These are deep waters and many are the social and demographic scientists who have delved into Third World population trends. The matter is not only complicated by the lack of reliable census figures but also by constantly shifting politics. Even in developed countries, the public doesn't listen to scientists very much and the sight of an aspiring leader telling the male members of a typical African electorate that they must cut down on their nooky is unlikely to materialise. The bare facts are obscure, anyway, and whether one is talking about East Africa or South Africa or Nigeria, no one knows within a few million what their populations really are. Does it matter? Yes, but there doesn't seem to be anything one can do about it. The world will probably keep turning on its axis for the foreseeable future, though it may not be as nice a place as it used to be.

What was the drawing power of East Africa for the bwanas and their memsahibs? Well, for starters, it was a beautiful country with varied scenery, which ranged from palm-fringed beaches and high-altitude forests to vast lakes and plains teeming with game. There were tropical lowlands and cool highlands, with enormous mountains and incredible features such as the Rift Valley. The towns were hospitable places and the local people were colourful and friendly. There may not have been much arable land expressed as a percentage of the total area but what there was had great potential for successful farming. The way of life was captivating, too. Where else in the world could one lead an existence that mixed the sophisticated with the primitive in such proportions? One could spend a long hot day, for example, driving along an earth road which passed through formidable scenery, freely inhaling dust and keeping a wary eye open for corrugations, potholes and washaways. Primitive tribesmen and wild animals might be in evidence and filling stations would be few and far between, being limited to the widely-separated towns along the route. Covered in dust or mud by the time one reached journey's end, one would then find oneself quaffing excellent beer, enjoying a hot bath, dressing smartly for dinner, and subsequently dining at a well-laid table in front of a log fire.

There was always this eternal contrast. As a young surveyor, one knew that the initial stage of a safari would mean being away in the bush for a couple of weeks, sleeping under canvas, bathing occasionally in brown river water, eating corned beef and baked beans, doing one's calculations at night by the light of a paraffin pressure lamp, and getting bitten to hell and back by mosquitoes. When the job was done, however, and the 3-ton truck lumbered back into town complete with loads of firewood and covered in dust, it was like re-entering Paradise and that very same night, one could find oneself at the local club or at a dinner party. With no television, people were intensely sociable and entertaining in the home was a normal part of life. The larger towns had a range of good restaurants and there were excellent nightclubs in Nairobi, Mombasa and Dar es Salaam. Bwanas and memsahibs danced frequently and each town had an amateur theatrical society, which staged many excellent productions and always put on a Christmas pantomime full of local humour.

For some reason, characters abounded in East African society. Maybe there was something in the air which encouraged eccentricity or maybe it was the effect of living on the equator, often at high altitude. Drink may have had something to do with it, too, but there was undoubtedly a higher ratio of extraordinary people among the bwanas than one would find in other groups of organised society. One well-known family in Tanganyika, for example, kept a couple of tame leopards on their property, an elderly scion of a noble house was renowned for drinking whisky out of his teapot, an agricultural officer collected snakes in the bush and then let them loose in town, a resident in one of Dar's best suburbs used to take his tame cheetah out for a walk, a white hunter wrote scurrilous poetry—the list goes on and on. The tale is still told how a professional crocodile hunter painted a baby crocodile pink and let it loose at 2 o'clock in the morning on the bar of *Ocean Breeze,* the premier nightclub in Dar. It caused an absolute sensation, as you might expect, and several hardened old topers even signed the pledge, thinking they were in the early stages of *delirium tremens.*

It was the complete antithesis of life in Europe. Even in the bigger towns, most people knew each other and there was as much privacy as living in the proverbial goldfish bowl. If one of the wives got pregnant, gossip would immediately be directed at identifying the party at which impregnation had occurred and if someone had an affair, it was all over town in a flash. Scandal was meat and drink to most communities and you had to be very circumspect if you were to avoid becoming the subject of discussion. You didn't even have to do anything—just looking as if you were going to do something was enough. Somewhat bizarrely, too, there were relatively few elderly people in East African society because they retired at an early age and went back to wherever they came from. It was unusual to see an old person, and children would only see their grandparents when long leave came round.

If you believe in the precept that Africa was, is, and always should be for dark-skinned Africans only, by all means condemn colonialism. At the same time, you must admit there wasn't much visible progress on the continent before colonialism kicked off. Africa's leaders have not made an outstanding success of it since colonialism came to an end, either, and there is a considerable body of evidence suggesting that independence came thirty years too soon. Why this happened is debatable but there is a strong case for deeming the premature and abrupt termination of colonial rule to have been motivated by self-interest.

For the window of stability afforded by colonialism, one must thank the generations of bwanas and memsahibs who worked, played, loved, drank, and gossiped throughout the sunlit years. Every single one of them felt a great and abiding affection for East Africa. *Lala vizuri, mabwana!*

Lightning Source UK Ltd.
Milton Keynes UK
UKOW05f1845290813

216212UK00001B/243/P